REMEMBERING THE FARM

Remembering the Farm

Memories of Farming, Ranching, and
Rural Life in Canada,
Past and Present

ALLAN ANDERSON

Macmillan of Canada
TORONTO

Canadian Cataloguing in Publication Data

Anderson, Allan, 1915—
  Remembering the farm

ISBN 0-7705-1572-X

1. Farm life—Canada. 2. Farmers—Canada—Biography.
3. Canada—Rural conditions. I. Title.

S522.C2A53   630'.971   C77-001627-8

Printed in Canada for
The Macmillan Company of Canada Limited
70 Bond Street, Toronto
M5B 1X3

This book is primarily for Betty, who helped me with it from the beginning, and who is my companion and my love.

It is for my sister Jean: kind, generous Jean.

It is also for my children: individuals all, with some of whom I do not always agree, but all of whom I admire and will always cherish: John, Robert, Alec, Susan, and Pegeen.

It is also for Mona: though separated, we are friends, and I hope will always remain so.

Contents

Author's Preface

I am writing this on a calm, hazy July morning, when all nature is bursting with the glory of summer. I'm typing at an old, red table under a maple tree that spreads its branches low all around me so that I can just see the far ridges of hills on the horizon from south to west. We are on a hilltop fifty miles northwest of Toronto and I always say that on a clear day we can see Saskatoon.

A sense of totally satisfying peace permeates the countryside around me. Someone is weeding in the garden back of the house. There are smaller gardens scattered through the orchard, and beyond the big maple there's a line of cherry trees. Although all's well with the world, a cherry emergency has been declared. It's us against the robins. A moment ago, an overstuffed robin had the audacity to land on the grass a dozen feet away with a rosy-red sour cherry in its beak. Not far away, Betty is sitting on an aluminum stepladder, picking cherries that hang in a shower over her head. In thirty years on these four-and-a-quarter acres, we have never had such an abundance of cherries. I should be up a ladder, too, but in truth there are enough sour cherries for the robins, for us, and for our friends, just as earlier there were enough sweet cherries for a flock of cedar waxwings and for our family.

You can tell I like the country. Although I have spent thirty years as a broadcaster and, on and off, as a writer, a book reviewer, and a lecturer, and although, of necessity, I have spent much of my time in the city, I am essentially a countryman. I feel unhinged somehow when I'm not in the country, and the older I get (and I'm hard at it these days) the more the city irritates me.

I believe there is a profound attachment to the land rooted in the Canadian character. How could there not be? Less than seventy years ago there were more people on the farm or in rural places than in urban centres. That is not long ago; my father and mother weren't even married then. In fact, I believe that farming is the single most important factor in the Canadian experience. The fur trade involved relatively few people. So did lumbering and fishing. Farming involved almost half the population.

Each farm was a little self-contained community, and a family worked long hours to keep the farm going. When I first started collecting the material for this book by asking people about their memories of the farm, I would say: "Didn't all that hard work get you down?" Invariably, their answer would be: "We didn't expect anything else. We knew we had to work hard. That was it." Farm work at times was monotonous, but it also had great variety. The cycle of the seasons meant different tasks. There was genuine satisfaction in seeing the obvious achievement of your labours: the hay in the barn, the jars of preserves in neat rows on the shelves in the basement.

Farm experience has been imprinted on Canadians, I have said, as have few other ways of life. I recall a woman who has worked in school administration in a big city for decades telling me, "You know, my husband and I still talk about the days on the farm. Almost every weekend we like to think about something that happened on the farm that we hadn't thought of for some time, and we laugh and talk about it and enjoy ourselves." I heard that same comment over and over again, all across Canada.

And the longing to be back on the farm! That is the most powerful impression I came home with from all those hundreds of interviews. Margaret Atwood has argued with me that these people are looking back on their farm life through rose-tinted glasses. That is balderdash, and this book proves it, although Peggy and I will no doubt continue our friendly argument for years and years.

Survival is not the basic tenet of Canadian life. We are not victims of nature, lucky to be around at all. What is overwhelmingly important about the farm people in this book is that they *coped* with all the trials and tribulations, the tragedies and disasters, the disappointments and heartbreaks. Certainly homesteaders failed, and farmers gave up. That happens in all walks of life. But what bright-

ened my work, through the three years I spent on this book, was
the cheerfulness of the men and women who had been touched and
forever changed by their farm days. I talked to young people, and to
real old-timers who, at eighty and ninety years of age, were still
husky and lusty and bubbling with laughter, and what pleased me,
because it happened over and over again, was how relaxed and
friendly they were, and how plentifully they were supplied with
dry wit and humour.

You see, it's terribly easy to drive along a paved road and here
and there look at dreary run-down farms and wonder how in the
world people ever put up with that life. What you don't see is the
relationship within the family, and outside it with the neighbours,
the busyness of life on the farms, the sense of a tiny, established,
relatively safe world.

Farmers have hung themselves from barn beams, just as stock-
brokers have jumped out of windows. Yet, in all my meanderings
across Canada, I met only three people who truly hated the farm.
One was a woman who couldn't stand the isolation, another a
woman who feared animals, and the third was an Englishman who
really never intended to farm and got shunted onto one, more or
less by accident, and soon left it.

Now, I'm not saying that there is a farmer in every Canadian.
Morley Callaghan once told me years ago that he was always glad
when summer came to Toronto and people in Rosedale went off to
their cottages and left the city to him. I can understand that: Morley
is completely a city person. On the other hand, I lived in Rosedale
for a year or so, and I wrote an article for the *Toronto Star* at that
time in which I claimed that I hardly ever saw people on the streets
of Rosedale, but since I did see dogs wandering around, and these
dogs must have owners, that therefore one could rationalize that
people did in fact live in Rosedale. All that hush-hush, well-
behaved anonymity of Rosedale horrified me, but I can listen to the
roar of the night silence in the country and be vastly contented.

It's my opinion that the vastness of the country and the small
number of people engaged in farming, even at its peak, made for a
qualitative difference in the Canadian farm experience as against,
say, that of the United States. The climate also added an extra
measure of toughness. It's difficult to argue a philosophical issue

like this, but I think it's important. A greater degree of loneliness perhaps made children more contemplative and self-reliant. It also meant that socializing was very necessary, and visiting, when possible, a happy duty. There was a compulsive need to visit—so much so that it was sometimes overdone. Some farm wives were glad when winter came, for then they wouldn't look out the window and see more damn friends coming down the lane in their buggies.

Sturdiness, a certain amount of eccentricity and even crankiness, and a strong sense of the need to do it yourself are characteristics of Canadian farmers, in the past and in the present. I'm talking of the small farmers, the men and women on the traditional family farms, not the big soil miners who cruise around the land in monstrous machines, perched high in an air-conditioned cab, listening on stereo earphones to raucous music. These soil miners aren't farmers: they are businessmen, they are accountants, and they talk like businessmen and accountants, and I avoided them like the plague.

Maybe I did just get in under the wire. Maybe this book does wrap up a hundred and fifty years of the most glorious era in Canadian farming: The Years of the Family Farm. Maybe we are seeing the last generation hanging on grimly. And, yet, I don't know. I bought this place on the fifth concession of Tecumseth Township in Simcoe County exactly thirty years ago, and of course some farms have gone and commuters are living all around us, but if you go two miles to the west along the concession (not quite as dusty as it used to be, they keep it in better shape now), you'll find the two Elmer families are still there—and the Davises—and the Wallaces. They were all here thirty years ago. Two more farms changed hands some while ago, but they're still family farms. That's not bad for two miles along a concession. And if you go to the east, the Flemings are still there, and the Ransoms down the sideroad. Some of these places are Century Farms, there since before Confederation. That's not a bad record, and it makes me wonder what's going on when I hear all the hollering about the family farm vanishing. If you drive away from the big cities, through good farm country, it's as delightful and rural as it's ever been. Some farmers do have to moonlight and take local jobs, but they're not the only ones doing that.

I know the farms are huge in the West, and that many people have drifted away from marginal farms in the Maritimes, or from rockier parts of Ontario, or from wherever it's been just too much for anyone to manage with prices going up and up. But if you look in the census records — and I often find them fascinating — you can see clearly what's been going on, and what hasn't been going on. The 1911 census shows that there were almost four million people on farms in Canada. Those were rural dwellers. The urban population in 1911 was just a shade under the rural total. From then on, steadily, of course, the number of people on farms declined. In 1971, less than seven per cent of Canadians were farming. That still meant, however, that there were 1,419,795 people on the farm, and that's thirty-six per cent of the 1911 figure. Now, I don't care how many people there are in the cities . . . that's their problem, not mine. But with almost a million and a half people still farming, I don't think the end is in sight by any means. Add to that the fact that there were almost four million rural dwellers in Canada who were classed as "non-farm" in 1971. Six years later, there are hordes and hordes more of these people, and they are crazy about gardening and about horses and cows and goats and sheep and dogs and cats and trees and anything rural. Some of them have tractors and work very hard. I was up the sideroad yesterday and the Joneses were haying and the teenagers were hauling the bales around, and that's farming, isn't it?

Most farm work moves steadily along, but once in a while machinery comes apart or accidents happen or animals are unexpectedly sick. Even when you take these maddening events into account, however, life on the farm is much simpler and less complicated than city life. The tensions and the intrigues of the business world are not found on the farm, nor is the utter tedium of office life. The psychological stress and strain is of a sort you can deal with and, let me tell you, good farm food and fresh air help immensely in easing the burdens.

It's possible that I enjoy an overly romantic view of farm life. But I made one trip right across Canada and another one across most of it and I heard a refrain that became very familiar: "If only I could go back to the farm . . . ", or "If only my children could understand what it was like to grow up on a farm, how wonderful it was . . ." How can you romanticize farm life when you keep hearing that sort of thing from Canadians in province after province?

Let me tell you how this book got started.

As a freelancer, I have always enjoyed the great pleasure of getting off to a slow start in the morning, and one morning three years ago I suddenly leapt to my feet and cried out for all to hear: "I've got the best idea I've ever had! I want to do a show called 'Remembering the Farm'!" I talked to Bob Weaver at CBC, a man I admire more than any other, and who for decades had made it possible for freelancers such as myself to roam the country putting together one- and sometimes two-hour programmes with Canadians in every part of Canada. Bob Weaver bought the idea and it became a two-hour programme and was on the air July, 1976. It was one of the last of the major Canadian public affairs documentaries on radio.

I started taping for that programme in the Maritimes and when I got back home I thought I had the makings of a book. Fortunately, Doug Gibson at Macmillan also thought so, and was able to persuade others at Macmillan that I had a good idea, and so the book was launched.

I travelled by car, bus, train, and plane across Canada. Boxes of tapes piled up in a room in my home. These I edited for the essential material, taking my questions out and splicing together the words of the people themselves. I always got people to tell me their memories of the farm in such a way that their talk would flow right along without me having to make up words to bridge their accounts. I don't like the phrase "oral history" — I find it a very stuffy term. I think of the process as People Remembering Their Past, and the reason why much so-called "oral history" comes out in such a dull, pedestrian way is that most interviewers haven't the foggiest idea of what they are doing. Interviewing is an art, and I have been at it for thirty years, and I have learned my trade. You have to draw people out, you have to stir up their memories, you have to provoke them or charm them, you have to bully them or be patient and kind to them or humour them along, depending on circumstances, but in most cases, interviewed properly, people are simply busting to tell their stories. I have always said Canadians were and are a most articulate people, and this book confirms that claim.

I owe these marvellous, generous Canadians in the book a debt of gratitude I can never repay. I interviewed them in hotel rooms, in their own homes, in cities or towns or villages, on farms, and sometimes out in a field. I badgered Agricultural Representatives mercilessly, because they always knew the men and women in their areas who could talk well and who were good storytellers. Many of these Ag. Reps. would take time out weekdays or even weekends to drive me to farms. It's true in most cases we all would have a good time and enjoy ourselves, but it still was most gracious of them to go to all that trouble for me, and I thank them most kindly.

My edited tapes were transcribed by Mrs. Christine Binkley, to whom I owe an incalculable debt for her patience with me, for her constant effort when she was busy with other material, and for her unwavering, intelligent interest in the book. Mrs. Binkley handed me back, over the course of time, 1,557 pages! Those 1,557 pages boggle the mind, but I had two very conscientious and sharp-minded editors, Ralph Beaumont and John Denison, who were unflaggingly cheerful and perceptive. Betty Tomlinson and I then made certain additions, and did further obsessive polishing; throughout the project Betty often helped me when life was becoming impossible, even though it meant taking time out from her own work as a broadcaster. Finally, and most importantly, there is Doug Gibson, the editorial director of Macmillan, who took all the edited material and stayed up day and night, neglecting his health, his wife, and his other work, to slave on this book and make it the cohesive entity it is. I am a real disciple of Doug Gibson's: I believe he is unequivocally the best editor in Canada. Such an editor makes a tremendous difference to a book.

I must add that "Remembering the Farm" is in fact a two-part book. It is also "Remembering the Ranch". The ranching part of the book I taped mostly in Alberta and British Columbia, and I will talk about that in the introduction to the ranching section.

If this book helps in some way to give back the farm to all those Canadians who miss it as much as I know they do, then I am repaid for my work a thousand times over. I regret very much that only a portion of the material I taped appears in this book. There simply wasn't room for everything.

Every item in this book is genuine. Every province is represented in the book and, except where they wished it otherwise, all the contributors are identified in an index in the back of the book, story by story.

Now I really must get busy and help pick the cherries.

ALLAN ANDERSON
R.R. #3, Tottenham, Ont.
July 5, 1977

ONE

All Kinds of Farms, All Kinds of People

*The New House . . . The Barking Dog . . . On the Buzz Saw . . . A True
Rancher . . . I Miss the Farm Very Much . . . A Bunch of Hicks . . . Born in a
Sod House . . . High in the Pecking Order . . . Politics and Ploughing . . . An
Evening's Fun . . . Last of the Big Spenders . . . Who's in Charge Here? . . .
Respect for Mother Nature . . . An Awful Character . . . Stone Houses . . .
Just a Two-Holer . . . Full of Fun . . . Grandfather's Kettle . . . If It's Not One
Thing, It's Another . . . Moonlighting . . . I Hated the Farm . . . Deep in the
Hay . . . Dousing . . . Always Look for the Best . . . A Little Dip . . . A Wonder-
ful Feeling . . . Very Efficient with Her Work . . . A Lesson*

I travelled fifteen thousand miles throughout Canada to meet
and interview the Canadians whose memories of farming and
ranching make up this book. I had a glorious time. A young woman
talked to me glowingly about her days on an isolated homestead in
the Peace River country. In St. John, New Brunswick, an Irishman
with a lilting brogue told me the tale of the Phantom Farmboy
Skater. On Vancouver Island, on a farm still rocky but brilliant
with spring flowers, an Englishman who had been here for decades
but kept a bit of England going on the Island gave me a brisk
account of his misadventures with a buzz saw. An old-time
rancher drawled out yarns in a dowdy hotel room in High River,
Alberta. Writer Joan Finnegan recounted without a pause her
memories of herself and her family on an Ottawa Valley farm. A
group of young people in Saskatoon remembered their recent yes-
terdays on prairie farms, and a husky young Manitoban explained
how he used to make moonshine. Peggy and Harry Holmes in
Edmonton regaled me with an hilarious, detailed account of
homesteading in northern Alberta (a Guards Officer and a beautiful bride fresh from England stumbling into one incredible adven-
ture after another on the frontier).

1

I keep thinking about them. One I've forgotten to mention is Peggy Sproul, who came from a farm near Viscount, Saskatchewan. I met her when she was working in a campaign office during a political election in New Brunswick. She gave me an enchanting and poetic account of her days on the farm, and she talked to me for an hour and a half and never repeated a story.

I talked with people all across the country: retired ranchers in Calgary from ranches scattered throughout the foothills recalling the old days; young people in Vancouver and Edmonton trading stories from recent years; old-timers in Goderich and Chesley, Bruce County and Glengarry County in Ontario and from around my own home base at Tottenham, Ontario, telling what the farm has meant to them; a group of men and women from the Newcastle and Chatham area in New Brunswick, staying late in the evening in my motel room, laughing and laughing as they reeled off stories; a sturdy young man in Vancouver telling me of almost drowning as a child in the well on his father's farm near Quebec City; a gnarled farmer near Alberton, Prince Edward Island, explaining about digging mud for the public (you'll find out about that later in the book); a fruit farmer in the Okanagan recalling the tough early days of one disaster after another until finally he had his orchard established — on and on they went, in that fine articulate style at which Canadians excel but to which they will seldom admit.

They talked about everything that happened on the farm or ranch. Everything. At one point, I broke their stories down into a hundred and seven categories, but as I taped more and more people, I gave up trying to keep track of the categories.

This first chapter is a preview of the rest of the book, and is made up mostly of shorter pieces. I just wish I could tell you about all the people I met. That, of course, is impossible; but, still, you'll meet a good many of them in the next three hundred or so pages. I hope you'll be as taken with them as I was.

THE NEW HOUSE "We always wanted, and talked about, a new house. 'Is this going to be the year for a new house?'

And so the crops would come up good in the Spring: you can't believe how it is to watch crops and know that everything depends on what happens to what's out there in the fields. So we would watch the crops. And if by the end of June things were going well, and we had rain when we should have . . . if into the middle of July it hadn't hailed and the rain had still come, and it was progressing beautiful, a few cautious words would be said about maybe this'd be the year for the house.

And then all through July you would watch the sky because it often either got very dry, and things dried up then, or it would hail. And you'd have to watch the sky.

Then into August, we would have to watch because we usually got frost. That's the trouble with the Peace River country: usually the frost comes about two weeks earlier than the rest of Alberta. And so there would be that terrible tension of 'Is it going to freeze tonight? Is the wheat far enough along that the kernels won't be too badly affected by the frost?'

But inevitably the frost would come. And we would say to Dad, 'It wasn't bad, was it, Dad? It wasn't bad.' But we would know by looking at the garden where the potatoes were all limp and everything was all sort of brown . . . we would know it was bad. But we wanted to say, 'No, it wasn't.'

And so that's how our summers would go. And then by the end of August we'd know, no, it wouldn't be a house this year."

THE BARKING DOG "I was working for the Power Commission at one time and I had occasion to call at farmhouses in the course of my work, and I found the farmers in New Brunswick exceptionally hospitable. For instance, you'd go there during a cold winter day and they'd practically hem you in and make you stay for a hot meal.

One day I was in this farmhouse and to show you the humour of them, I was sitting there eating my meal and it was one lovely meal. They served the best, I must tell you that—just the old staple food, which is the healthiest you could get. However, while I was eating, this dog kept yapping at my elbow, and he made such a clamour that I said to the farmer:

'What the heck is wrong with that dog?' And the farmer laughed and he said:

'Oh , don't mind him, he always barks like that when anyone is eating out of his dish.'"

ON THE BUZZ SAW "The doctor tells me I should live for another twenty years so long as I don't give up my politics. But in those days — this was '46 or '47 — we used to saw our wood in four-foot lengths and then we'd get the buzz saw to cut them in three pieces. That meant two cuts on the buzz saw.

Well, this particular day there was a man next door was helping, and I had gloves on, and I said:

'Now for God's sake, don't touch anything on that machine until I've taken my gloves off.'

But before I had time to take my gloves off, he had put his foot on something, God knows what it was, and I had lost my right hand. But the wife was away, and the daughter was away, and we were two hundred yards from the house, and I had to walk to the house, and I could see the hand hanging by one tendon, and I got to the house and my daughter-in-law was here and I shouted at her:

'Bring me a sheet and don't argue, bring it.'

And so she brought it in and I wrapped it up, and in those days there was no such thing as an ambulance, and the only thing you could do was go to the police station and they had a nurse there, and she was supposed to do what was necessary, which was to put a tourniquet on me. But unfortunately for me or for her, I don't know which, she fainted, and they had to take me into the hospital, and they fixed me up that night."

A TRUE RANCHER "This man, he was working for my brother-in-law, who was milking cows at this time, and he couldn't bear the thought of milking cows. Of course a true rancher wouldn't. And he used to, after milking, get a basin of soap and water, and carefully wash down the legs of his blue jeans to get any bit of milk off them. He couldn't stand the thought of cows."

I MISS THE FARM VERY MUCH "I'm Joan Finnegan, and my mother, May Horner, grew up on a farm about a mile off the Ottawa River on the Quebec side, just above Shawville, in a little place called Glendon Centre, and I've spent as much time as I possibly could there. I adored my grandfather, and every morning, the minute his foot hit the floor at five o'clock, I was up because I knew the day held wonders.

And my grandmother would say: 'Oh, child, why does she never sleep in?'

Why would you sleep in on a day like that? I mean, if the day had started at two in the morning, I would have been up. And I would go down and we would sit at the big, long pine table in the kitchen and we would have our oatmeal porridge with dark brown sugar and cream. And then I would go out with him.

It was a huge farm, it had seven hundred acres and there were seventy head of horses at one time when I was a child there. It was a mixed farm. There was a barn for cattle, and a barn for horses, and a barn for pigs, and a granary, and a whole complex of buildings. We used to swing out of the hayloft, and I've often wondered how we weren't killed. You know, we would climb up the ladder and then just jump down feet and feet and feet from the rafters into the hay, endlessly.

We were allowed to a certain extent to help with some of the chores. They'd let us feed the pigs maybe, and that kind of thing, so we were sort of useful, but kind of underfoot.

The farm was real. You know, you got your feet in the manure; you got your hands on the fresh-laid eggs—they were warm. You could feel the grain in the granary; you could go down to the creek and sink your feet in mud, and it was cold, and you know on a July day it was gorgeous, and everything about it was just real.

My grandmother had a cupboard off the kitchen where she kept all her spices and her flour, and you could feel it and smell it. It was a great big bin; you could put your hands in it. You weren't supposed to, but you could. And down in the basement you could put your hands down in the sand and feel the carrots and the turnips, and everything was there.

I miss the farm very much. I would really like to go back to the land—I think I probably will. Probably I would go back to the land because I want to become self-sufficient in terms of producing, and I want my children to have some land because, you know, that's one thing I want to give them, and also because I know, looking back at it, that that is the place of creativity and tranquility."

BORN IN A SOD HOUSE   "I was talking to a woman one time, a very nicely dressed woman, and she said that she had lived in a sod house. I was taking her out and talking about sod buildings. In fact she said she had been born in one. She said it had been raining all day and the roof was leaking all over the place. She said they had to hold an umbrella over her mother while she was being born."

A BUNCH OF HICKS   "I think the thing I appreciated most was when we were playing ball against a city team and they'd bring out a bus to the country town that I used to play ball at. And they'd be calling us a bunch of farmers and a bunch of country hicks. And it just so happened that we probably had one of the best ball teams in the country at that time. Beating those city kids about ten or twelve or eighteen to nothing in these ball tournaments and provincial playdowns was really satisfying. I never really felt inferior to the city people at all. And I don't think I've ever really thought about it much, except for them coming out and calling us a bunch of country bumpkins or something. And then being able to whip the pants off them."

HIGH IN THE PECKING ORDER   "When we moved into the house, we had our settlers' effects. We'd brought my wedding gifts from England, which were no good at all on the farm, you know, and the dishes we had were Royal Doulton. And the chickens had to eat out of Royal Doulton whether they liked it or not."

POLITICS AND PLOUGHING   "When a man's out there ploughing with two horses and the walking plough, or three horses on the riding plough, or if you're sitting in the tractor and the radio going, and the heater going, you're still thinking about something else all the time. You watch that furrow to see that you keep in it, and you keep looking around to see that the furrow is turned the way you want it to be, but you're continually thinking about something that's going on, especially a man in political life. He has so many things to think about that he is continually planning all the time.

And I can remember when I first started into politics that my wife said if I spent as much time thinking about the farm as I did about politics, she'd be a rich woman."

AN EVENING'S FUN "Do you remember, Olive, when we used to get together, oh, maybe twenty-five, thirty-five of us for an evening and play cards and sing in homes? One weekend it would be at your family's home, the next weekend at ours. We had wonderful times. Singing was a means of getting together in community gatherings, and contests and games and singing provided an evening's fun."

LAST OF THE BIG SPENDERS "The rumour that designates farmers as penny pinchers I think is all wrong. I don't think there's a better spender in the country than a farmer, providing he has the money to spend. He won't necessarily get into a big debauchery or something like that, he won't do that. But he will go out and have himself a good time, and he probably will maintain a fairly expensive hobby that city people couldn't even look at.

As a matter of fact, at the present time one of the more popular events that is taking place is tractor pulls, and some of these men have got as much as $30,000 tied up in a so-called modified tractor that isn't good for one other thing but going to fairs and events and pulling a weight. And that's all it's good for. You couldn't call this man a penny pincher when he's got $30,000 invested; and even if he got first prize at every event he went in, he wouldn't have any more than enough money to buy his gas and tires."

WHO'S IN CHARGE HERE? "I've heard it said that if you're driving through the country and you see a barn and all the outbuildings in real good condition and painted up, well, the man is the boss there. But if it's the house that's all in good condition, well, it's the woman that's the boss on that farm."

RESPECT FOR MOTHER NATURE   "I was raised on a farm in southern Alberta, close to the foothills, about eight miles from the U.S. border. Our farm was a small, mixed farm right in the southern area of the province. You could say between Whiskey Gap and Mountain View.

We raised cattle and hogs and a certain amount of grain. It was rolling land, very hilly and difficult to farm.

I guess looking back now on being raised on the farm, I can see advantages and disadvantages to it. As far as advantages go, I think that it broadens a person's scope very much. You get a touch of carpentry. You get a touch of mechanics. You learn a certain love for machinery and animals. You're in closer touch with nature, possibly, than your counterparts in the city.

Yet for myself, too, I learned that nature can be pretty harsh and cruel, too. It can be beautiful, but when your bread and butter depends on it, you learn a certain amount of respect for Mother Nature: it's much different from having a garden in your backyard."

AN AWFUL CHARACTER   "This Sandy was an awful character. After the house was built, he left home and went to western Canada and he wondered how much his family thought of him. So he had a letter sent back home saying that he had passed away and the body would be coming in on the train at Chesley at midnight. So the neighbours gathered at the old stone house and they sent a team into the train to get the body off the train when it came in at midnight. The train came in, but Sandy slipped off the other side of the train, and when there was nobody there, the team and men came home, and they were all sitting in the stone house mourning about the loss of Sandy and about one o'clock Sandy walks in the front door. He wondered if they thought enough of him to give him a decent burial."

STONE HOUSES   "In Bruce County, there are a lot of stone houses in certain areas. Now on the line that we live on, the seventh of Elderslie, there are several stone houses now. You can go to other lines where you hardly see a stone house, but I guess we have so many because we had a lot of stone, and stone masons lived in this area. There are not too many stone houses built today because it's a lost art.

The advantage of stone houses is they're nice-looking structures. They're cool in the summer; they have high ceilings. The ceilings in this house are 10½ feet high, some of them. The disadvantages in this day and age of an energy crisis is they're darn hard to heat. It costs us close to seven hundred dollars to heat this house with oil. As I say, there's eight bedrooms here, but we don't furnish them all. Some of them are closed off, but with big rooms and big halls your heat escapes on you.

I sometimes wish this house was in the city of Toronto or Montreal—it would be worth a fortune and I could retire."

JUST A TWO-HOLER   "And behind the house was the outhouse, which we had to go out to in all kinds of weather. Myself being younger, maybe I didn't always have to go out there, but usually I did, and we had lots of catalogues out there and you would tear a page out and rub it in your hands and make it nice and soft. And a special treat was to get the little orange papers that used to come on apples, in the crates of apples and crates of oranges that we used to get; and we used to take them out there, lay them all out flat and put them in piles in the outhouse, and this was a special treat because they were so soft.

It was just a two-holer, and it was not too far from the house. It was very cold in the winter time. I can remember getting all bundled up and going out there and, oh . . . I don't know how we did it. I don't know how the older people did it—it was so cold. And I can remember it was all frozen down below. You didn't have to worry about the smell in the wintertime because it was frozen solid as a rock. I can't remember ice on the seat . . . oh, I can remember putting the paper on the seat to sit on, probably it would make it a little warmer to be able to sit on it. I can remember putting paper on the seat."

FULL OF FUN   "Well, I would say that in the West there were a few characters; of course a frontier attracts characters, and Jack

Morton was certainly one of them. He was one of these ex-
hibitionists who drank a great deal and was full of fun.

He took a badger into a restaurant on Ninth Avenue once and put
it on the counter, and the badger ran all the way down the counter
throwing off all the dishes, got to the other end and looked down
and couldn't see anywhere to go, turned around and came all the
way back and into the sack. And this is the kind of thing that Jack
Morton did."

GRANDFATHER'S KETTLE   "Over the years they added different modern conveniences to the house, and one of them was quite a
nice modern bathroom with toilet and bathtub and everything; but
I can remember my grandfather, when it came time to shave in the
morning — the hot water that came out of the hot water tap somehow was not quite the same as the hot water that came out of the
kettle on the big range in the kitchen. And therefore, every morning, instead of taking the hot water out of the tap, he used to go
down to the kitchen and get his jug full of hot water out of the kettle
on the stove and take it back up to shave, and that was just his way.
My grandfather certainly wasn't going to have anything to do with
the new-fangled plumbing."

IF IT'S NOT ONE THING, IT'S ANOTHER   "The one incident I
can recall was the time the young bull mistook my brother for a
young heifer. It went after him, and it jumped him and give him a
pretty rough time. And I can recall my father was standing around
laughing at my brother's predicament, trying to get out from under
this bull.

The other story had to do with the same brother. He had to do
most of the chores and milking and cleaning out the barn. And I
recall the time he went to clean the udders on the cow. Instead of
going in from the side, for some reason this time he went in from
the back, and I can just recall watching him feel that first plop on
top of his head—he had a big hat on, eh? And I can just recall seeing
the cow lift its tail and watching this thing drop. He just froze. And
the stuff piled up on top of his head before he had the nerve to get
out from under there."

MOONLIGHTING "One lady, she always seen that the potatoes were planted by the moon and they were taken up by the moon, and all the planting, and she practically dictated the procedure on the farm, and it was all done by the moon. But no, as far as the rank and file of the farmers were concerned, they never paid a darn bit of attention to it. Her potatoes weren't any better than anybody else's, they didn't taste any better, and they wasn't any better crop."

I HATED THE FARM "I married a farmer and we farmed eight hundred acres near Harris, Saskatchewan. It was wheat and mixed farming and we had livestock. I hated the farm. My parents were city people and I was always more or less city-oriented. But, anyway, we lived on the farm there and we had to make do the best we could.

I hated the farm every minute I was ever on it. I hated the fact that we didn't have too many close neighbours. Our farm wasn't isolated, but it was in a low place and there were trees all round and you couldn't see any of the neighbours. And that was one thing that bothered me because I came from a big family and I'd never been alone in my life until I was married, not even in broad daylight. And then it seemed I was alone so much of the time, and that was the main thing I hated about the farming after I was married. I thought plenty about leaving the farm but I didn't do it.

The work was terrific, you know. Our farm was just the right size so we needed a lot of help, and we couldn't afford it of course because we were just starting to farm, and it was just a little bit too big for us to manage by ourselves, so we really had quite a job trying to manage our farm, and I hated all that hard work. I disliked most of all the heavy lifting — carrying pails of water — and being tied down, that was another thing I hated.

We live in Saskatoon now and, believe me, I haven't missed that farm."

DEEP IN THE HAY "I think the thing that I remember most as a young boy on the farm is that because we were close to a small community, the barn and the hayloft in our barn was sort of the community recreation facilities for all the kids in the community.

We used to have endless hours of fun in the old haymow—building forts, and swinging from hay-cables, and falling into piles of straw. We had great fun in building very intricate tunnels and forts deep into the hay. And then when the second crop would be piled on top we used to be twenty or thirty feet down."

DOUSING   "As far as dousing is concerned, it's absolutely impossible for me to detect any underground water, but those that do will lead you to the inevitable conclusion there has to be some type of power there. One of the tests given is to put your finger under the wand and feel the immense amount of pressure that comes on this wand through this man's hands.

Many of these dousers use either a forked stick or a piece of clock spring or a piece of No. 9 wire, and always there is a point which is in a horizontal position. And when they pass over a water vein, this point will turn down toward the earth and point straight down. And one of the tests we gave it was to put our hand under the point of it as they crossed a known source of water, and there you can feel the pressure. To me it would be inconsistent to say that they were turning it with their hands. No man would have that amount of grip on a piece of No. 9 wire—too fine.

I have seen dousers with a willow branch, a forked willow branch, hold it so tightly that the bark twisted on the wood of the branch, in their hands."

ALWAYS LOOK FOR THE BEST   "You like to see the crops grow. Of course when you plant, you always have a vision of a huge crop—it's always going to be a grand crop. It doesn't always turn out that way. I think it almost necessary in farming to have that belief anyway that the good Lord is going to fill your bins for you, and if it doesn't happen, why then it will the next year, and that's the way it's been all my life. We always look for the best and, oh, pretty near all the time, we get it too. It's been wonderful, if one thing isn't good, another thing is, and it all evens up.

I've seen years when the grain crop would be very poor, and we had a neighbour down the road said:

'Well, there's one thing to be thankful for, the threshing bill won't be so big this year.'

So you've always got something to be thankful for anyway; usually if the grain is no good, why the hay is good or the corn is good or something like that. And there's always something to compensate, at least in this country where it's mixed farming. Now on the prairies or some place like that, where it's all grain farming, if you lost the grain crop, you lose everything. But not in Ontario here, where there is a mixture of crops, and it's very seldom that you lose everything. So in that respect, it's not too bad a place to be, and I've enjoyed every year that I've farmed.

I never did feel as if it was a burden to get up and work. The nastier the job, I was always the happier when I got it done, so it compensated that way, and I think I worked harder at a job I didn't like than one I did like, such as picking rocks or something like that —going around the field, lifting up these rocks that you plough up, you know, and they seem to grow, they seem to come every year. I've been picking them for the last sixty years and they're still around yet. But when you've got a field picked, why you know that's finished her up for another year at least. That always made me happy to get it done. I think I'd work harder at a job like that when I was younger — of course now I'm getting close to my eighties, and that is slowing me up some—but I'd work harder at an unpleasant job than I would at a pleasant one."

A LITTLE DIP "These sheep had to be dipped, on account of ticks. And we had a dip vat rigged up, and we were dippin' a thousand head of sheep. And it was hot, hard work, and they were razzin' me because they always said you had to dip the herder along with the sheep or you wouldn't get rid of the ticks. And, by golly, when I was pushing the last sheep in, I fell in. But after a thousand sheep had gone through it, well, it was a little thick."

A WONDERFUL FEELING "It's a wonderful feeling to be snow-bound in the midst of a real winter storm. Your family seems to come so much closer together. They have opportunities to play family games. It's a time when you can read, knowing that you won't be interrupted; it's a time when it's fairly important that all members of the family work together to protect what you have, food and stock; the cattle have to be carefully cared for — the water supply is tricky."

VERY EFFICIENT WITH HER WORK   "We lived on a party line and we had a neighbour who ... I guess she must have been very efficient with her work, because she had a lot of time to spend listening on the phone. And she was a bit hard of hearing, and if she didn't hear it she would say:
   'What was that you said?'
   This got to be a real joke throughout the community, but it was taken for granted that she listened on the phone, and so that was just accepted.
   It was a big joke—but you'd repeat it, yes."

A LESSON   "I remember a story that my husband tells about a driver they had, which had a bad habit of just stopping when she thought she didn't want to go any more. And you could try as you like, you couldn't get that animal to go. And someone told him that the good idea would be to build a little fire under it, and that would teach her a lesson.
   So of course, having tried almost everything else, he decided to try that, too. He made a little fire. But the horse moved ahead only long enough to have the fire under the buggy instead of under the horse."

TWO

The Weather Controlled Our Lives

The Weather Controlled Our Lives . . . No Salvaging of Anything . . . Better Luck Next Year . . . There's a Flood Coming . . . Ice on Their Noses . . . Hail in the Butter . . . A Really Dumb Thing To Do . . . The Joys of Farming . . . An Act of God . . . Gumbo . . . Darkness at Noon . . . A Visit from a Tornado . . . Sophisticated City Fellows

I t would be possible to put together an entire book about the effect of climatic disasters on farm life. When I was travelling across Canada interviewing, I found that stories poured out of people about blizzards and tornadoes, sandstorms and floods, fires caused by lightning, frost damage to crops, snow half-way up the telephone poles, and a range of natural disasters that encompassed the spectrum of human experience.

The opposite side of the coin, of course, is a child lying in the grass in a state of innocent delight, watching the scudding cumulus clouds pass across an immense sky.

But on the farm you watched the weather carefully: it could be breath-takingly glorious and tranquil or it could be an uncontrollable demon that descended on the farm as if its special fury had been saved for that little group of people alone. Fine weather and enough rain at regular intervals could mean good crops and prosperity; bad weather — a late frost, a four-week wet spell or a four-minute hailstorm — could wipe out a year's crop, and a year's hopes and dreams.

15

THE WEATHER CONTROLLED OUR LIVES "We were very aware of the sky all the time because it meant changes in the weather. And the weather controlled our lives. Completely. In the summertime if it looked like rain, well then certain things had to be done, and certain things had to be brought in. The wash had to be hauled in in a hurry if it looked like it was going to rain. And then you had to fear for hail. So you'd be watching the sky. We were terrific sky-watchers always, and usually on a functional basis again, although in our early days we used to do the things that kids do — you know, lie around and watch the clouds and figure out what the shapes are."

NO SALVAGING OF ANYTHING "Most tobacco growers are a different type of an individual. I don't know how I got involved in it, but I liked it. They're an excitable type of person and lovers of hard work, I must say, because it's about the hardest thing you can get into in farming. It shows no shortcuts, and if you do, well you're short at the end of the year.

I think this applies to any farming. There is no shortcut to farming. It's tricky. You have to become a professional. You've got to know how to handle a greenhouse and prepare and get the fields ready for planting, and the fertilization has a tremendous bearing on your crop at the end. Too much can keep it green; too little will immature it. And in the harvest time, you've got all your eggs in one basket and you're working on borrowed time, from the time you start your harvest. You start about the fifteenth of August or maybe earlier, it depends on what the season has been prior to that, how it's grew it and got it ready. If you've had a cold, wet summer, then you're later. If it's been a good warm summer with adequate rainfalls, then your crop comes in earlier, so you start the harvesting earlier. But if it's been a bad summer, you've got all your eggs in one basket and it's nothing to lose twenty thousand dollars in a year. Frost is a constant threat to you.

Normally you start to plant tobacco in around the twentieth of May, twenty-fourth of May, and lots of farmers that have twenty-five acres plant it and lose it with frost. Of course you have your greenhouse there that you sow the first part of April — if you lose your crop out in the field, you just can't go out and say:

'Well, I'll buy some more plants.'

That greenhouse only produces so much, and if everybody is running into the same unfortunate frost, well, then you've got a problem. I've had bad luck in over eighteen years, and yet fortunate too. I've had frost in the spring without too much planted, maybe about eight or ten acres, and have been able to replant it and finish my crop.

And I've had the frost in the fall when I just had a very few kilns on, maybe eight or ten kilns and the frost would just wipe the whole crop out overnight . . . well, not overnight, a matter of minutes in the morning the frost sets in, and you go out there and your whole crop is ruined—no salvaging of anything. You don't know what to do, whether to run or stay with it, because first of all, you nine times out of ten will be into the bank for about ten or twelve thousand dollars by this time, and you're hoping for a carryover. So you start into the next year's crop with maybe a ten or twelve thousand dollar overdraft, plus this year's expenses coming up, so you know this year, all you're doing is to pay off your overdraft, if you can do that. And this goes on and on and you're up and down and it's a very tricky operation.

You either come out a wealthy man out of tobacco or you come out with just what you've got on your back, and that's about the size of it with your profits, your losses, and your misfortunes."

BETTER LUCK NEXT YEAR   "I practice law in Toronto now, but I grew up on a farm in Dearwent, Alberta, which is a hundred and thirty miles northeast of Edmonton. One of the most vivid things I remember on the farm was the sand storms they had in the post-Depression years from about 1935 to 1939, and it was a period that for days or even months the sky would be black with sand. You couldn't see more than ten or fifteen feet away from you. You couldn't see the sun in daylight. There was dust everywhere — in the kitchen cupboards, in your pillows, in the bed, in the water and food, in your clothes, in your shoes, in your ears and your eyes — and there was nothing you could do to get it out.

These sandstorms were so fierce and continuous, mostly because of the dry weather, that there were sand drifts across the roads from one rural fence to the other, and the drifts would be anywhere from two to six feet high, so you couldn't use these drifted roads. The farmers would cut the fence in and cut into the neighbour's field and drive along the field beside the drifted road and cut back in there a mile or two down the road.

These sandstorms never did really get to me. The reason for it probably is my Ukranian background — they came down as pioneers and opened the land and settled on it, and they were hardy, hard-working, patient people, and I guess they passed it on to their children. If it didn't work out that year, they would say:

'Better luck next year.'"

THERE'S A FLOOD COMING "We had just finished cutting a little field of registered oats, and it was stooked, and we didn't have such a heavy rain, but east of us, along the Rosa River, they had a downpour, and the morning after the rain somebody phoned me from that way and they said:

'What's your river like there?'

And I said: 'Well it's not bad.'

And they said: 'Oh, I hear there's a flood coming.'

I went out and I told my husband, so we stood out on a hill and we could hear the roar of water. It came down the river and it came down a little creek, ran through the farm, and we walked up on dry land and we didn't walk a quarter of a mile, but before we got back, we were walking in water about a foot deep. And after that flash flood passed we had one stook, no, we had three stooks left out of approximately five hundred in that field of registered oats. It was only a small field of registered seed for the next year.

The rest all went down the Rosa River. And Mennonites, who had just come to the country about a year before, they crossed the river and they caught all those stooks that went down and threw them out on the bank at the Main Street. They didn't get them all, but they got a lot. And there was fields around the river that that happened to, more than ours."

ICE ON THEIR NOSES   "On our farm at Virden, Manitoba, that year spring had been early with most of the snow gone and the sloughs full with water. Now this morning dawned cloudy and windy with a skiffle of snow in the air, but my brother and I ran across the fields to school. We had a mile to go. We just got close to school, when suddenly a furious wind and snowstorm broke. My father phoned the school to tell the teacher to let school out, and to phone the parents of the children who were there and to advise them to come to meet the children, because he was concerned with the fury of this spring storm.

Dad turned up at school in about half an hour with the team and the sleigh. Going home the first half mile was okay; we were on a road and it was fenced at one side, so we were able to get down to our own property half a mile away. Now visibility was absolutely minimal; you couldn't see much more than ten feet ahead of you, but we made our own fields and got into a gate and started across the fields the last half mile towards home.

Now we had to cross three fields to get home. We made the first field without any problems. Crossing the second field the visibility became practically zero, and my father turned wrong.

My brother and I told him he had turned wrong, and he insisted he hadn't. Subsequently we came across our own sleigh tracks — we were going in a circle. So then we really were worried. It would be about ten above perhaps or zero (Fahrenheit), but the big thing was the intensity and fury of the storm, the wind was furious, it was carrying sleet and snow.

Now the horses' eyes and noses would freeze over. This doesn't seem possible, and I wouldn't have believed it, but it is true. The horses would fall to the ground right on their sides, gasping for breath. Dad would have to get out and take his fist and hit them right over the nose and the nostrils and break the ice, and then they would start breathing, and then he would go to their eyes and hit with the flat of his hand and break the ice that was surrounding their eyes, just like they were looking out a window. It was horrible.

They would eventually get to their feet as soon as they got their wind, and stagger on a few hundred yards and then they'd go down

again, and this process would be repeated again and again. It was
terrifying, I can tell you, it haunts me even today. Finally our sleigh
got stuck. The horses were lying down and this time they were
absolutely exhausted. We knew we could go no further, so
Dad said:

'We're going to have to unhitch the horses; we can't leave them
out here.'

And I wondered if we were going to be out there too. And
suddenly the storm lifted for a few feet, and I saw a fence and an old
plough, and I knew where we were, and I pointed it out to Dad. So
he got the horses to their feet, unhooked them, and we started along
the fence; we came back to the gate, and then we had one more field
to cross.

Now this was our pasture, and here there wasn't any stubble to
hold the snow, and the wind there hit us with a terrific fury. My
brother, who was then about eight years of age, he got cold, so my
father took off his coat, and put it on my brother, and of course my
brother would step on the coat every couple of steps, fall on his face
and cry, so you can imagine the problem that my father had. Now
I'm not trying to make a hero of myself. I was old enough that I
didn't cry. My main concern was for my younger brother.

The horses were in a little better shape because when they were
loose and not pulling anything, there wasn't quite the strain on
them. I've heard people say:

'You know, if you get lost in the storm, give your horse his head
and he will take you home.' As far as our horses were concerned,
they'd never read that story. All they wanted to do was to turn their
rumps to the storm and wait it out. If they had their behinds
towards the storm, they could breathe easily, they could see, and
they didn't want a thing to do with going into that storm—which
we had to do. We had to go north—right into the teeth of the storm.
But we did get to our own barn, with my brother being dragged
along, falling and crying, and the horses wanting to turn around.
We got into the barn; we knew we couldn't possibly get out to feed
the stock that night, so while we were there we fed all of the stock—
horses, cattle, pigs, and hens. We also knew there was no way we
could water them, so we cut blocks of snow and put it in the

mangers and left it there. We knew it would melt and they would get some moisture from that.

There were about a hundred yards to go to the house, so we started out for it. Now this wind was blowing and we couldn't see, but we knew the general direction of the house. I saw it loom up in front of me, but my brother went right past it, and he would have been going yet, I suppose. So I ran after him and grabbed him, and between me and my father — he was terror-stricken — we got him back and got him into the house, otherwise he would have been blown away by the fury of the wind.

About ten miles away, two or three people lost their lives in that storm — the worst Manitoba blizzard I've ever known."

HAIL IN THE BUTTER "I want to tell you about the hailstorm. This was really something. One day we had the table all set and butter was on the table and everything, and the hail was pounding on this great big window by the table so hard it broke right through the window. And they were as big as moth balls. I can remember them landing in the butter. And they were landing all over the table and bouncing around on the floor, and they broke right through the window — and that's really hard when they broke right through the window."

A REALLY DUMB THING TO DO "One Sunday afternoon we were hauling some junk out from the yard, and it was early spring, and the wind was blowing from the south, and the grass was fairly dry, and we had a great big pit out near the edge of the field that we used to haul all our junk into and burn.

And I took it out there and I lit it on fire and I drove the tractor back to the yard. And just as I got back I thought, well, gee whiz that was a really dumb thing to do, that blaze is going to go. So sure enough by the time I looked back it had already started to run through the grass.

And it just so happened that this pit was on the south side of the farm and so all the buildings were downwind from the fire. So off went the fire and I went out there with an old sack and some pails of water and tried putting that fire out.

It was getting up towards the barn. And the only thing that really saved the farm was the old tractor trail that used to run out to the field past the barn. It hit that and it didn't jump across, and basically the whole farm was saved.

But the thought that runs through my mind now looking back at that is, there's probably nothing more frightening than a fire that you can't stop. It just goes, and the smoke is choking you, and there's that helpless feeling of a brush fire or a prairie grass-fire running. And you hit it with a sack and it just seems to flame up more, and you're there by yourself and you've got no help, and you can't do anything at all to stop it. It's a frightening experience."

THE JOYS OF FARMING   "I started in '28 and I farmed for fourteen years and never got a crop. It started in with the dust storms, about three or four years dust storms; then it started in with the grasshoppers; then after the grasshoppers were through, it started in with the rust. We went through all those years without anything, on a $14.40 cheque from the government to keep four of us for the month. We was hailed out two years in a row, never had a chance at all of getting ahead. We stuck it out, because the times would break if we stuck it out long enough, but it went fourteen years and it never did break."

AN ACT OF GOD   "When we were first married, we lived in a two-roomed shack, and when they hauled the grain in the wintertime, they hauled lumber out to build a house. Then in the spring, we had the house where we wanted and the cellar built, and in those days you didn't hire somebody to build the house, the neighbours all came in and helped build.

I remember my husband and some of the men got the horses onto this two-roomed shack and pulled it up close to the house site so I could make the meals and have everything ready for them there.

So this day the house was all built up, they had just gotten to the top of the roof, and I was in this shack, oh, perhaps a hundred yards from the new house, and I felt the house shake and I wondered what it was and shut the door and the window. And then it shook that way and I looked out, and I saw this cyclone coming, and do you know I guess it was just an act of God, because it came between the house and where I was in this shack, and it moved the shack a bit, you know what I mean, shook it, shook the dishes off the walls and that, but didn't hurt anything . . . anybody.

The buggy was out in the yard, and we always kept our chickens fenced in, six feet high, and I saw this thing lift the buggy right up over the top of the fence right into the chicken yard. And then as it went along further, there was a shed roofed . . . you know a shed roof they built for the cattle. It took the roof right off that. That would be about . . . oh, perhaps it would be thirty or forty feet long —it took that right off and carried it maybe fifty feet.

There was a horse tied in there, and always after that, any time you went to put the saddle on her, if you put your hand on her back like that, she would crouch right down to the ground.

The chickens got scared enough too, I guess, and they didn't lay any eggs—that's for sure. They took a rest for a few days."

GUMBO "In the Red River Valley here is what they call gumbo. It's clay—it's not the yellow clay, it's black clay—and when it's wet, it's very sticky. I've seen cars going down the road, and it would pick up and jam in the fenders so that you'd have to stop and clean it out so the wheels could turn.

In the fall, if you were hauling grain with wagons, the wagon wheels were three-and-a-half inches wide and they would cut a ditch in the road three-and-a-half inches wide, and I can remember that we bought a car in 1917 that had four-inch tires on it, and when they run in this three-and-a-half-inch rut of the clay, baked just like bricks, it would chew the side of the tires right out. A set of tires would only last one year. Then you'd have to buy new tires.

One fall in harvest time, it was so wet that they couldn't have the machines on the field. They would take them on the grass on the side of the road and set the machine there and haul the sheaves out. They threshed as long as they could, and then they quit, and the rest of the grain was stacked and wasn't threshed until Christmastime, after the ground froze. The grain was all right, it was the ground was so wet you couldn't get on it.

Another year I remember I saw an awful lot of what they called stoneboats—it's just a flat drag for hauling stones off the field in the spring. But the field was so wet this fall they couldn't use wheels, and they'd got two posts with a little bit of a curl up in the front for a runner, nailed a few planks across it, and that's what they used to haul the sheaves from the stooks to the threshing machine in the harvest. The stoneboats were pulled by horses — it wasn't so wet that the horses couldn't walk around in it — but it was the wheels and the load that would sink in so because the ground was so soft.

Another fall we had flax and it was wet, too, and you couldn't drive the binder in the field. My father waited until the ground froze, then he got the blacksmith to put shoes on the horses with spikes in them for the horses to walk on the ice, and he cut the harrow teeth off short and bolted them to the bull wheel of the binder so it would turn, and that's the way he harvested the flax.

Heavy land, and it's hard to work, but it grows good crops and it holds moisture for a long time, much longer than the sandy soil would. I've seen some years, if the season is dry, the wheat roots would grow long and reach the moisture. They're always out looking for moisture, they'll go down and they can stand a good deal of drought after that. But another year maybe, when the plant is first growing, you have plenty of moisture, and the roots don't reach out to the same extent; and then if it gets dry after that, then your drought affects the plants much more than it would if they had been nurtured first under dry conditions."

DARKNESS AT NOON   "During the depression years in the thirties, this country was very dry, and we had dust storms that would last for days. On the ranch I have seen so much dust in the air that you would think it was nearly night, and the chickens would go to roost at four o'clock in the afternoon."

A VISIT FROM A TORNADO   "My mother phoned and she said:
'My God, we've had a tornado.'
And I said: 'What happened?'

And she said: 'It came through the yard, the machine shed is gone, the barn is gone, the pig barns are gone, and trees are gone.'

And I said: 'Mum, we'll be out in the morning.'

As it happened my husband was working down in Dryden, Ontario, at the time and I couldn't get hold of him. And Elmer, my brother, was out visiting and I got hold of him at two o'clock in the morning. His car wasn't working that well, so I said:

'Okay, we'll take our car.' At that time our car was just a year old, so we packed the kids in the car, and out to the farm we went. We left Winnipeg about six in the morning and we got out there at eight, and it was quite a terrible sight.

The combine had been taken. The tornado had come into the yard, had left the yard and come back in again, and my brother had about sixty head of cattle in the yard at that time, and it didn't hurt one cow, one chicken, one pig. No animals were killed, but it had taken all the hydro wires down, and the previous night these wires had been sparking. The wind had taken the combine out of the machine shed, brought it across about five hundred feet over to the house, and had twisted this combine so that it was not repairable. It had also taken the roof off the machine shed, over the top of the house, and laid it on the garden. The garden was wrecked. The pig barn and the barn itself and the other buildings — the roofs were either taken off, or they were smashed, but they were a complete disaster. They were not usable.

And it took the doors very neatly off of the hinges of the upstairs bedrooms and laid them on the bed. The wind had done this. And it had also brought branches in from the trees, and mud. The eye of the tornado had picked up water with this dirt and as it come into the house like this, it put mud all over, and it seemed to imbed it into the wood and plaster. It was such a force, I suppose, that it just imbedded it, and when you opened the cupboards up, which had been closed, the dishes were just literally full of mud, muck, even leaves were in there, and it was just unbelievable how this could happen and the house stood. The only thing I think was wrong with the house, I believe they had to put new shingles on, and the chimney was leaking. And right in the middle of the yard, my brother had a truck full of bales, and it never touched one piece of hay on that truck of bales. It stood there through the whole thing.

They seen this funnel coming and realized it was a tornado, and my mother was watching it as she was doing the supper dishes and she said to my brother:

'It's going away. It's not going to bother us. It hasn't done a thing.'

It came from the southwest, the funnel came into the yard; it went back again out of an opening in the trees which we had to the west, and it veered to the north, and my mother said:

'Thank God it's gone.'

And she was washing dishes at the sink at the time with the window above the sink, and the second time she looked up, the thing came back into the yard again, the funnel which is smoke, mud, you name it, and she said:

'Oh my God, Harold, it's back in the yard.'

And he said: 'Down in the basement we go.'

And as soon as they got into the basement, they heard crash, boom, and this hissing, which was almost like a jet motor when it's revving up, and it lasted about two minutes and it was over.

There was three of them in the basement, my brother, a brother-in-law, and my mother. The first thing that my brother said when this was all over, he said:

'I hope my cattle are okay,' because he had just taken over the farm two years previous, and then a thing like this should happen. And when he went out, everything was fine. There wasn't even a chicken that was killed.

So the next morning when we did come out there—it was eight o'clock when we got there — there was no power, there was nothing. I believe we had brought a barbecue so that we would have something to cook on, and by ten o'clock there was hordes and hordes and hordes of people coming. We finally had to take wire and wire off the yard so that they couldn't drive in, because the barn was sitting at a forty-five-degree angle and people were leaving their children go into these buildings, which could have collapsed at any time. So we made them get out. But they were walking across the garden, the little bit of garden that was left—they didn't think, what are these people going to do, they have nothing. But they never thought of this. They just kept walking and walking and walking, and finally we got very upset, and we took tractors and we took broken trees and put them across so that people couldn't get in.

I believe this happened about seven o'clock on Saturday night, July 20th, 1968 — I believe it was a Saturday. Fortunately it didn't take that long to clear up. My brother Elmer stayed out there and people from two hundred miles around came to help my brother, and in one week they had all the buildings rebuilt. They supplied the meals, the women, the wives of these men, who came from as far as Steinbach, Manitoba, which is two hundred miles from our place, from north, south, west, they had the whole thing built within one week. They supplied all the meals and everything. It was just wonderful.

This was the worst one as far as anyone could recall that ever hit that part of Manitoba."

SOPHISTICATED CITY FELLOWS   "You know a blizzard can come up very quickly in that country with little warning, and the roads can become impossible, you can't find your way. This night everyone was worried about getting home and some of them had already left, when there came a knock at the door, and it was a young fellow with summer coat and no hat, about half-frozen, and he and some friends had been coming across country to go to a dance somewhere else, and they had got caught in the blizzard. But my Lord, it wasn't any more than two miles, but my dad and my brother went in a stoneboat and they had a heck of a time going out to get those fellows, it took them half the night to find them, and they were freezing to death in a boxcar, I think they tore up some of the floor of the boxcar to try to keep them warm. They still had summer clothing; they weren't prepared for a blizzard at all.

And I can remember them being brought home and staying the night, because I was big-eyed and quite impressed because they seemed quite sophisticated city fellows to me. We had to bed them down all over the house, one sleeping in the leather chair, another one on the floor — we didn't have that much spare space. It was quite a worry. It was really quite tragic because we heard later that one young fellow had died as a result of the strain of the exposure to that storm."

THREE

Schools and Schoolteachers

A Very Good School . . . The Schoolroom . . . Boarding the Teacher . . .
Around the Bear . . . On the School Bus . . . Shells in the Stove . . . Christmas at School . . . The Fence Post . . . Chester . . . The Schoolwork
Slipped . . . Like One Big Family . . . Hats Off to the Teacher . . . The Inspector Calls . . . The Last of the Little Red Schoolhouse . . . Quite a Nice Girl

F olk mythology is hard to explain sometimes. In old postcards
after the turn of the century in Canada the schoolteacher
is nearly always depicted as prim and spinsterish, given to wearing
a pince-nez and whamming unruly students across the knuckles
with a ruler.

The schoolteacher in the little red schoolhouse or the sod hut
was quite a different creature. She was very often young and a
charmer, and she had more dates than she could contend with. She
was more likely to be high-spirited than mousey, and sometimes
she could give the family she stayed with a hard time, demanding
oranges and other luxuries and special treatment. But ordinarily
she was a fine example of healthy womanhood — intelligent, able
to cope with surroundings which were alien to her and people who
at first were total strangers — and she was, as this chapter shows,
very, very, marriageable.

Right across the field from us when we came here to the fifth line
of Tecumseth was a little red schoolhouse. I have a picture of the
class of 1952 — exactly twenty lively, grinning farm kids and the
pretty teacher. She was something like eighteen years old, and it's
hard to tell her from one of the older girls. That creaky little
schoolhouse was familiar to kids and parents. It had a narrow,
little rectangular lobby and then, plunk, right inside was a pot-

bellied stove and then the rows of battered desks, the little platform
where the teacher's desk was, and a world map that pulled down. It
had the happiest look of clutter I've ever seen in one room.

A VERY GOOD SCHOOL "There was no school, but the children
were growing up; finally a house that had been abandoned for three
or four years was fixed up for the children to go to. They got a
teacher. This old abandoned house was made out of logs, and it had
a sod roof and two little windows in it and a door in the middle. The
farmers got together and made some desks and benches out of
rough lumber for the children to sit on for studying.

But whenever it rained the roof leaked and the children brought
jam cans or lard pails and the teacher put those out wherever the
rain drops came through. And the children used to have to move
the desks away from where the rain was falling, so that their books
wouldn't get wet or their clothes, and the teacher had to move her
desk too. But they really had more fun and they weren't annoyed
and they thought it was funny because the raindrops made such
musical sounds in the pails.

The teacher was a young girl, and she was very pretty, and the
girls used to wish that they could have such pretty clothes and they
tried to imitate her hairdos, but most of the children—about eleven
or twelve of us at the beginning—came to school barefooted, they
couldn't afford to buy shoes. We never had school in that district
very long, only about four months every year; they couldn't afford
to pay the teacher, and the children tried to study at home.

It was a very good school. The teacher did her best and we
learned fast from her because we were interested in what she had to
tell us, and what she wrote on the board really fascinated us,
because we hadn't seen a school or a teacher and we were all about
eight or nine years old already, and we were very much interested
in studying and learning something."

THE SCHOOLROOM "You went into an unheated cloakroom with nails on the walls to hold the coats. Near the back of the schoolroom there was usually a great pot-bellied stove and a beat-up coal scuttle. There were rows of very scarred, inkstained desks fastened together, smaller ones on one side for the younger children, larger desks on the other side, facing the teacher's wooden desk and chair, which sometimes was on a raised platform. The furnishings were sparse. There was usually a small shelf of old books, the Alexander Readers in 1914 and later and Canadian Readers in 1924. There'd be an old globe on a pulley, and over the blackboard there'd be a long, dusty rolled map. Most schools had a piano or an organ, usually out of tune, a banjo clock, and the Union Jack high on the wall. The banjo clock was called that because it was shaped like a banjo.

There was a water pail or a crock with water and a mug or a dipper, and sometimes there was an enamel basin for handwashing. Lunches were carried in the bottom of lard pails and usually consisted of a jam sandwich or a hard-boiled egg. Children wore what their parents could afford, or what mother could sew. Some children walked miles to school or rode horseback, and the only sure way to miss school other than to help with the harvest was to get measles or chicken pox or scarlet fever. Then the doctor hung a quarantine poster on your gate post or on your house.

The subjects taught were history, geography, agriculture, nature study, hygiene, drawing, and composition and grammar. Reading, writing, arithmetic, and spelling were stressed. There was no electric bell to call the children to the lessons, but a hand bell which was clanged by the teacher after recess to call classes in."

BOARDING THE TEACHER   "One of the days we were driving to school my father happened to be the driver. Well, since we boarded the teacher, we usually took most of the children, and some of the children would walk to us, and we had about thirteen, I think it was, in the sleigh box that morning. It was during the spring break-up and the water was rushing down through the field that we had to cross. It had a good track across it all winter, but of course as the spring run-off came, the track wore away.

And just as we were crossing it, the water caught the sleigh box and took it right off the runners with all of us in it, and away went books and kids and everything down the stream. While most of us were long enough legged to get out, there was one little girl I remember, just a little mite, and my father saw her bobbing in the water and he grabbed her by her long scarf that we used to wear in those days and lifted her out of the water with it, and she went home and told her mother that Mr. Catley tried to choke her.

But the teacher's books were found years later, way down in the Qu'Appelle Valley. They had floated right down into the Qu'Appelle Valley, all her lessons and everything, quite a loss in those days because girls came out from Normal—what they usually had was a Grade Ten and one year Normal School, without much money, and the wages were poor . . . oh, I think sometimes only three hundred a year, and teachers always bought their own books. Our schoolbooks, the readers, were supplied, and for some reason each pupil was allowed to keep their readers at the end of the year, because I have my collection of old Alexander Readers, and then as it changed to the Canadian Reader, but as later years came, those books had to be turned in and used as they are now.

From May until freeze-up was the season of teaching. We boarded thirteen teachers in ten years. I guess our home had the best meals and because of that the teacher had oranges every morning and everything. And when the teacher went to visit, she was always given a good meal.

Well, our teacher didn't like eating rabbit, and mother always had to have something else. But when she went to the neighbours', she'd come home and say she'd had the loveliest mutton dinner or lovely pork dinner and you knew right well it was a rabbit dinner, but she hadn't known it. But she wouldn't eat rabbit at our place, because she saw us skinning them.

My mother received twenty-five dollars a month at the first and then thirty dollars a month, but in the thirties more often than not they couldn't pay it.

Boarding a teacher I think could be explained this way: the homes that had the best facilities were chosen, and we happened to have the plumbing put in our home in 1918, and so it was a logical place. Oh, they had boarded in other homes that I don't think had plumbing, large homes that were large enough to take in hired man, hired girl, and the family, and have an extra spare room that was definitely the teacher's alone, because the teacher always had to have a room by herself. So this was what had to be in the district was a house that had a spare room that could be held just for a teacher.

The teacher was very much the idol of the district for all the boys. There'd be a different one every night that wanted to take her out. There was some prestige about teachers. I remember being at a dance one night, it was a local dance, and all the boys had rushed and picked up the teachers first and then with long faces would come to pick the rest of us up to dance with.

And every district put on a play every winter, and the teacher was always given the star part of the play, regardless of how pretty or how nice some of the local girls were. The teacher always had the star part in the play."

AROUND THE BEAR   "I often wonder now how our parents could ever send us off to school, because we had to walk a mile down to the bus. And you never knew if the bus was going to come during the winter, either.

And I remember the time that my brother and I came around a corner, and there was a big black bear. And I just loved school. I wouldn't miss school for anything: that was the highlight of my day, certainly. It wasn't for my brother. So we had this conference.

And he said he wanted to go back, and I said: "Oh, come on, we can go round." So these two little kids — and we must have been approximately nine and seven — went around the muskeg, just a little bit out of the way, and around this bear, and carried on to school as if it was nothing."

ON THE SCHOOL BUS   "Riding the school bus took a great part of the day. We'd get on the bus about eight o'clock in the morning. We only lived about four or five miles out of town. But we'd have three or four sideroads to go down, you know several miles, to pick up some other kids who lived further away from the highway. And I don't know how our bus drivers ever stood us, because it must have been really hectic for them.

We had a lot of fun, you know, screaming and sitting around with our best friends, and all the rest of it. Every once in a while somebody'd be late for breakfast and they'd be eating their toast as they came onto the bus or something like that. But we'd just talk and sing, sometimes try do our homework or whatever. And mostly bug the bus driver, I think.

We've had fights break out on the bus. And the bus driver'd stop and kick the kids off and make them walk home or something like that. Or if everybody was really really noisy, one time we had a bus driver, you know, stop the bus in the middle of the road and refuse to move until everybody was quiet again. And I really feel sorry for the bus drivers now. We thought they were kind of picky then.

The people in the bus were usually really good. Like I remember when my Dad died. I was thirteen, and my brother and sister were both younger than I was. And all the kids on the bus collected money and one of the kids brought the flowers over to the house for us, that they'd gotten from the money the kids on the bus gave."

SHELLS IN THE STOVE "The teacher used to get pretty mad when one of the boys would think it was smart to put a .22 shell in the stove — it was one of those pot-bellied stoves with the red railing around, which was usually full of drying mitts, things drying in the heat. They'd stick a .22 bullet in there, perhaps two or three, and they'd go off with a wham and the whole stove would jump."

CHRISTMAS AT SCHOOL "Christmas at school, we always put on a little play. Our teachers always made up a Christmas concert, and all the parents came that night to see the children perform. There were different concerts, you know, different little plays that they would put on, and we'd all bring things from home to dress ourselves in, make-up, costumes from home from old clothes and one thing and another. We never had too much to work on, but we had a lot of happy memories. We used to make popcorn and make popcorn balls and string popcorn to decorate the Christmas tree, and cut up the coloured pages out of catalogues to make some paper garlands for the tree."

THE FENCE POST   "When I was teaching north of Beausejour, I really learned what gumbo was, because our farm in western Manitoba was bush and sandy loam soil and not anywhere near as hard to work in some ways. I think they always figured they could always pull one more plough bottom further west than they could near the city. But this time at Eastertime my car had been in Beausejour and we were eight miles north, and Joe was to take us down to take the train to go on Easter holidays. His mother came out and carefully saw that everything was loaded properly in the wagon and:

'Joe, you've got lots of hay, and use the feather bed to put over your knees and keep warm . . .'

It was a chilly morning. You know what Easter is.

'Joe, you got the fence post?'

Now I wondered what that was, but I didn't dare say while his mother was there. So as we got down a little further I said to Joe:

'What's the fence post?'

He said: 'You wait a minute.'

We went another half-mile and Joe gets out, fishes out the fence post that's in at the edge of the wagon box, and pushes the mud out from between the wagon box and the wheels and from between the spokes of the wheels, so that the horses could really pull the rig. He did this about three times in the eight miles, and that was a wagon, not a buggy with a fine wheel, but a wagon with a good, wide three-inch wheel.

That gumbo is rather hard on cars, too, because you know school teachers are supposed to be there on certain days, and I loved to be away on the weekend. So coming back more than once I ended up with broken springs on the front of a Ford coupe, Model T, and to get back to town, you carefully tied in with wire a two-by-four to keep the radiator from coming down too hard on the front of the car. I could even fix those occasionally."

CHESTER   "The first year I had fifteen students and they were all grades, but they were anxious and keen to learn, and they were good youngsters. I don't know what they were like at home, I don't know anything about that, but when they were under my supervision we had a lot of good times together, had our Christmas concerts, and we would decorate the school, and make wreaths for to trim the schoolhouse. And we had what we called an examination day, and all the parents would come to the school that day.

And I remember so well this young boy in this school. I asked them questions of course. So I said:

'Chester, tell me some of the organs of the body.'

And Chester said: 'Liver and lights.'

So anyway his mother was sitting there, and I thought she would have a fit of some sort. She roared and laughed — it was just like bedlam, but it sounded so funny and he was so serious about it. That's what made it funnier."

THE SCHOOLWORK SLIPPED "In fall time you were always harvesting, so you'd come home from school and get on the combine or the tractor, and after you'd finished harvesting you'd be ploughing till heck knows when at night. And then during the winter of course there was cleaning the barn and slinging the manure out and bringing in wood for use in the house. We never had anything but wood heat at that time, so we'd have to split wood and bring it in every evening, and bring in water from the well. And that was mostly my work. I was the only child at that time, all the rest of the boys had left home, so that was all left to myself. My father had a bad back, and couldn't really do much, so all that was left up to me.

I also had some schoolwork and possibly didn't do as well as I could have when I eventually did finish Grade Eight and then had to catch the bus into Selkirk to go to high school. My grades weren't very good at all, and sometimes I felt it was because I didn't have time. I was kind of conscientious about my work, and at times it really depressed me that I couldn't really do well in school, because I had, you know, combining to do and you just had to do it, it couldn't wait till tomorrow, so you did it today and the schoolwork slipped."

LIKE ONE BIG FAMILY "The atmosphere in our country school was like one big family, the teacher knowing all the children, and she usually knew all the parents. I have an old school picture taken in the early fifties, where about twenty children were attending and the teacher was only eighteen years of age, straight from high school, and it amazed me how marvellously she was able to cope. Most of the teachers were very good and kept good discipline in the classrooms, but I think some of the older ones were a little stricter than others, which didn't go down too well with the boys."

HATS OFF TO THE TEACHER "When I was a kid going to school, our teacher would try to teach us to be polite to her, to take off our hat whenever we met her on the street. In those days toilets were out at the back of the school, and one day we saw her going in there, so while she was in there we all lined up on the path between there and the school and when she came out we all took our hats off to her."

THE INSPECTOR CALLS "The inspector would turn up very unexpectedly until the telephones came in. After that, the Tregarva one would warn the Kennell one, so this helped out a little bit there. But up until then it was usually very unexpected and he was a very stern man, and maybe more stern possibly than he was.He just had every kid so scared that they didn't whisper one word. The teacher got a good report on good discipline. We were scared stiff, we wouldn't even stir in our seats."

THE LAST OF THE LITTLE RED SCHOOLHOUSE "I'm twenty-two now but I spent the first six years of my schooling in a one-room schoolhouse, a little red-brick schoolhouse just barely half a mile up the road. My brothers and sisters and I all walked there, or during the nicer weather we'd ride our bicycles. The teacher was an older lady, and I had her for all the six years I was there. There was such a close relationship between all the students and the teacher that we'd often forget, and instead of calling her Mrs. Falconer, we'd often call her Mum. But with all the students we all knew each other's relatives—it was one big family. Recess, we loved to play out of doors. We had the biggest swing set in the whole of Ameliasburg Township, and we loved to get the swings right up parallel with the top bars and jump off and see who could jump the furthest. I'd be scared to death to do it now.

The only severe discipline would be the strap, which was given only occasionally. Somehow she had good control of us anyway; we seemed to all behave very well. She was quite a lenient teacher. She loved art and music, which of course we all did, too, and we spent a lot of time on that and Christmas concerts and lots of parties. We had parties every St. Patrick's Day, Easter, Valentine's Day. I never remember it being too hot, but I can remember in Grade One we were allowed to get out about half an hour earlier than the rest of the school and we never wanted to go home. We'd hang around until the rest of the kids got out. And noon hours, many of us could have gone home for lunch, but we never did.

The education I got in the one-room schoolhouse is the very best I've ever had. I've had the opportunity to go to college and now university afterwards too. I think it all began back in that little schoolhouse. It was the stimulation of having the older children there. If we finished our work early the younger students would listen to the older students and learn ahead. We knew we'd be taking it some year anyway; or else we could help the younger children with their work, teach them to read or go ahead. There was a great amount of sharing, and often the older children would be called upon to help the teacher and listen to the younger ones read, to help them with their math.

A great deal was lost when I moved on to central schools, and I think maybe the most important was the great rapport we had with our teacher. I remember all of us being eager to please and we wanted to do our best, and the bigger schools are much more impersonal and I think a lot of that element is lost. The little red schoolhouse had the same end as every other one in Ontario. The government decided to consolidate all of them"

QUITE A NICE GIRL "I remember my teachers. They were lovely women, but I hated going to school. I'd much rather go in the field. I'd do anything — I'd work my heart out on the farm rather than spend time in the schoolhouse. But I never went to school till I was seven, and then the teacher put me in the fourth grade and I was only there five years and I got my ninth grade. I didn't want to go to school—I wanted to educate myself. I got all the education I thought I needed.

Well, I married a schoolteacher. I just took her driving. I seen that she was a good singer—she used to sing in the choir and I used to play my trumpet with the organ in the church, and I used to have to go to pick her up to take her around to rehearsals, you know, and she was quite a nice girl, good company, so I married her . . . just a back-country girl; her home was in Kentville."

FOUR

The Kitchen

*The Stove Was the Centre of the Kitchen . . . Wood for a Winter's
Burning . . . Chimney Fires . . . Our Smokehouse . . . Cooking on a Wood
Stove . . . Very Good Food . . . The Spirit of All the Home-Cooked
Things . . . Rabbits All Over . . . Too Fond of the Cream . . . Canning
Sausage . . . Well Cooled . . . Gingerbread with Whipped Cream . . . Moose
in a Barrel . . . The Mounties' Dinner . . . The Native Fruit*

The kitchen has always been the heartland of the farmhouse. In the old days in winter it was warm and cosy and
full of odours, delectable and otherwise. Keeping the stove supplied with wood was a constant chore, but in every other respect
the stove, with its warmer at the top, its water reservoir at the side,
and its various moveable shelves and other gadgets, was an orna-
mental and utilitarian triumph. There usually was a chrome bar
below the oven on which one and all rested their feet. After meals,
the oven door might be open to let the heat out, and that was a
handy place for the feet, too, which meant that sooner or later the
springs in the oven door ceased to be of too much use. Everyone sat
around the stove in a half-moon arc and yarned, delighting in the
sense of comfort and solid pleasure. In the course of my travels
for the book I was in some farmhouses where a wood stove was
still going strong, while nearby there was an electric range, unused
and cold.

The summer kitchen was a back porch, really. For instance, we
live in a farmhouse built in 1920, and our battered old back porch
was the summer kitchen. You can still see the round hole, now
covered over, of course, where the stove pipe went out the wall. The

point of the summer kitchen was that on warm days it got the
family away from the excessive heat generated by the wood stove.

Now let us talk of ambrosia and nectar — farmhouse cooking!
First: a farmhouse breakfast was meant to give a person a solid
start on the day; it might well be a heaping plateful of bacon, fried
eggs, and fried potatoes, followed by apple pie. Dinner at noon (not
"lunch") was often roast pork, with roasted potatoes or roasted
parsnips. Mashed turnips were a standby. There was sauerkraut
sometimes. With the pork perhaps there'd be red-currant jelly. With
roast beef, the relish dish might contain a tasty mixture of horse-
radish, beets, and cabbage, while corn relish and bean relish were
both common and popular. Cold nights the family would often lard
into homemade baked beans, homemade bread, and churned butter. From a "go" of jam (an expression still used by one of our
neighbours — it means a batch of jam), the jam dish would be
replenished constantly.

And what desserts! At noon perhaps preserves, and pies at
supper: sour-cream pie, Dutch apple pie, cherry deep-dish pie,
especially pumpkin pie with whipped cream, and, if you were
really lucky, blackberry pie, made from the wild blackberries,
sometimes called blackcaps, that grew in the bush. One woman
told me that her Uncle Milt's favourite of all was rhubarb pie with
maple syrup poured over it. Now that is something! A container of
maple syrup was left on the table as long as there was maple syrup.
The kids revelled in taffy, chocolate fudge, and maple cream.
Drinks: well, there might be home-brewed beer, sometimes ginger
beer in summer, tea much more than coffee (the tea could be green
tea, bought from a pedlar, which was milder than ordinary tea).
There was also a black-currant drink.

Farm wives have always gloried in providing good meals, and
their families have returned the compliment by happily stuffing
themselves. They need the food; they've earned it with hard work
and the never-ending round of chores.

THE STOVE WAS THE CENTRE OF THE KITCHEN "The old black wood stoves, there were several makes, and they were more complicated. Of course they had more things to them. There was the reservoir, a great thing — you had warm water as long as you had a fire on. Now the stove has none of that, we don't need it. And they had a big warming closet, warming oven, and this was a great thing for the farm wife because she'd have a meal warm for her husband when he came in — he couldn't always be in at the right time. They were a great place to store on top the mitts, socks that always got wet, rubber boots, the children's galoshes, you name it; they were all piled underneath.

There was quite a country aroma in our kitchen. In fact under the stove, the boots of various kinds were arranged there, the children's wet galoshes, and Andy's rubber boots.

In the spring, we often had a little lamb in until it was able to stand on its wobbly feet, and on different occasions they became pets of our children. In fact, they didn't want to part with one particular lamb called Pete. And Pete grew to a good old age. We couldn't sell him. Sometimes these animals were put on the open oven door until they warmed completely, and then they went out to the barn. Oh, we've had goslings in until they were able to be put outside, maybe about six or so; and we've had little pigs in various stages.

The stove was the centre of the kitchen, and the kitchen was certainly the centre of the house, and oh, on cold days and cold nights, we'd all be gathered round. I can remember before we had hydro, the table would be pulled over to the stove, so we could see from the old oil light, and we'd keep warm at the same time. And when neighbours came in, that was the first thing, get warmed over the stove. It still is that way in the wintertime."

WOOD FOR A WINTER'S BURNING "We still use wood entirely on this farm. We've a wood-burning stove, a wood-burning furnace and all our wood comes from our own woodlot, with the exception of a few slabs from the local sawmill. Years ago, when we first started farming, it was cut with a cross-cut saw, all the large wood, then we had the circular saws, and now of course it's mainly done with a chain saw.

It was quite a job when we did it with a cross-cut saw. My neighbour and I used to try to put up six to eight cords a day, that is, cut our trees down and block it into fourteen- or sixteen-inch light wood. The smaller trees were put up in piles, thirty or forty cords, then we had a local wood-buzzing bee with a circular saw. We'd have six to eight of the neighbours at each of these wood bees. Incidentally, these are almost a thing of the past, since the chain saw has become so popular.

The first days of cutting wood with a cross-cut saw were pretty tough, but it was like everything else, you soon got used to it, and I don't know whether we could afford as much food as it required to pull one of those today. Sometimes when we had pretty bad aches, Sloan's liniment was a pretty regular around the farm, plus some homemade remedies, mustard plasters. Certainly we got over them."

CHIMNEY FIRES   "The old wood stoves really didn't give too much trouble, but if you didn't keep the pipes clean, they filled up with soot, and it was quite common to have a real wild chimney fire. We've had lots of chimney fires, never a real serious one . . . I mean the house never took on fire, but it would scare you in the night sometimes when you'd hear the roar, and you'd see the pipes red from the stove to the chimney. Oh, I remember wakening up and hearing the roar, and we'd run down and we nearly always kept sulphur on hand to throw in, and that would certainly check it . . . throw in about two handfuls of sulphur and make sure that the drafts were all open, because if you didn't, it would put you out of the house very fast. It was a suffocating smell, the sulphur. You couldn't stay in the room, but it certainly would extinguish the fire.

Sometimes we'd have to use water. The wallpaper would start burning near the stovepipe where it went through the walls or ceiling. I remember once the curtains getting a little bit on fire, but we've been fortunate all the years, we never had a fire.

Sometimes my heart was in my mouth, particularly if Andy was at the barn or maybe away from home, and the children were small. But we always were able to put it out."

OUR SMOKEHOUSE "In the yard outside our house we had a smokehouse, which was used for curing meats, a real substantial little building made of fieldstones, with a wood-shingle roof. It had small openings in three sides, which were really just slits in the wall, too small to be called windows, I guess. And a doorway to walk in. And this doorway had an ingenious type of lock on it so that you had to know the secret in order to be able to open it.

Inside the smokehouse were rods on which the hams and bacon and sausage could be hung for smoking. You made a fire and then covered it with sawdust. And you used apple or maple or hickory wood. And this fire would sometimes last for several days, just smoldering under the sawdust, and giving the proper colour, texture, and flavour to the meat. Some types of meat, of course, had to be left in the smokehouse longer than others. Such things as bacon would be finished smoking in just two or three days. Hams could be left a full week or more, because they were much thicker.

The smell in the smokehouse was a very strong smoke odour, and would remain in the building for years after. The walls were completely blackened from the smoke.

It was an interesting little place, and I remember one time a man coming into our yard who thought this had been an old Indian fort because it had these little slits in the walls. He thought that's where the people could go in case of emergency, and just using the little slits to point their guns from, they would be safe in case of an attack. I think when we told him it was only a smokehouse it punctured one of his illusions about pioneer life."

COOKING ON A WOOD STOVE "In the summer I do not use the wood stove, but I'm always glad when the cooler days come and I can light the fire again. It's always comforting in the kitchen, and I bake everything but bread. I use my electric stove for the bread. I prefer cooking on the wood stove because it is slow cooking, you can cook meat beautifully, bake beans — it's just better all around. But in the summer, you have to go back to the electric stove."

VERY GOOD FOOD "The baking was really something to re-member. We had cream pies, all kinds of cakes. We had dried apples, stewed prunes, and there was an egg-and-flour mixture we called knepp, and it was eaten with browned breadcrumbs poured over it.

And we had shoofly pie, which was a great delicacy in those times, and we never seemed to get tired of it. It was made of either molasses or a corn-syrup base and a crumb topping which all blended in together in the baking. We ate it quite often at break-fast time.

We had very good food. We never wanted for anything. We were not quite in the Mennonite tradition as they say 'seven sweets and seven sours'. I don't think we followed those lines, but we had a never-ending supply of good food. And baking was done once a week to last for the whole week, something we wouldn't think of doing today."

THE SPIRIT OF ALL THE HOME-COOKED THINGS "After the pigs were butchered, my aunt would take whatever the entrails are and they were washed, were soaked in salt water and then blown up and the sausage meat went into them. Those were the casings for the sausage as we knew it.

And the head of the pig was always cooked, and all the different parts of the head went to make headcheese with the gelatine and the natural jello, and I remember there would be nothing wasted. Some of the grease and the fat that came from the pig would be made into soap, and that soap would be used on washdays.

And my aunt had a special formula for making soap; and it was just a matter of making use of everything when you butchered a pig.

I remember my aunt making butter, and it was a cylinder-type churn, a wooden pounder, and you kept turning the pounder and pounding the milk until this turned into butter or whey or whatever . . . I guess it would be whey. And then you would take that whey and you would let the kind of juice or whatever drip out of it, and what you had left in that hand-like scoop with the holes in was the butter. And you would take that and you would knead out all the water or the milk or the juice that comes from the milk, and then you would add your butter colouring, and add your little bit of salt, and that was your butter.

And my aunt made bread. My uncle would take the wheat to the flour mill and she would use that wheat to make whole-wheat bread. I keep referring to my aunt because my aunt was the spirit of all the home-cooked things.

My aunt would make the butter, and we didn't have any refrigeration, but we did have a good cold basement; even in the summer months it was cold and it was well protected, and leading from our kitchen was what we used to call a dumbwaiter, which was part of our kitchen cupboards, and it was worked on the principle of pulleys and weights. And you would cover your food and keep your butter covered or wrapped up, and then you would lower it into the cold area of the cellar, and then you would close the doors, and then when you wanted something from that particular dumbwaiter, you would just lift the ropes and the weights would do the work and bring the dumbwaiter up, and that would save you going down and up.

We had a root cellar where we would store our beets and our carrots and our turnips and our potatoes, and all the things that we would store for the winter months to prevent us from buying things that we would grow on the farm. And this root cellar was beside what we called our fruit cellar.

The fruit cellar was where we kept our wine and our butter and our jam, and it was like a cool part of the basement, while the root cellar had to have an earthen floor, dug into the earth, to make it even colder.

We had quite an orchard. We had Spy apples, Delicious apples, Duchess, different types that sometimes you don't even hear about now, but the one that we would keep most for winter supplies was the Northern Spy. The Northern Spy we would just pack in bushel baskets. We never wrapped them in tissue paper and we wouldn't wash them, but we'd make sure that they were all in firm shape before, because if you have one bad one, the fermentation starts right through. So you'd have to have good apples packed in bushel baskets and store them in the fruit cellar. And my aunt would go down from time to time and bring up some of these apples and cut them and dry them; and I remember as a young girl having dried-apple pie. And I imagine some people have experienced that, but it's a very delicious treat, a dried-apple pie.

And those apples would last into January or February. From time to time we'd have to pick them over. If there was one that started to ferment, you'd have to take that out and keep rotating them — you have to keep doing that because one bad apple, that's where you get the saying.

The same with tomatoes. And there was a great canning experience, you know, in the late summer. You would can so much in the jars — canned tomatoes, canned beans, canned beets. When I say canned, they were always in glass jars, because you know there was in those days, there was no such thing as a can ... in those days there were the old crown jars and the old beaver jars that are so valuable today. I wish I had some of them."

RABBITS ALL OVER   "It's difficult to mention the rabbits without seeming to be a most unrestricted liar. People can hardly believe how many there were. I've stood on the doorsteps at my friend's house in a winter night in January and shot them from there, and the surface of the ground would almost seem to be oscillating with white rabbits running all over white ground, you know. And our first two winters in the country, if it had not been for the rabbits, in all probability we would have run short of meat."

TOO FOND OF THE CREAM   "I was too fond, I think, of the cream. I didn't have it in the house all the time because if it was here in the fridge, I'd be using it anyway whether the rest did or not, because you couldn't beat it on fresh strawberries, and it really made a cup of coffee taste good, and on top of pumpkin pie, whipped cream was a must. So I'd always be tempted to have cream with something. This way I'm probably better off without it, but I do miss it. The cream would just whip without any effort at all; all you did was take it out of the fridge and beat it a little, and there you were with a mound of lovely, fluffy whipped cream. It was gorgeous.

When we were shipping cream, the cream went into the cream-ery in six-gallon cans—that was about the size of the can—and we got around seven dollars or eight dollars for a can of cream, de-pending on how it tested. So when you think of going into the store and buying a little half-pint carton of cream, and what you pay for it today, you'd get a lot of pints out of one of those five or six gallons, wouldn't you?"

CANNING SAUSAGE "My mother used to do up about fifty or sixty quarts of the stuff and it was always a favourite with us kids and to us it was as good when it was raw as when it was cooked. My older brother wanted to sneak some of this sausage and didn't want my mother to know, so instead of opening one or two sealers and eating the contents, he opened up every sealer and took a piece out of every one and ruined the whole batch. I don't think she's ever quite forgiven him for it."

WELL COOLED "On our farm we used to keep our butter and our milk, buttermilk or anything like that, down the well outside. Dad had a little trap door on the top of the well, and there was ropes there and we could tie a pail to the rope and lower it down into the well. It didn't touch the water, but it was still cold enough it kept the milk and the butter and that nice and fresh."

GINGERBREAD WITH WHIPPED CREAM "The first thing I remember was Dad always lit the fire in the morning. He always shaved little pieces of cedar and had a little pile there ready for the morning, and when it would be time to be waking up we'd hear the kitchen stove lids rattling and Dad would be putting the fire on. That was the signal for us to get up and there was no problems in getting up, it was time to get up and everybody got up. And mother always cooked the breakfast and everybody for sure had a good hot meal before they started off to school.

You went off to school well dressed and ready for the weather. Most of the time we walked. There was a man across the road from us who was a gentleman farmer, and so he gave us rides on the days that weren't good, because he didn't have as much to do and had one daughter. But, most of the time we were expected to walk.

We were also expected to walk home on time. We could dilly-dally some, and when we'd come home, Mother would usually have gingerbread or maybe there'd be hot bread and a johnnycake, but we always had something to eat when we came home, which we enjoyed. To this day we can think about it with real pleasure . . . specially gingerbread with whipped cream on it. I can remember those things so well."

MOOSE IN A BARREL "We didn't cook rabbit, no. The moose was very important to our diet. And the garden. But every fall Dad would try to get a female moose. And during the winter you could keep it because you kept it outside in a barrel and sort of sawed off a piece whenever you needed it."

THE MOUNTIES' DINNER "Deer meat was a delicacy, and of course it was much more a delicacy when it was out of season. I can remember one time when we had this deer meat and along came the Mounties. There had been an accident on our farm, and the Mounties were out to investigate it, and all we had was deer roast in the oven. Well, we didn't know what to do. So we phoned while they were in the front room taking down notes — we phoned my aunt and told her our predicament and she happened to have a roast of pork in the oven. So out came our hot roast and onto a little sleigh, and up came the little farm sleigh up the road and they met my brother halfway with their pork roast and he took it and put it in the oven and out came a pork roast for the Mounties' dinner that day."

THE NATIVE FRUIT "We always used the native fruit. Saskatoons were very plentiful — you see our farm was a bush farm at Snow Lake, and there were saskatoons, there were pin cherries that made jelly, the most beautiful jelly in the world unless you have a cranberry. I have made them all. I still do — my one concession to canning is native fruit as jams or jellies, and a very nice young lady pleased me much last winter. She brought me enough saskatoons

The illustrations that follow (here and in the
next eight-page section) consist of postcards
taken from Allan Anderson's extensive
personal collection. All of these postcards
date from roughly the first twenty years of
this century, when Canadians were crazy
about postcards. Many of these cards bear
their own captions, which reward
the careful reader.

Farm on St. John River

Ox Team Ploughing
Annapolis Valley, N.S.

FEEDING THE CHICKS, CANADIAN RURAL SCENE.

IN THE COUNTRY.

PUBLIC SCH.
CHURCHVILLE.ONT.

Canadian Farm Life.
"The Merry Milkmaid."

102,353 UV

No Cold Storage in Canada.

Afternoon Refreshment

· CANADIAN ·
HOMESTEAD LIFE

Canadian Rural Life. "Preparing for the stern work of the Morrow."

Market, Napanee, Ont.

POLICE HEAD QUARTERS

FARM SCENE, PORT ELGIN CANADA

Raising
Hogs in
Canada.

for to make about four pies. I had been away in the summer at saskatoon time and I hadn't done up many and she knew that I like them and brought them to me—a choice gift.

We have two cherries on the prairies here. The chokecherry is black and grows on a stem. The blooms are open now the end of May and just looks like a finger of white flowers, but these become a black cherry and the name explains them. They're chokecherries, they're very dry tasting, your throat and your mouth all pucker up from it. They won't jell of themselves, but with crab apples or with pectin, and you can make a jelly. In fact it's quite a choice dark-blue jelly.

The pin cherry grows on the end of a stem in a cluster, and, oh, they're a little bigger than the heads of these pins that you pin on a corsage with a stone in the middle. But when they grow in clusters and groups you can get them, boil them, strain them, and they make a perfectly beautiful light scarlet jelly. Other wild fruits, we have a few sand cherries, which like the choke cherry is puckery, and cranberries; we get wild raspberries, saskatoons, and when we were youngsters, we used to pick wild strawberries. Now if you go out and find a cupful you're doing well, but when we were youngsters there was a hill slope down to the lake, and you'd pick berries for an hour or two, lie on your back and count the clouds, and go on and pick again and come home with several quarts for three or four youngsters of real wild strawberries, the taste of which, you know, is the most perfect berry in the world.

Just outside our door, where my husband and I live now, is a piece of prairie, it's a ridge and it's a bit sandy, and this particular part has never been cultivated. At one end of it is what has been called an Indian mound — we know there's been a burial of some sort there—and coming down from that and across the road and in other parts of our area are fields of our provincial crocus, the provincial floral emblem.

I saw a man this spring stand in the midst of those, a man of well over sixty saying:

'I have never seen these growing.'

And if there was a thought of worship of nature, it was right on his face that day."

FIVE

To Every Thing There Is a Season

Such a Variety of Things . . . A Harvest Excursion . . . The Back End of the Train . . . The Harvest Crew . . . Stooks . . . Harvest-time Refreshments . . . The Lindsay Syrup . . . A Real Winter Storm . . . Hunting the Mud . . . Beautiful Apples . . . In the Fishing Season . . . Learning to Plough . . . A Showing on the Field . . . The Potato Crop . . . Priming Tobacco

The cycle of the seasons makes a regular, unchanging demand each year on the farm household. Far from being regarded as an endless routine by the farm family, the arrival of each new season is welcomed as a change of pace in farm life. There is also, I think, a deeper, more profound reason for this welcoming attitude. Farm people are so attuned to the climate and so linked to the earth and its rhythms of growth and fruition and decline and death that there is a psychological urgency for the shift of seasons. The seasons are natural and right, and on the farm the solstices and equinoxes are of a significance far beyond the understanding of city people.

So these stories recall how it was off to the woods in the early spring when the sap was running; and how in the full heat of late June it was haying time (with, so often, a hot spell, and the men sweating it out in the fields); and after the full, rich summer there would be harvesting and threshing; and in winter all the repair jobs to machinery and the tinkering around (and time for curling?). Every thing had its place, and to every thing there was a season.

SUCH A VARIETY OF THINGS "I lived on a farm until I was sixteen at Unionville, just north of Toronto. We were always aware of the seasons, and now that it's spring I can remember the awakening of life.

We always had chickens that would hatch just before Easter, and we would have small turkeys hatching just before Easter, piglets, and these small animals were part of the awakening of spring. And we would collect pussy willows in the bush part of our farm. And my aunt always had the traditional hams for Easter, and the raisin buns that were homemade, and all the other things, and of course the church services. We were much involved in our church.

And then as the summers came on, it was haying, and black-currant time and preserving and all the things that go with summers, and taking the black-currant drink to the farmers in the field, my uncles and their hired help. And then as the fall came on it was putting things away. We had beautiful flowers and we had to take up the bulbs and prepare for winter.

And then as the winter came there was always the fun of skating behind the barn on the layers of ice that would form.

We would prepare for Christmas with homemade popcorn strings on our Christmas tree—and incidentally we would cut our tree right on the property, and that would be a big event. We would set up our Christmas tree in our living room and that would be maybe a week or two before Christmas, and our families would talk about the Christmas plans, and my uncles and my aunts would come over in double cutters for Christmas Day. They had no other forms of transportation, but that was a big event — the double cutters were always ready for Christmas Eve and Christmas Day.

The awareness of the seasons was so vivid because we grew so many of our vegetables and so many of our own fruits right on the farm. In the spring we'd collect the dandelions and we'd have our glass of dandelion wine, and in the fall it would be the wild grapes along the fences and we'd have our wild grape wine. And all during the summer there'd be wild strawberries, and the things that we had that were wild.

And in the summer, the late summer, we would collect black walnuts from the trees along the fences, and then we knew, when they were dry, my aunts or my mother or my grandmother would be making homemade fudge. And we knew we had to let those black walnuts dry so that we would have them and enjoy them in that lovely maple fudge in the fall and winter months.

And you'd get these black-walnut stains on your hands, and we had pumice stone, I think that's what you call it, and Snap, and you'd try to get this black stain off.

And then there would be butchering time, when my uncles would do the butchering of a pig, and we didn't like to see all the details but sometimes we'd sneak around behind the barn and see them going through the actual stabbing the pig and letting it bleed and then hanging it up in the tree and letting the blood run out. I know some people have blood pudding and they save that blood, that wasn't part of our tradition.

And then the anticipation of this lovely fresh pork, and then my aunt would cure the hams in a homemade way with her salt, and we had a house that was called a smokehouse, and that ham, we would eventually have for Easter — the next spring, you see. And that would be in the fall.

We had an ice-cream machine and it was one of the kind that you had to roll by hand, and put your ice in around it and then keep putting the salt in, because that keeps it melting and keeps the friction so that it will freeze the cream. And of course the cream and the eggs were all from your farm. And then for variation we'd have the wild strawberries in it and sometimes we'd put the wild grape jam in it, and you know some of the strawberry ice cream and the black walnut and the different kinds of ice cream they have on the market today, we had, just because they were part of all those things that grew on the farm. And we had such a variety of things, that every time we made something, we'd always try something different."

A HARVEST EXCURSION   "In the early twenties and before that, the railroad put on a cheap rate for the harvesters to get out West and help with the harvest. They put on rates of fifteen dollars to Winnipeg and a half a cent a mile from there on out, and thousands of boys and men in Ontario and other provinces went out West to help with the western crops.

I went out in 1923 with three or four others, and we got four dollars for stooking and five dollars for threshing. I went West in '23 on the thirteenth of August, 1923, and I went C.P.R., boarded the train at midnight, and happened to get a very good coach with a real good bunch of fellows in it. There were four fellows from Bethany, Ontario, right set across from us, and one played the violin and one the mouth organ, and one kept time with spoons on his knee, and they all happened to be good. But we walked through to the lunch counter at different times and there'd be a lot of rowdyism and drinking and even breaking windows. But our coach had a real good bunch of fellows and it took us from Monday night at midnight, Toronto, till Wednesday night to get to Winnipeg. I'd been warned about pickpockets on trains, so my wife sewed a pocket on the inside of my undershirt, and my money was in there with a safety pin over it. So I says, 'Anybody that can get that will do.'

When we got to Winnipeg we set around in the hotel, the C.P.R. hotel there till morning, and then we went across to a Chinese café and had our breakfast and walked up the main street in Winnipeg till seven o'clock, and the next morning we left for Stoughton, it's near Weyburn and ninety miles east of Regina. And a fellow came on the train and he hired the four or five of us—he didn't want us all for stooking but he wanted us all for threshing and he would place us around with different farmers, but we was all to come to his place when the threshing-time come.

So we stayed with a farmer by the name of Alfred Barnett through the stooking and then for the threshing we was all together and the other man, A. W. Howe, had a big caboose that held twenty-four men, and we stayed in that nights.

The wheat was pretty much No. 3 grade that year, and they got around eighty cents a bushel, but we got five dollars a day. I drove a stook team and would load up, and two pitchers would pitch it on, and the spike pitcher, when you got to the machine, he would help you. He pitches into the machine, an extra helper and he got one dollar a day more than we did, for his job was pitching into the machine all the time. They didn't all have spike pitchers. Some-times you had to just unload your load alone, but if you had a spike pitcher, why you'd get it off that much quicker and you were ready to go for another load.

We worked from whenever we started till dark. We had four meals a day. The third meal was brought out about four o'clock and we didn't have our supper till after everything was done."

THE BACK END OF THE TRAIN   "I went out to Manitoba, it was on an excursion. I think it was ten dollars . . . wasn't that standard price? Colonist cars. My pal and I were very lucky that the car we were in didn't have a lot of drunks in. That was something you had to look out for in those days . . . because if a bunch of those fellows would see an old horse tied or a wagon tied out there handy to the train stops, they'd go out there and tie it to the back end of the train, you know, and that's the last of that. That happened lots of times."

THE HARVEST CREW   "There wasn't enough accommodation in the house, bedding space for to bed these people, so many places they had old bunkhouses on the farm, or if they didn't, they had an empty hayloft that they used for that purpose. There was always the attendant risk of having the barn burn down with somebody smoking.

But we were fortunate in that most of the men had homes within ten or fifteen miles of us and we didn't have to put up with them that long during long periods of rainfall. Invariably there'd be a beautiful Friday and Saturday and Sunday, and then they'd come back Sunday night from home and Sunday night about dark it would start to rain, just pour down the rest of the night. We've had that experience many times, so it was pretty hopeless. If it was real heavy rain they'd have to go back home again and sit it out till it got dry enough again."

STOOKS   "If the stooks are well made — and that's quite an art, believe it or not, to make a stook that will stand up for two or three weeks and be more or less waterproof — they could stand quite a good shower and inside of eight or ten hours they would be okay again. But when you got a long drizzle, quite a heavy rain for two or three days, then you're in trouble, because it would soak in eventually right through the sheaves, and it would take two to three weeks sometimes to dry."

HARVEST-TIME REFRESHMENTS   "I can remember going out to the fields where my father was, taking him a drink, and what do you suppose it was? It was water and oatmeal. And he called it 'crowdy', the Scottish people called it that, I believe, and it was apparently better for you than drinking straight cold water.

We didn't have ice then; except a neighbour would put ice away. Ice harvesting was very important in those days; if you were going to keep your milk and cream in the summertime, or be able to churn, it was almost a necessity to have ice. So one of the great times at night in haying and harvest-time would be making homemade ice cream. It was made in a wooden bucket with this crushed ice around it and salt around on the outside with a crank being turned, and the ice cream would be a mixture of cream, eggs, sugar, vanilla, and a custard made of that, and then this was churned and scraped down at the side till it would be a solid mass of ice cream, and it was very, very delicious."

THE LINDSAY SYRUP   "My father had the first maple-syrup outfit in our district. We had a fair-sized bush on our farm and I suppose they must have tapped, oh, perhaps nearly a hundred trees. You'd have to have the horses and the sleigh to go around and put the sap from the trees into the big vat, and they had to drive along very carefully not to spill the sap, and they made certain tracks in the bush for the horses to go along.

And you would take the sap to a little frame house, a small place, and in that we had the evaporator, a big evaporator, and it took so many hours to boil down that syrup to have it the right thickness. It was all done in a very, very clean way, then the syrup was strained, which meant that people were very anxious to get the Lindsay Syrup.

And we'd have a party. We'd ask the neighbour people in and

have a great time. We never did it just like a taffy pull; we'd be making pancakes, go into the big house making pancakes and maple syrup and anything they wanted.''

A REAL WINTER STORM   "If you're on a farm, there's a wonderful feeling when there's a big storm. I can recall when a big storm came up at night, you could hear the wind, and look out the window and see the snowflakes hitting against the panes. All good managers went to their barns about ten or ten-thirty o'clock at night to check on their stock, and you'd take a coal-oil lantern and wade through the drifts, following an old path probably until you got there. And you opened the door and you went into a hot, steamy stable, and saw all your animals lying down, all's quiet and all is in order. You know there's a big storm outside—there's a real feeling of isolation and you have a great feeling of well-being, that everything is right with the world and you're looking after it.

And the next morning, after one of those storms, the roads were blocked; there would be six to eight feet of snow, and if people had to get out, the young chaps, boys in their teens, would be sent out to make two tracks down the road through the bigger banks, then they would come back and they'd get a horse, just using a halter and a rope to lead him with, and try to get him to come through these banks, and of course the horse being so much heavier, he sank down and eventually would tire out, and then he would lay down. Sometimes we'd have to tramp all around him and get the snow hardened down so he would get on his feet again.''

HUNTING THE MUD   "Prince Edward Island at that time needed mud to grow clover and grain crops. There was no other way of getting lime in that day but from the mud beds, old mud beds that have been there for a thousand years, growing from the bottom of the river. The mud was in the river, in the channel, all around the bridge. You see all this place down here, well all that was solid mud, a bed here and a bed there.

We had a long fork handle—it was twenty feet long, the fork in the bottom, a great, big, iron fork, and there was a capstan and of course a horse on the capstan. And he wound around until he brought up the fork full of mud and dumped it in sleighs for the public, and they hauled it home and spread it on the field with a shovel, all day long, and they never gave a man time hardly to eat.

Everybody was hunting the mud; the whole country turned out to load single sleighs and double sleighs. A lot of diggers, in fact, there was one hundred and four diggers on the river. In 1904, they were counted, one hundred and four diggers, until about 1920 and '25, they commenced to get a little scarcer, and by '39 or '40, mud digging was about over, and at any rate the mud in the rivers was pretty well dug up.

The farmer that hauled the mud put on about ten or twelve loads, perhaps more to the acre. Sometimes many of them mudded over the second time, but the first mudding was the best. When the mud was put on you could grow as much as two tons of red-clover hay to the acre. Without that mud, you couldn't get nothing like that. It also helped the timothy; it helped the oats and it helped every crop; in fact it was hard to grow much without it."

BEAUTIFUL APPLES "We used to grow beautiful apples. We had Bishop Pippins there as big as your fist, and we used to pick them by hand, you know, and they'd keep all winter. Oh, the trees were hanging right to the ground, the limbs with beautiful fruit. We crushed our own apples and made our own vinegar, cider vinegar, and it was delicious."

IN THE FISHING SEASON "We had the farm, and we couldn't fish the year round so we'd fish in the fishing season and then we'd go to farming. Farming I liked equally well, but there was more money in the fishing.

My grandfather was a cripple and my grandmother, we had to maintain them and my father said:

'I'm afraid there ain't a living here for all of us.'

I said: 'Look, don't let that worry you. If you want to work, we can get a living here. There's a bay here right full of fish. Now,' I said, 'I'll get a boat and we'll go out there fishing.'

I bought an old skiff; she wouldn't float unless I kept her in a pool of water all the time. We'd have to haul her to that pool, and then we'd go out there. And I bought a lot of old traps for ten cents apiece. The ends were rotted out of them. I got twine and new ends put in them. Then we'd take those traps out there and dump them. We'd turn out at two o'clock in the morning and be out there on the bay, we'd pull our traps, take our fish right into the breakwater there and sell them, and when the season closed, we only fished one month one spring and we had three hundred dollars fishing in that old tub.

People said: 'You're going to get drowned there.' Some days it got pretty rough, but that old skiff would run on them seas. She'd move fast, but anyhow we managed to survive. We tried to keep her right end to as she broached, or she'd turn over. I was out there fishing when two big gasoline boats rolled over there. I was there one day when a fellow was drowned right long side of us. The next morning I had to haul him out of the water.

I never was upset. I was fortunate. I had a good boat and I knew how to handle her. The feller who owned her before we did, they run her ashore one day, jumped out of her, and left it there. They said they couldn't shut her down, they had to run full speed. Well now that was the whole trouble. I used to get over that engine, just feed her the gas, you know, just keep her going, and she'd ride them seas like a duck."

LEARNING TO PLOUGH   "I guess I was a tomboy really. I wasn't much for dolls. I played in the role of a farmer's son really. When I was old enough to manage a horse, I had a single horse attached to a plow. My uncle would help me put the harness on, because they are pretty big, and he had enough confidence in me that I could plough a single furrow, even though I was only nine or ten, and it may not be as straight a furrow as he would do, but he would encourage me to practise and to do a straight furrow. And he would get back and he would say: 'No, look at that, now can't you improve it?' And it was quite crooked, just in and out, in and out, and you see the idea was to aim for that straight furrow. He had a lot of pride in his ploughing. We didn't have a tractor—two hundred acres and every inch tillable, and we had only horses as I told you, we had ten horses and we had no tractor in the sixteen years that I was on the

farm, so you can imagine the back and forth going. So he encouraged me to learn to plough so that if I could learn to plough straight,
I would be a help to him, and my sister the same.

We had a horse that was what you call a furrow horse. He was a
big horse, but they walked a certain way and they know that they
have to keep in a furrow. And the horse does the work—you do the
guiding, you know, there's no work that you do other than walk up
and down, all you do is guide it. The ploughshare is set at a certain
depth, you know how deep you want it for your field, and it's set on
a gauge, and the horse does the work and you do the guiding, but
you do the walking also.

I was very nervous when I started, when my uncle gave me the
reins . . . but you know, I learned, because he gave me so many
opportunities to learn.''

A SHOWING ON THE FIELD   ''When I was going to school, my
father and uncle just had walking ploughs. They had what they
called a gang plough, but they never used it very much, didn't have
much faith in it. And the other implements was just a common disc,
horse disc, and a harrow. And I've seen them going out into a field
with a bag of grain—part of a bag of grain in their hand, tied over
their shoulder — and throwing the seed out on the field and then
passing over it with the harrow to cover up the seed.

A walking plough was the main implement of getting the land in
shape for a crop. And I remember when I started to plough first, I
don't know what age I would be, around fifteen, sixteen. We were
very fortunate that the northern part of Glengarry, where we lived,
was a clay land and we weren't bothered with too many stones. The
big run of the country through that part, all that neighbourhood,
was a clear land where you would work all day and hardly hit a
stone. The walking plough it just turned about I'd say an eight- or
ten-to-a-twelve-inch furrow. It'd turn a strip of sod or ground over,
turn that upside down, and it'd be only that wide, and you had to
keep going up and down the field while you kept turning it all over
in ridges. And to get that done in the fall was the main thing,
because the spring didn't prove out so good on ploughing.

You walked holding the long handles that was attached to this plough. You walked there with the team of horses, one horse walked in the furrow you made the previous round, and the other horse walked up on the top of the sod, the part that still wasn't ploughed. And you steadied the plough and steered it to turn this even amount of sod each time.

And you had the lines, or the reins of the horses — you drove them with the long lines tied around your back—and you steered them with that. You could handle a good old team with very little pressure or anything on the lines; they knew what you meant.

It was hard work, and, oh, your arms would be tired, but your legs would be tired, too, because by the time you put in a full day from seven o'clock in the morning till up to chore-time in the evening, you travelled a lot of miles. And if it was a little bit wet, you were carrying a load of clay or mud on your boots, too, at the same time. You walked right in the furrow, where you had turned the ground over. But it took a good long day to cover an acre of land; on a good day with a little extra time and a good fast team you could do an acre and a quarter, probably.

When you would strike a real bad stone, and the horses happened to be walking fairly fast, if you didn't have a good hold, sometimes you'd see the plough handle going by the side of your face. And it gave you a good feeling of being careful for the next stone.

When the evening came, when you looked back on the strip of land that you had ploughed, you got a good satisfaction, and you said you turned out a good day's work. And it made a showing on the field."

THE POTATO CROP   "I never knew a crop on the Island, on Prince Edward Island, to be what is called a failure. Sometimes you'll have a good crop and sometimes you'll have a poorer crop, but you'll always have some kind of a crop, you'll always harvest a crop.

Even if we didn't have the acreage that required more help than we had with our own family, for the digging of them we'd have to have extra help, for whatever length of time it took. In them days, with a one-row digger, we could dig about four acres a day, and we'd have to have a crowd for to haul them from the field and that kind of thing, which is all done today by a truck that's equipped. And one or two men now would do the whole job that a whole lot of people took to do in them days."

PRIMING TOBACCO "We found the tobacco farmers in Delhi was hiring men there and I got up to them and they said:

'Have you ever worked in the tobacco fields before?'

I said: 'Oh sure, I've picked tobacco, lots of it.'

So he hired me and he kept me and I was one of the last to leave in the fall. When I was leaving he said:

'I knew you hadn't worked in tobacco fields before.'

I said: 'How did you know that?'

'When I asked you if you had worked in the fields before, you said: "Oh yes, I've picked tobacco before." You never say picking in tobacco—it's all in priming.'

I've never done any harder work on a farm than working the tobacco fields, starting down at the ground level with the priming leaves and working up, you know you're bending . . . touching the ground, walking along all day with a stoneboat between the rows, working two hands, one row each side of you. I can't say I liked it, and you couldn't stand up at the end of the day.

It's pretty difficult to describe just how tough it is when you step right into priming tobacco as to how you are going to stand up at the end of the day. It's most difficult, and when you go to bed at night just absolutely every bone is aching. That was the ultimate in farming, and I decided that farming wasn't for me."

SIX

Courting

Young Man, What Are Your Intentions? . . . Girls Had a Marvellous Time . . . Stocking Feet and Tuxedo . . . The Only Time He Asked Me . . . Courting a Girl . . . Like a Lady . . . In the Family Way . . . Okay, to the Milking . . . The Way They Met . . . Catholic Boy, Protestant Girl . . . We Got Along . . . Good Girls, Bad Girls . . . The Course of True Love . . . Under an Apple Tree . . . And So It Went On

Perhaps I ran into a bit more reticence when asking about courting than I did with any other subject. It may be that some of the older people I talked to were naturally guarded about certain happenings in their youth, and yet I have no doubt at all that in most cases very definite rules were followed, since marriage was looked on as desirable, and courting a necessary prelude to it. In few cases was there any talk of girls becoming pregnant before marriage, but of course that happened, and, as long as marriage followed, little must have been said about it. Society accepts what it has to accept, and always has.

In days gone by, it must have been painful for young men to make conversations with girls they were taking to a dance or a box social, for farmers didn't need to do much talking. When you were out behind a team and a plow, you might be thinking, but you weren't going to be babbling aloud.

Some farmers, of course, were natural wits, and courting has very often meant lots of fun and flirting. Country people may be proper, but they are very seldom stuffy.

YOUNG MAN, WHAT ARE YOUR INTENTIONS? "My father took great delight in questioning my boy friends and I always wanted him to be on his best behaviour. One of his little questions was inquiring what their intentions were. And one time I had a young man who invited me out to the movies and I was upstairs getting ready, and I heard Father at the front door letting him in and I thought, 'Oh, I'd better get down there in a hurry.' I was coming down the stairs when I heard Father launching into his speech:

'Now, young man, just what are your intentions towards my daughter? Are they honourable or dishonourable?'

Most times when he said this, the young men were always very shy and got all flustered and said:

'Well . . . nothing really, just want to take her out.'

But this young man was really up to the occasion. He looked at my father and said:

'You mean I've got a choice?'

Father never did repeat that little one again."

GIRLS HAD A MARVELLOUS TIME "In Saskatchewan in the early days, there were very very few women. Not many of the schoolteachers who came in our district ever left, because they married one of the bachelors and settled down. When it came to the girls, we had such a choice of having any young boy that we wanted to go out with that I can just tell you the honest thing — I was brought up just a regular brat. Because there were five and six boys to every girl. So you went out with a boy if you wanted to. And if you didn't want to, you just threw him over your shoulder and you went with the next one. And we had a marvellous time."

STOCKING FEET AND TUXEDO "I remember the night Sally, my sister-in-law, dressed all up in her Sunday best, her formal, to go into the big city. And the city slicker came in, and first of all I guess he didn't realize that the lane would be plugged, and he had to park out on Dufferin Street, and he had a good six-hundred-foot walk through drifts in a tuxedo and dance shoes. Well of course we didn't know when he would arrive and we couldn't help him get in, and he slogged his way in, and by the time he reached the door, he was still in his tuxedo, all right, but he had sock feet, and apparently somewhere along the line he had lost his shoes. So all the five girls, including Sally in her long formal, we all went out to look for this fellow's shoes and finally found them and sent them off on their way. Oh, it was funny to see him in his stocking feet there with his tuxedo.''

THE ONLY TIME HE ASKED ME "I remember when I was a young girl, we always went to church and Sunday school on Sunday, but at night in the Presbyterian Church we had Christian Endeavour. And one night I was coming home and a boy came up and asked if he could walk home with me, and I was so surprised I just took to my heels and I ran. I ran all the way home, and before I got home, I had to go between two hotels, but I didn't take the sidewalk, I took the road. I had on these high-laced boots, and when I got home my shoelaces were flying, but I had no time to stop to tie them up. That was the only time he asked me.''

COURTING A GIRL "I have been asked many a time what did you do in those days when you were courting a girl? Well, any place that I went I was always welcome to go in the house. But I can remember going with a schoolteacher one time that was boarding at a farmer's, and I didn't like to go in his house because it wasn't her home and it wasn't my home, and we used to go for long rides in the buggy. I'd let my horse walk maybe eight or ten miles while we enjoyed ourselves talking back and forth, and I think we had just as good a time as they do today.

The cutter especially, I can remember the cutter, because the cars were not running in the wintertime, and it was a narrow road, and we really had a good time riding in those old cutters. There used to be pitch holes four feet deep. The horse would go over them, and if you would let him go he would go too fast, because he was afraid of the cutter hitting him. There was no trouble in those days to get a young lady to go out in a horse and buggy or a cutter and no trouble to get permission from her father and mother, either.

A young farm boy could pick up his next-door neighbour or a girl two or three farms away, or probably as long as she was in the church and the people knew her. There was a distinct frown on going with anyone you had never met. That was completely out: 'Don't you go with just anyone you've just picked up at the dance.' But as far as meeting a girl, picking her up, taking her home from the church, and then going and getting her the next time and taking her away, the parents used us a hundred per cent. We certainly enjoyed meeting the parents, and we had a lot of nice times together.

The schoolteacher was always considered a good catch. When a schoolteacher came into the area, about five or six young men immediately set their caps for her, and the one that got her was usually considered pretty lucky. And I know of several communities where schoolteachers came in to teach and in two or three years they were married and were permanent residents of that municipality, and they made real good citizens. They were smarter, you know. I don't mean there wasn't girls from our area that went out and taught in other schools and married away, and they were smart. But a schoolteacher was rated a really, a top catch; or a nurse was too."

LIKE A LADY "Now as far as chaperoning was concerned, our parents didn't come along with us. But we were trained very well at home to know exactly what standards were held by our parents. And the way my father always explained to me how to act in the company of a young gentleman was: 'If you keep yourself in your place, you'll never have any trouble keeping the boys in their place.' And I can honestly and truthfully say that is a fact. Boys know exactly. When you act like a lady, they treat you like one."

IN THE FAMILY WAY "As far as morals go, I guess a lot of us were very little different than what they are now except that the things that were going on were more covert. If a girl became pregnant, it was generally expected that the father of the child would marry her — it was expected by everyone. She was kind of looked down upon — I don't think they are so much today. The young man generally did marry the girl he got in the family way and then everything seemed all right. He had given the baby a name and had done justice to the girl, I suppose, and took some of the shame away from it by marrying her. And after they got married, the people would forget about it and there would be no shadow over their marriage."

OKAY, TO THE MILKING   "I had a lot of astonishing uncles, who were younger than my mother, so that they were young and they would get all dressed up at night and go out courting girls . . . and I would just stand there and look at this transformation. You know, in the daytime they had been going around in old gum rubbers and old pants and here they are all decked out and they've got the horse all rigged up and they're going off to court some girl, and my grandfather would say:

'What is he doing? She lives on the Fifth Line.'

And what that meant was he wouldn't be back till dawn—it was so far away. And he would come in and my grandfather would say:

'Okay, to the milking.'

And he'd be up all night and they'd just go out to the barn and take over, because they knew they had to milk all these cattle by hand."

THE WAY THEY MET   "I think courting, at least back in the horse-and-buggy days, most of the young men met most of the girls at garden parties, which were very often sponsored by church groups, or they met them in church, or they were a close neighbour, or even not so close. Then they would probably meet at a dance and be introduced there, and probably the young chap would ask permission to take this girl home from the dance—she may have come with her parents to that dance because parents would be also at the dance. Or he may have been introduced to her by some of his friends, and then they'd have further arrangements, or got a date with her, drove her home in the buggy or drove her home in the car. This is about the most common way they met.

Communities had plays, and very often through some role you

played in the play, you became infatuated with one of the characters. That was so in my case and I married him later. A 'character'
either way."

CATHOLIC BOY, PROTESTANT GIRL   "I recall an instance
when a Catholic boy came to pick me up following church, and I
knew I wouldn't dare get into the buggy and ride away from the
church, so I went home with my parents and he followed, came
later to the yard. But when I went in to ask my father he said: 'It's
much easier to stop now than later,' and I didn't get going with him.

And through the years, I hadn't seen him until this spring, which
was some forty years later, and he came to my door one day this
spring, and I asked him if he recalled, and he said: 'I most certainly
do, but I understood your father and I understood my father.' They
were always the best of friends, but because of Protestant and
Catholic relationships in those days, it was very understandable.
But my son who was visiting me at the time, was just standing
there, and he said to him: 'You know, your mother was my first
sweetheart,' and gave me a kiss and left, so that was to make up I
guess for the forty years in between."

WE GOT ALONG   "My Mother and Dad and the family didn't
approve of me marrying a non-Japanese. I can remember them,
pounding into me that our family could be traced back for twelve or
fourteen generations and what not, and this would be a kind of a
blot on the name and so forth and so on. But, however, I took the
bull by the horns and I left home, and this was right in the middle of
the Depression, but we survived it. We were fortunate, possibly,
that we were not living in the prairies; we had chances to get fruit
and vegetables for nothing, if you had the energy to and the acumen
to go out and get it, right in the Okanagan, and you had to go out
and look for work. We got along."

GOOD GIRLS, BAD GIRLS   "Where I grew up in the Maritimes,
mothers didn't seem to tell their daughters about sex. I should
make it clear that the girls I'm talking about are country girls, girls
out in the country, not girls from town but farm girls.

My Mother never told me anything. I found out from friends, you know, as a teen-ager. Sex was just sort of not talked about, sex or pregnancy even was not talked about. If a girl was pregnant, the only way you would find out was if you seen the girl and seen for yourself she was pregnant—not a word was said about it. We never kidded about sex in high school. About the only people I ever talked to about sex was my close girl friend, but other than that in my day, you know, we never talked about sex the way the kids do today. And I was in high school in the sixties.

Usually we met our guys at dances, and you'd always go driving, and parking afterwards, so if a girl was going to get pregnant it was while she was parking after a dance or ... well really any night of the week, you always ended up parking. Girls never tried to prevent getting pregnant. You know, back then, I didn't even know there was such a thing as a birth-control pill until after I had gotten married.

Of course there was always your good girls and your bad girls. You knew it was bad to get pregnant, but nothing was said about it. I mean it just wasn't talked about, but those were the bad girls. And the good girls, well they just really didn't go parking I guess that much. A lot of teen-age girls did get pregnant and they were anywhere from fifteen to eighteen years old, even though I do know a girl, a friend of mine, was pregnant when she was twelve. The girl would usually keep on going to school and it was just accepted by the parents. They would very seldom give the baby up. It was always kept, and it was either a brother or a sister to the girl, like depending on how young she was. But I don't know of anybody who gave their baby up.

The girls usually end up getting married because they're pregnant or shortly after they've had the baby, and for the child's sake. And they're usually not good marriages ... they don't usually end up divorcing each other, but the husband has another woman, and the wife has another man ... usually. And a lot of times, after they've had about two or three more kids, then the husband will take off and live with another woman who has already got kids, and the wife will live with another man with all her kids from her husband.

As far as abortion goes, nobody really ever thinks about having an abortion. They don't hate the child. They usually love the baby. They keep the baby. They don't even think of getting rid of it.

I think a mother should tell their daughters about sex so that the daughter can prevent pregnancy. But as far as whether telling her about sex is going to help her to be a good girl or a bad girl, she's either going to be good or she's going to be bad, no matter what you tell her. If a girl just has one baby before she is married, you know that's accepted, but if she has more than one, she's regarded as a whore.

The boys aren't usually blamed for any of this. You know you're either a good girl or a bad girl, and nobody pushes you into having sex. The guy doesn't push you. If you don't have sex, you just don't go out with him again, and usually the girl knows what kind of a guy he is anyway. You know if he's a bad guy, because there's bad guys and good guys, and if he's a bad guy, he just doesn't take you out any more — you're not his kind. And if you are his kind, then you go out with him. And the girls, I guess at thirty years old, they don't think back to what they should have done or regret what they did do. That's just the way . . . it's life, you know. They don't have any regrets, really."

THE COURSE OF TRUE LOVE "When a young man got interested in a girl, he would be bold enough to call for that girl to go for a drive, and if the parents approved, that was fine. But if the girl's father and the young man's father were bad friends, if they didn't approve of the marriage, they met secretly just the same. And finally they had to go to the manse secretly and get married. As long as they had their licence and were of age, they could get married.

You had to own some farm property before you got married. The eldest son usually inherited the farm, you see. All through Glengarry, the eldest son was eligible to have the farm. The father handed it down in his will to his eldest son."

UNDER AN APPLE TREE "I was walking down to the orchard one night, and I could smell bacon frying in my orchard. I felt this kind of odd — I'd never smelled it before in my orchard and I wondered where it was coming from. Well, just like a bear, I sort of get the scent and I walk towards it, and what do I see? I see a young couple sitting underneath a tree with a blanket all spread and a little stove, a Coleman stove, I guess, and they were making something to eat. I didn't like the idea of having them there, but this couple weren't doing me no harm. They were just sitting there, so I just would make sure they weren't staying there all night, and I asked them what they were doing there, and oh, they were tired driving, and we're going to leave here, we're just making a little bite to eat and we'll be gone and we won't bother you. And I took their word for it. So I left.

But next morning, and I always get up early in the morning, I went down to check up my orchard again to see that they were out, and I could still smell this bacon again and I said:

'By Jesus, don't tell me they're still there yet.'

By this time I got a little annoyed and I went over there and sure they were all in the blankets, they were just coming out of the blankets, had the bacon frying laying in the blankets, you know. So I got kind of rough with them, a little bit, and the girl said:

'Mr. Farmer, please be polite with us. This is our honeymoon, and we made up our mind that we were going to spend our first night in an orchard under an apple tree.'

So of course I couldn't say much more. I left them alone until they were ready to go."

AND SO IT WENT ON   "This day I was on an errand. Our neighbour kept a dairy farm and I crossed the field — not noticing the cattle in the other quarter — when out came Mister, and with his head down, chasing me. I took to my heels, for I could run then, and I jumped over a fence.

I was so frantic to get away from the bull that I didn't see where I was jumping, and I landed on a young man who was out shooting. And he was lying down in the pasture there, waiting for the sea birds that come up on the land to feed.

Well, this almost got me a husband eventually.

I was surprised and so was he. He was laughing heartily after he

saw that I was safe. The bull went back to the cattle when I got far
enough away. I was terribly frightened; I've been frightened ever
since of bulls. We laughed so hard.

I hadn't even met him before this. He was of the next farm, and he
was a young man growing up there, but I hadn't even met him. He
saw what had happened and he laughed heartily about it. And then
I asked him and his sister if they would like to come to our
Sunday-school picnic, which was at Rocky Point, just across
the river.

He and his sister came. And my brother and myself, there were
four of us. And it ended up four or five years later with my brother
marrying his sister.

And I was supposed to marry him.

But his father thought I wouldn't make a good farmer's wife. I
was too small, I was too tiny to make a good farmer's wife. I needed
to be strong, and hearty. His interest after that was in me, but it
didn't end in marriage. After that he thought he'd like to come back
again. And again. And it ended up in a courtship. But not in
marriage.

We went on sleigh rides and buggy rides, and parties, and
dances. I admired him. He was an open young man. He was a kind
of a young man anyone should like to have. His name was Ben.

The reason I didn't marry him was his father thought that I
wouldn't make a good farmer's wife for his son, and he did everything to shut it off. Well, I let him finally. I didn't want to go into a
home like that.

I went West. He married a good farmer's daughter. Not big and
strong, but strong and healthy, I suppose. And so it went on. We
were unhappy for some time. And forty years later when I returned
to Prince Edward Island, he was the same gentleman. I liked him so
well, and he liked me, I bought an acre of ground off him and set up
a home, living next door to him. And you would have thought that
nothing had ever passed between us.

He had two children. We had three.

I met a young man, out West, who was principal of a school I was
teaching in, and I married him. He was one of the finest scholars

from Ontario, a classical man, Latin, Greek, and ancient history. We later ended up in Hamilton Collegiate, where we stayed for twenty-seven and one-half years.

I had no regrets. I'm not sure that it worked out for the better. But it worked well. He married a beautiful girl whom I took for my very best friend later in life.

Would you believe for years afterward I would have nightmares of a bull chasing me? And I just got away in time."

SEVEN

The Old Homestead

An Old Quebec Farmhouse . . . There You Are . . . How to Build a Sod House . . . Only the Willow Stakes Grew . . . A Toast to the New House . . . Still Standing . . . The Buffalo that Dropped In . . . Power to the Sod House . . . Go to the Aunt . . .

T*he sod house, the original homestead, the home farm; so many people gave direct accounts of the first dwelling their fathers built or the homes in which they were born which are now gone. There is something haunting about an old deserted farmhouse — a place a man spent weeks or months of hard toil putting up, and a home a woman took pride in and did her best to make pretty.*

I remember, one Sunday in August some years ago, coming down the five-hundred-mile stretch from Hay River to Peace River on a high-lift car with a railway superintendent. There are no passenger trains through that beautiful country, only freights and ore trains, so I was privileged to be able to see, here and there in the bush, forsaken and crumbling sod houses. I thought of the men who'd cut the sods and lifted them up one after another, and of how, when it was all done, they had their first home, miles and miles from the nearest neighbour. We stopped for a while and I explored one of these old sod huts, and it was like stepping into a dream of hope and a nightmare of hard work at one and the same time.

The first home could be a centuries-old farmhouse in the Province of Quebec or it could be a log house that went up by-guess-and-by-God but stood well against the elements as an act of will more than a triumph of architecture. However it was built, and wherever it was, it was a visible manifestation that a start had been made, a family established, and a country on its way.

73

AN OLD QUEBEC FARMHOUSE   "The farm was called Burnside, from the Scottish word 'burn' I guess, because there was a small stream that ran through the property. There was a large stone tablet leaning up against the front steps with this engraved on it, Burnside, and I can always remember because we used to whitewash it and paint it every once in a while.

The farm was on the northern outskirts of Quebec City, well within the present-day city boundaries. I think it was considered a large farm, perhaps two hundred acres, about that size anyway. It was a very pretty location and I think they did all sorts of mixed farming.

It had belonged to my grandfather and his father before him, I believe, was the original farmer in the district. We moved there in 1940.

The farmhouse was typically Quebec. It had a verandah that extended around three sides of the house, with steps going up front and back, a large sloping roof on all sides with dormer windows. And in the back, there was a sun porch that was used in the summer for flowers and plants. And along the back of the house was a large room they called the summer kitchen, and it was used for large get-togethers in the summer and also during harvesting and haying more particularly, when the farm help used to eat in the summer kitchen.

It was not really very far from downtown Quebec City, and to give you some idea of its age, on either side of the front steps coming up to the gallery there was a cannon ball that evidently they had found in the fields somewhere back.

And downstairs was the creamery in the basement; and there were these huge thick stone walls always whitewashed, where they kept the milk and the butter, things like that.

I can remember the room upstairs that we slept in had hard, bright red, flowered wallpaper, and I think with nosey fingers we found seven or eight other layers of wallpaper underneath it, all just as colourful. I can still smell the smells of the special raisin buns that my grandmother used to make, and they were always on the table, breakfast, lunch, and supper, always on the table, and they were always good.

Today the farm is completely gone. It is now a playground for an orphanage, I believe. The river is gone, althought it was a natural drainage river; they put pipe in and it is all levelled over, all the huge beautiful elm trees have vanished of course. The house is gone, and the last time I was down you couldn't really tell where it had been—it's just gone, gone, disappeared."

THERE YOU ARE "When we went in there we didn't have a team or anything. We did like so many other people; we got a man in town here, a pioneer who said: 'Yes, I know where that is.' And he took us out there. He took what little goods we had out in two wagons, our neighbours and ourselves went out there together in two wagons — that was it. And he took us out four days into the bush and dumped the neighbours off a mile or so from our place and dumped us off and said: 'There you are.'

Well, Dad didn't know what he was doing too much. This was October. No Canadian would ever dream of going out to a homestead in October, but we just had to go on from there, and the result was that though Dad took out what he thought was a lot of food, we ate a lot more food than he dreamt of, and on about January or February of this terrible winter of 1897 and '98, he was forced to come back in to try to find some work in Edmonton to get some money to get food. It all worked out very nicely in the end.

Now the sort of thing that he did, thousands of others of the homesteaders did the same thing. I would say they were courageous; they were ignorant of what they were going into but they were capable enough of getting by, once they found they had made a mistake."

HOW TO BUILD A SOD HOUSE "You got your sod by ploughing the sod in the bottom of a dried grassy slough, where there was lots of roots, and this furrow rolled up in a long ribbon behind your plough. You had to try to plough fairly carefully, the right depth and the right width. The sod would be about four inches, and it would roll up in a long ribbon. You cut it into lengths approximately two foot in length, and you'd lay these sods — we did in western Canada, and I think all over the States—you laid this sod grass-side down. Most of them had two layers, side by side. That would make a wall about twenty-eight inches thick.

You'd lay your first two layers around; you'd lace your corners in for stability, and you'd take a sharp spade again as you laid your sod grass-side down, you'd fill in the cracks, you'd level it off.

I've heard of one family they came out on the homestead and they lived in a tent all summer, a father and a mother and the three little girls. It came along towards the fall and the neighbours figured something should be done about this, so they called a sodding bee, and the whole neighbourhood flocked around and built that sod house in one day.

They'd brought along a lunch—it was a community effort—they brought along a lunch and there was a few poles they had brought with them. You laid these poles at an angle from the sides of the roof up the central ridge pole. You covered these poles with hay or light brush and laid your sods on top of that. This made a very warm building. We used to have a saying of course, if you had a dirt roof, if it rained all day outside, it would rain for about two days inside. But it doesn't rain very much in the West, not usually.

People very often ask me, 'Didn't the sod walls wash out with the strong rains?' But if you picked a grassy slough with lots of roots in it, they held. As a matter of fact, we had a sod house out at the old museum site that we put up and it stood for at least sixteen years, with no trouble.

I've been asked sometimes how long did it take a man to build a sod house, and I have to counter that by saying: 'Well, it all depended how much work you could get out of your wife.' But if there was husky kids around and everybody pitched in, I suppose it would take about two weeks. But we had more time than money. A sod house of course was just a crutch to lean on. You figured that a lot of homesteaders were forty or fifty miles from town, and the mere fact of going to town with a team of oxen and hauling a big wagonload of lumber back was quite a proposition, to say nothing of the money; but it was pretty tough going, and these sod buildings, they were an integral part of homestead life.

It depends, of course, how big your family was how big your sod house would be, but we'll say approximately, oh, twelve-to-twenty to twenty-four foot length, and you didn't have partitions.

They tell me that when you built in some of the river valleys, flowers would grow on the roof, the morning glories, and that the sod roof was just quite attractive. But they weren't damp. They kept off the rain when it took a little while to dry off. But we're talking of dirt roofs and dirt floors, of course, and this dirt floor could be packed hard and swept out fairly clean, although of course there was always a little dirt sifting around. Some women got building paper and papered the inside of the sod house. Oh, it was too dry for bugs. Mice would come in now and again, but there weren't many mice on the prairie. Of course, one of the biggest enemies to the sod buildings would be the cattle. The corner of a sod building was very nice for a cow to scratch on and rub her neck up and down. But that was heck on a sod shack."

ONLY THE WILLOW STAKES GREW "We landed at Victoria, and they placed us on a farm of seven acres, five acres of which were under water on the first of July, and the rest was bedrock. Being Englishmen we had to have a run of beans, so I found a place where oak leaves had dropped for the last two thousand years and put them in, and then I had to find me some place where there was some stakes. There were some willows there so I cut them down and sharpened them and put them in and waited patiently, and the only thing that grew was the willows.

So then we made contact with the superintendent of the settlement farms and said: 'Listen, we want something better than this.'

So he gave us a list of farms all the way up to north of Duncan and we went with a shovel and a pickaxe. You couldn't swing a pickaxe because you'd hit a stump, and you couldn't put a shovel in the ground because it was rocks. We finally landed this twenty acres right where we are—it looked pretty nice and we thought we could make a job of it. We thought we'd have it ploughed and we had a man to do the ploughing. And every ten feet he hit a rock that probably weighed three hundred pounds, and we had to have a team of horses to take every rock out. On one of the rocks we had to use a team of horses and block and tackle, but we finally got it off the land. So we just took it as part of the punishment...having been stupid enough to get here."

A TOAST TO THE NEW HOUSE   "Well, I helped on the building. I had to peel the logs and then we'd put them up as high as we could. We'd decided on a very big house, which was very foolish. You know, we thought we'd have a real home. And it had to be very large with gables and everything.

Well, when we got so high up, that was it: we'd had it, couldn't manage any more, so we had to buy ropes. Harry would throw these ropes over the building; and I would have the team at the other side of the building. And he'd give me the order as the log rolled up, and he put it into place. That's how we put the high building up alone. It was a two-storey building.

The logs went up very well, but when it came to putting the roof on, well, we had to live in it all the winter without a roof. So we put the top floor on and put a tent inside. And that's how we lived when it was sixty below zero—in this tent. Without a roof.

But when we did come to put the roof on, the next year, we had to get a proper roof, and we put shingles on. And as we finished it we were so delighted—I was up there shingling with him—we had a nice meal set on the table, and were sitting down thankful that we'd done it, when the thing caught fire. And we had to race out, and Harry had to put the fire out."

STILL STANDING   "When my Dad decided to build their first house, he went to look at another house, another log house on an adjoining quarter, I suppose. He had never built one, but he figured he could just go look at it and do it. So he looked at it, came back, and he and his brother started in to build their house.

And they did. They just piled the logs one up on top of the other, and they only made it about six feet tall. It was no taller than it had to be. And then they put a straight-across roof on it that they put dirt on. And they had a lot of trouble with that dirt roof until finally about five years later, when my mother came into the picture, they put a slanted roof on it, and that did keep out some of the rain and some of the critters that used to come through the dirt roof.

But Dad found out years later that he had notched the logs entirely the wrong way around, and I don't know which way is which, but he had apparently done it exactly opposite. And to this day that little place still stands. So even though it was wrong, it worked.''

THE BUFFALO THAT DROPPED IN   "There was another sort of sod shack called the dugout. You'd excavate a hole in the hillside and build up the walls around them. These were warmer yet. I've heard of early-day settlers in the very, very early days, that owned these dugouts, they just ran off the prairie. I've been told of a buffalo falling through the roof of one of these shacks and being terrified, just as terrified as the people, and dashing out the door and taking the doorframe with him. This was one of those stories, but I think it would very likely be true.''

POWER TO THE SOD HOUSE   "There was a friend of mine built a sod house and lived in it fairly comfortably, and when the power came through, about 1940, they were just in the process of building a lumber house, but the power came through and they were still living in the sod house, so they thought they might as well have power in this sod house. Bill used to claim that his was the only sod house he had ever heard of that was wired for power.''

GO TO THE AUNT...   "I can think of one remittance man who happened to be a bachelor, he never married. He was a very fine musician, studied music in Germany and Vienna and several other European countries, came out to this country, left money by his family, built a little home in the town of Baldur, Manitoba. He just had a one-room shack with an attic in it, in which he slept, but he had this beautiful grand piano on this ground floor. He played this thing at two o'clock in the morning sometimes.

Unfortunately, the building was right beside the Baldur Hotel. At that time they were surveying the land of the municipality of Baldur, and the surveyors were rather a hard-living and hard-drinking group of men, and they didn't like being kept up till two or three o'clock in the morning every day, so one night one of the

fellows got tired of listening to this concerto being played about 2
A.M. He went out and poured a little gasoline on the side of the
house, set a match to it, and up went the house and the piano.

The chap escaped all right, but he had the editor of the Baldur
Gazette at that time write an article in the paper about the sad loss
of the beautiful home, this wonderful estate, that had gone up in
Baldur. He cut the clipping out and sent it to his family in England
and one of his rich aunts sent him 250,000 pounds to replace this
beautiful estate. But he was smart enough to take the money and
went to New Zealand, and we never heard any more of him —
hadn't the faintest idea of what happened."

EIGHT

Horses

Personalities of Their Own . . . Prints on the Wall . . . To the Barn Door . . .
Speedy Irish . . . The Gate Was Open . . . Jealousy . . . Crying Like a Baby . . .
The Sign of a Good Horse . . . Old Bill . . . Runaway . . . Horse Trading . . .
The Glue Factory

O ne thing that came across loud and clear when I was putting this book together is that a farmer's best friend is his horse. That certainly used to be the case. Not too many farmers have work horses now, and those who do usually have put them out to pasture as honoured guests.

Farmers took great pride in their horses, whether in the fields or driving along the concessions. It seems almost as if a kind of mystic bond was established between man and horse. A minority of farmers were bad-tempered and would light into a horse if it displeased them, but I was told over and over again that a horse is what you make it, and that if a horse is ornery, then someone somewhere along the line mistreated it. Most farmers, of course, were kind to their horses, understood their little eccentricities, and unfailingly took good care of them. There was a relationship between man and horse that was eminently satisfying to both.

You can hardly have that kind of relationship with a tractor.

PERSONALITIES OF THEIR OWN "I think that animals very definitely have personalities of their own. I can recall as a child on the prairies, going to a one-room country school each day, and driving a team of horses. There were two in particular that I remember, that we used to drive as a team. One was called Queenie, and one was called Lady. And the personalities of these horses were quite different.

The horse called Queenie was a very aggressive horse, and would attempt to pull the entire load herself. She would always be straining to the utmost of the length of the traces. While the other one, Lady, would lean right back as far as she could, and just be pulled along by Queenie."

PRINTS ON THE WALL "One time one of my older brothers was teasing a young two-year-old horse. This young colt was drinking at the pump outside, and my brother thought he could tease it with a long straw. He went up to it and said 'Budzudzudzudzudz' and the colt gave a sort of kick out behind. But didn't do anything, didn't leave her drink. And after she was through drinking, and my brother was over near the door of the stable, she went over after him with her ears back. She reared up with her front feet and planted a hoof on either side of him. She left her prints on the wall, and he was in between. As much as to say, 'Look out. That's what you'll get next.' He never would tease her again."

TO THE BARN DOOR "I developed a great love for horses and one of my stories is the night my brother and I rode to the school Christmas concert on horseback. It was a terrible snowstorm just building up, and by the time we got out when it was over we didn't know which direction was which. So we sort of headed for home, and it soon became evident we weren't going anywheres near home at all.

The blizzard was blowing at forty, fifty mile an hour, snowing. We started following the telephone line home. We couldn't see from one pole to the other, and we didn't know where we were. So we tied the reins to the saddle horn. Within twenty minutes the pony had changed to the proper direction and walked us right up to the barn door."

SPEEDY IRISH   "Now take this one. This is one of the oldest, one of the best horses that we ever had, Speedy Irish, and won the Clarendon Plate, the Cup and Saucer, the Coronation Stakes, and twenty-three thousand as a two-year-old — all that except for the Plate. When he was sold to Mr. McCullough, Mr. McCullough put him in the Plate. All he had to do was to win the Queen's Plate and he'd've won almost everything. And he was in beautiful shape, his coat looked like gold.

So anyhow, Mr. Taylor had a horse, and it was one of the first horses Mr. Taylor ever put into a Plate, and that was a horse called Epic. So anyhow they were in the race there, and Chris Rogers was riding Mr. Taylor's Epic, and Johnny Dewhurst—poor fellow died here about a year ago — Johnny Dewhurst was riding our horse. Now our horse had a peculiarity about him, Speedy Irish would never go into a bunch of horses. As he's coming away around the back turn and out to the low turn, he would be behind them all, but as soon as he got on the level of the stretch, then he'd make his charge, and there's where he won all his races.

But this very particular race, it happened, he was in the race there, and what made him turn or do what he did, we'll never know till doomsday, but anyhow, instead of being where he should have been—at the back waiting for his chance to go around—he opened up a few yards like that, and Epic got in between him and the fence, and Epic got the Plate by two lengths, and our poor horse was knocked out.

But anyhow, after that Mr. McCullough died, and his wife said she didn't want to keep the horses. Well, Speedy Irish came back to the farm after they all had been sold, back to where he was born. And his coat was like gold, honestly he was a beautiful looking thing, he was. So old Tommy, the groom in the farm there, he said to me one day:

'George, let us put all the mares down out of the way, get them away from the sight of their own paddock.'

I said: 'All right, I'll get them out.'

He said: 'I'll tell you what I want to do—I want to take Speedy out and see what he'll do.'

Well now this is the fact, you'll hardly believe it. Speedy was in the barn by himself, you know, and all these mares were away out in the top field, and we thought they were all out of sight, you see, with the trees and that. So I went in and got Speedy out, took him up to the barn, dropped the bars down, and let him go into the paddock. And he run diagonal like that across, and when he got to the corner he looked up the field and he saw them and he whinnied . . . who . . . who . . . who . . . and down he jumped, and that was the end of Speedy Irish.

He'd won all these races, been trained down until he was just tension like that. He saw the mares up in the field and got so excited there that he went on his hind legs, and down he dropped dead, that was the end of Speedy Irish. He was only a three-year-old then. When Speedy Irish died, it was practically the end of Mr. Heffering. Mr. Heffering, the breeder, was taken away and taken to Oshawa General Hospital and put into an oxygen tent, and he lasted about two weeks, and that was the end of Mr. Heffering and the end of Speedy Irish too, the horse and the breeder. That was the end of the farm."

THE GATE WAS OPEN   "I was told several times not to ride the horses, not to go near the horses, and of course being eight or nine years old, I had no fear of them at all, and I didn't take my grandmother's advice. So one afternoon, when I thought everybody was busy and not noticing what I was doing, I went to the field and proceeded to try and ride this horse, Prince. It was a regular plough horse that they used for drawing the hay or for ploughing. It was huge across the back, and of course when you sat on him, your legs stuck straight out. And I spent around an hour trying to get him to the fence. I'd just get ready to get on him and he'd pull away. So I chased him across the field, and finally I succeeded. There was no bridle; there was no saddle; it was just the horse and I, and I was so excited about being able to ride the horse, I didn't shut the gate. So when I did get on, Prince and I, we were doing quite well until he noticed the gate was open, and back he went and broke into a gallop and I had no other choice but to hang on for dear life, and it's quite hard when your legs are sticking straight out on both sides. He headed for the barn—and they were threshing so they had the barn door open — and he headed right into the barn and into his own stall.

My grandmother, my aunt, my uncle, and everybody else were witness to this great ride, and all I could think of was my grandmother — I could see her face — and really I wasn't too concerned with falling off, I was concerned about what was going to happen when I got there. But we made it all right and I didn't get into too much trouble.''

JEALOUSY "They told me that a stallion would kill a little colt, and the first colt that come, when I went out in the morning, the stallion hadn't seen it. I think she had it down behind the gravel pit and I met her coming up with the colt walking along. And at that time I seen that the stallion and the rest of the horses were away over at the far side of the field. And they spotted the little colt, and of course they all come over to see it, and the stallion stepped up close and then he let an awful squeal out of him and he struck with his front foot, and of course I chased him off. The mare put her ears back and went to kick, but there was the danger of her going to kick at him and hit the colt and everything commotion.

Well, from then on, I always watched and kept him in the stable before there was any mares to foal—I didn't want to take a chance. I think he was out one time when the mare foaled and there was no trouble, but I never took a chance.

The other problem that I had with the stallion running out was when there was two mares in heat. One would get jealous of the other, and when he'd come to breed one, the other would come up, and if he didn't pay attention, she was liable to wheel and plaster him . . . kick him. And I've seen him at one time he was covering a mare, and this other wheeled and let blaze at him and I think knocked him off—there was never any accidents, but they will do that. If you'd take him out where there was two or three mares in season, you'll have to watch, for one will let blaze, and you can get kicked in between with them.''

CRYING LIKE A BABY "I remember we had about ten horses when I was growing up, and they were all named. Every one had a name. We had a beautiful chestnut team, and that was Dolly and Charlie, a male and female. Anyway, they were work horses and they were a beautifully matched team and they had the right . . .

you know how some are matched the way they can pull...the right weight. And my uncle, he cherished this team.

And one day when we were small, I must have been eight or nine, he came into the house crying like a baby and he said: 'Charlie has just dropped in the field.'

He had unhitched the two of them and brought Dolly back into the barn, and they got the vet and Charlie had died of a heart attack. Now this horse was only eight or nine years old. It was in its prime of life, and they could give no reason at all why Charlie died so suddenly. It took my uncle weeks to get over that, because when you attach yourself to a team and they work so well together and you call that your team, when that team is broken up, to a farmer, that's tragic.'

THE SIGN OF A GOOD HORSE   "We used to have an old lady stayed with us. Her name was May McKenzie, and she was probably one of the kindest people I think I ever knew.

And she was quite outspoken. If somebody happened to let a foul smell, she would say: 'A farting horse will never tire, and a farting man is the man to hire.'

Now the reason I tell you this thing is how important it was in teaming. Suppose we say you were riding along on a heavy load of logs, and you were coming along and coming to a hill. When those horses were going up the hill, they would invariably make manure and then there'd be this phht, phht, phht, every little while, farting all along, which was definitely the sign of a good strong horse. That was a mark of it. It was a farting horse, and it was a good horse.''

OLD BILL   "One day when I was eight or nine, on the farm at Cheviot, near Saskatoon, I had quite an experience driving to school. I had four miles to drive, and being so young, they gave me an old, old bronc to drive. He was no good for farm work, but he could pull the buggy.

This was summer, and we started out around half past seven to get to school at nine o'clock. And we had gone about three-quarters of a mile, when I saw what I knew was a cow. It was facing us so that just the head showed. It was light grey and it had long horns, and Old Bill, the bronc, didn't know what it was. So he reared up on his back legs.

And that is about all I can remember till I wakened up, under the buggy, in the ditch. And when I opened my eyes and crawled out from under the buggy, I can remember gathering up my books. And then I looked around and there was no horse. He had completely disappeared. I must have been knocked out for quite a few minutes for him to have disappeared.

But I could feel something warm on my face. There was blood running down. So I was really scared, and I started to cry. And I guess I was crying loud enough that when the folks at home, after seeing the horse run in the yard, were out looking to see where I was, they could hear me.

When they came, they were quite worried because there was so much blood. I had bitten right through my tongue and it was just hanging there by just a small piece at the side. But anyway, my mother told me: 'Put your tongue in your mouth and keep your mouth shut.' Which I had to do because there was no doctor around, and they didn't realize, I don't think, how serious it was.

So I had to keep my mouth shut, and be very careful. I couldn't eat anything. I drank with a straw without opening my teeth. And I don't know how many days that went on — and then of course it still hurt after I could open my mouth. It finally healed, but in the meantime, I was really upset with this old horse. I didn't realize that he was so frightened that he didn't know what he was doing.

And the day after the accident, he went down to an old manure pile behind the barn, and laid down. And died."

RUNAWAY   "I do remember in harvest time we had a big wagon and a team of horses and we were small children, very small, and we were all in the wagon in a rocky place—what they called a lane —and there were big boulders, stones, around and my brother was leaning against the rack on the front of the wagon that would support the load, and that rack broke down and went on the horses' backs and that's what started the race, and it was terrible. They ran away, they went about half a mile running away, just wild, just mad you know, because they got frightened.

And my brother, oh, he was about fifteen, I suppose, he was down on the part of the pole, down between the horses where the pole started, and he hung on for all his life till the horses ran into the corner of a fence and they were stopped. They broke something and they couldn't go any further. And he was all bruises, his head was all bruised and he was terribly hurt. There were six children on the wagon, we were sort of sitting on our knees, you know, and we were all bruises, and it was a terrible thing. My brother's face was all black and blue and he had to be taken to the doctor for fear there was greater damage being done. But he escaped, he escaped wonderfully.

I was on the wagon and my older sister was holding me so I wouldn't get hurt or fall while the wagon was jumping over the stones, so I wasn't hurt at all. But I can remember it so very plainly. I didn't have the sense to be scared. I was too young, but it was a terrible thing for my parents watching this episode. They were very frightened that we were badly hurt, but when they found out that we weren't badly hurt, we just got a talking to. We got enough spanking on the wagon."

HORSE TRADING   "I had enough wheat to pay my rent, my taxes, my threshing, and my wages, and some besides. This give me a good start. But the sweet clover, I sold it to pay for a horse which I bought when I went there, and the horse dropped dead the day I finished cutting wheat. This was a kind of sad day for me. He was in eating his dinner.

I know the horse must have dropped instantly because there was lots of straw around the horse and he never even had kicked. But I found out afterwards the horse had been sick once before I bought him, and the veterinary told the fellow that had him to get rid of him; and that's why he phoned to tell me he had a horse to sell."

DOLL   "We were very fond of horses out on our farm, and particularly our drivers. Of course we didn't have cars, and through our high-school days we had one driver in particular we called Doll. By a driver, I mean a horse who pulled a buggy and took us each week to high school. And not only did she pull the buggy, but on race days, Fair days, my dad used to sometimes race her, and mother would drive her home after the Fair. Everyone thought we should be afraid of her, but none of us were. She stood in the passageway in our stable, and anyone outside the family who attempted to go past her, she would crowd them out. She'd put her ears back, and everyone was terrified of her, but nevertheless we loved her.

This same gray driver would not like a car to pass her. They were new to her and she'd just put her ears back and take after it as fast as she could."

THE GLUE FACTORY   "My grandfather had an old horse that he was very, very fond of, and the horse got older and older. Finally one day it died, and it was the custom that when you had an animal die on the farm, particularly a horse I guess, you phoned the glue factory in Quebec City and they came and for a small fee collected your dead animal and took him away to the glue factory. My grandfather had such an affection for this old horse, that he said nothing doing, there was no way that he was going to sell the old horse to the glue factory. So he and several of the hired men that worked on the farm, they dug a great huge ditch and they buried the horse behind the barn."

NINE

Lives of Girls and Women

Alone in the Bush . . . The Facts of Life . . . Busy Seasons . . . The Best Hired Man . . . Craftswomen . . . Winter Clothes . . . A Water Witch . . . Hired Help . . . A Kicker . . . Isolation . . . Then Back to the House . . . A Good Frontier Cook . . . The Red Blanket . . . Nest-Eggs . . . Loafing Around the House All Day . . . High on the Ladder . . . A Hopeless Situation for Her

It's usual to think of "the farmer" as the mainstay of the farm, with the farm wife as a background figure. Nothing could be further from the truth. Farm wives have always needed ten arms with fifteen fingers on each hand to get their work done, and required the patience of Job to cope with emergencies or with the tedium of much of the work they have to do. In addition to this, the farm wife is chiefly responsible for holding the family together and teaching her children duties and responsibilities, and is sometimes at work from five in the morning until eleven at night, especially during harvesting.

On the surface of things, it would seem that she would inevitably turn into a hag and a nag, but the farm women I met (and indeed there were many of them) seemed to have thrived on it. Many of them were over sixty, or seventy, or eighty and they were mostly healthy and bouncy and vigorous and very good-humoured. Women have a way of taking up direct challenges and finding energy sources in themselves and turning that energy into enthusiasm. The baking, the sewing, the washing: they larded into it all. And, often, when left alone of necessity, they found great courage to face situations that must at first have appalled them.

I must point out that there was loneliness and isolation and despair, and sensitive women were trapped in situations that gave them no access whatever to cultural pursuits. One such woman lent *me a four-hundred-page novel which, years later, she had written about her days on the homestead when she felt smothered by an environment that was too narrow, too restricted. She simply had to get it out of her system, and writing a novel was the way she managed it.*

Nevertheless, for all the tribulations, the women were tough and resourceful. On occasion, they went out in the fields when the pressure was on and helped their menfolk. They still do. No wonder more than one farmer told me: "The best hired man I ever had was my wife!"

ALONE IN THE BUSH   "Mother, I know, had a terrific amount of courage, which had never been tested up to that point, when Dad had to go off and leave her alone in the bush. Dad was expecting to be away, oh, perhaps a week, but I think he was away about three weeks, and Mother and I lived in this tent. The weather was very cold, but that didn't matter. We had lots of firewood . . . I was just a baby of about a year or so, and I think it was the terrific loneliness of it, no neighbours, she didn't see anybody in that three-week interval, that was the thing that tested her courage. Some women might have cracked up under it.

When Dad left, he had three or four different kinds of guns, a shotgun, a rifle, and so on. He left these all there and he said to Mother: 'Now here's the guns if you want to use them.'

And Mother had never paid any attention to a gun before, but it snowed very heavily there for several days, and one night, she woke up with something crawling up onto the roof of the tent. It was just a little bit of a tent, and she was frightened to death. She had heard about bears and wolves and cougars and all this sort of thing, and she felt sure that the thing that was up there would come down and eat us.

Well, it disappeared in the morning and came back the next night and climbed up there, to get the heat from the stovepipe that went through there. On the third night, Mother couldn't stand it any longer, she was almost beginning to crack up from the general loneliness, and she took this big rifle of Dad's, a .303 British Army rifle, and pointed it in the general direction of this thing that was sagging down the canvas two or three feet above her head. As it turned out she missed it, but she must have scared it because it never came back again.

Now I can't imagine what that was. She thought it might be a lynx or a cougar or something. I suspect it may have been a rabbit or something that crawled up there for the heat, but nevertheless, the effect of this unknown creature two or three feet above her head on the canvas was nearly enough to crack her up."

THE FACTS OF LIFE   "In those days you couldn't keep the facts of life from kids living on the farm, but it wasn't supposed to be for girls. I wasn't even allowed to be around at the birth of a calf, never mind the beginnings. We learned, anyhow."

BUSY SEASONS   "The different seasons brought different chores for each day. In the seeding time, we always figured there's probably two weeks good weather and if you aren't up and at it, well, you're just not going to get your crop in in time, and so you're out early in the morning, probably you're out four or four-thirty, and then you come in and do all your barn work, have breakfast, back out in the fields till noon, and the same thing over in the afternoon, and we would work till nine o'clock or so at night, and come in and do our barn work then, milk cows, and it would be late. But then that didn't go on week after week — just while that certain type of work had to be done while the weather was good.

Most of the time when the men were particularly busy at seeding or haying or threshing time, you didn't have time to yourself. You really had to be doing baking or something in preparation for another meal. You had very little time in their busy season, you were busy too. As a rule you followed a pretty rigid schedule. You knew that there had to be a lot of baking prepared; in those particular seasons you had extra men for threshing, you always had ten or twelve men, meal after meal. For silo filling, you'd have as many as twenty men for two meals a day, and they were always starving; they were as empty as the silo, we used to say, because they were working in the fresh air, and I think their appetites were thus whetted. We thoroughly enjoyed the crowd as they gathered at the table and it was always a pleasure to see them enjoy the food. There were always stories told and lots of fun going along with it, and I guess it helped to pass the time for us and relieve us of our worries in connection with the meal.

For a farm woman had to always provide good meals, keep a clean house, and raise her family, and also be a helper right along with her husband.

And farming was mighty hard work, it was hard physical labour. There are so many things today that are done so much easier than was done in those days. For instance, in the harvesting of crops, today we put in a corn crop and we treat that corn with one of the many chemicals that prevents the prolific growth of weeds in the corn crop, and outside of cultivation in the early stages, that's all that happens to that corn.

In the olden days, we pulled that with a hoe from one end to another, and when that corn was ready to cut, again we cut it with a hoe, a short-handled hoe with a strap on it that you put around your wrist, so that you wouldn't lose it.

If you had ten acres of corn in those days you were doing pretty well. But that represented a lot of cutting with a hoe, and I still remember the first time they sent me out with a hoe, I just took about fifteen minutes until I cut my little toe in half, including a good pair of boots. This will happen.

Then when it came to haying time, they mowed the hay with a mower, and then it was raked into windrows, and then the farmers and their families, sometimes their wives — we're speaking of hard-working wives—came along and put this hay into coils, and it was left there to cure. These were round mounds of hay, the tops were raked down with the tines of the fork, so they'd be more or less waterproof. And when it came time to take these in the barn, this had to be forked on to a wagon, and when the load got away up in the air about six and seven and eight feet, it needed a five-foot handle in the fork to get it up. When it was gotten to the barn, it had to be forked off into the mow again before the days of the big hayforks.

And at harvest time, all grain was put into sheaves, then it had to be stooked or shocked in the field, left to mature, brought into the barn, forked into the mow, and then at a later time, it was forked out of the mow into the maw of our threshing machine.

The haying operation was always conducted in about June and possibly to the first of July, and it was mighty hot work, and during the morning sometimes the children would be sent out with a drink, and some of the local drinks that were sent out was raspberry vinegar, which was quite a tart, good-tasting thing. Probably the most popular drink in our area was the plain water mixed with oatmeal, a small amount of oatmeal, and this gave us a certain amount of nourishment as well as helping to quench the thirst."

THE BEST HIRED MAN "I think women would enjoy it better if they got out and helped their men farm. When I got married, I married at twenty-four and my wife was the best hired man I ever had in my life. She would really work and not only do a good job, but do it so willingly and so pleasantly that, why, it was a pleasure to have her. And it's something I'll never forget, and I think that she didn't lose anything by it; she lived a good long age and it didn't hurt her to work, and I think she got a lot of pleasure out of helping me. She mainly pulled weeds, picked stones and hoed in the garden, and stooked the grain and loaded the hay and helped pitch the grain on, unloaded and helped in the barn when we were stowing the crop in the barn and all that stuff, work that's not there now at all. We don't have that kind of work nowadays with our combines and what have you. There's not the same kind of farming at all. It's changed altogether."

CRAFTSWOMEN "I think of the farm women within our community, perhaps not as collectors, but as craftswomen, particularly talented with their hands, particularly good at crochet or tatting or good embroidery or knitting or some of them are painters. I know of several neighbour women who can sit down and do doilies for the evening or what have you and it's a sense of achievement when it is done. And this is relaxation for them."

WINTER CLOTHES   "The weather is a factor up there in the Peace River country. There's no getting around it. And in the winter my parents didn't let us walk down to the bus if it was more than thirty below. I mean Fahrenheit. And that used to just kill me. I used to negotiate. You know, if it was thirty-five below, I'd say: 'That's just five more than it was yesterday; can't I go?'

And even if it was under the thirty and we went, the clothes that we had to put on! It was so incredible, and they were awful clothes. We always had to wear long underwear. And this would all get all bunchy around you, and it used to chap you. Oh, it was awful!

I always hated being a girl on the days that it was terribly, terribly cold, because the boys would get to go out and dress in front of the heater. There was no problem. But my Mother being the Presbyterian that she was, I had to stay in the back bedroom and get dressed back there. And the underwear would be so cold. And the dumb clinking garters — I'll never forget them. They always just sort of froze you right up at instant touch. So I always resented being a girl at that time.

Spring was the favourite season. You were so glad to see the end of winter and to be able to walk out without having to put on boots and socks and these awful ski pants, and to get the underwear off. Spring meant such a liberation to us that we looked forward to it. And of course, spring was the beginning of growing things, and that was our whole reason to be there."

A WATER WITCH   "Water witching is very interesting. I had a cousin who came down from Saskatchewan and carried a water-witching stick in the trunk of his car. And of course each time he visited his relatives, he displayed his ability to witch for water, and we'd go in and out our lane and each of us tried it. And my husband couldn't . . . the stick had no effect when it was in his hands. My brother-in-law tried it and it didn't have any effect, and of course I didn't expect it would have any effect when I would take hold of it, but I could walk in and out the lane, and as soon as I would come anywhere near the well, I couldn't hold the stick—it would twist in my hands just as it did in my cousin's hands. So I was very delighted that I could do something that the men couldn't."

HIRED HELP   "The girls that worked at our place lived in. We were on the farm six miles from town. She had her own room and we were warned that was somebody else's room, not ours, and she lived there, had time to do her own sewing, used our sewing machine, and perhaps her wages were a little less than a man's wages at that time. It seems to me they got twenty . . .twenty-five . . . thirty dollars a month and the girl would have been eighteen to twenty dollars, and if you had a good girl you paid her well, because the neighbours knew about it, and you just didn't always want your girl to go to the neighbours. They didn't always do the same things the same way, and I don't know of any of the women that would have appreciated having their particularly trained girl going to someone else's home and having the other lady say she didn't do everything perfectly."

A KICKER   "As a boy on the farm, I can recall that most of the men were recognized as the boss of the family. They made the major decisions and did the hardest work and did the heaviest lifting and all this. This is not to belittle the farmers' wives, but the farmers made the major decisions.

But we had a neighbour who was a very timid man, and he was very timid particularly with horses, which was rather odd for a farmer. And one day our neighbour had traded horses and got a different horse, a big horse, and he'd hitched him up in a team to rake hay. And as soon as the rake started to trip, at the end of the windrow, this horse put his heels right back beside this farmer's head. After about three of these, the farmer tied the team up to the fence and stood there looking at it and my father went over to him and said: 'What's wrong with your team?' And he said: 'I've got a kicker.'

And then all of a sudden, both men noticed this farmer's wife

coming from the house, clad in overalls, one of the first women I
had ever seen in overalls, and she was carrying a blacksnake whip.
And when she got there she simply asked her husband what was
wrong and he, white in the face, said: 'I've got a kicker.'

And she simply walked around and untied the team from the
fence and started down the field sitting on the seat. She tripped the
rake and back came the heels—and up came the lady onto the frame
of the rake with the whip, and she licked that horse through to the
far end of the field, and I don't think I've ever seen a hayrake go
faster in my life. And I don't ever recall that horse kicking again
when she got through with it."

ISOLATION   "My mother once went eighteen months without
going to town, and six months without seeing another woman. And
of course going to town, what did it amount to when she did go
after eighteen months? You could have thrown a rope around the
place, you know."

THEN BACK TO THE HOUSE   "In the early days the wife and I
used to cut a tree down and if we couldn't land it on a nickel, we
figured we'd made a bad job of it. And then we sawed fence posts
and we'd split them and we'd work out there for two or three hours
in the morning and a couple of hours in the afternoon, and then the
wife had to come back to the house to get supper ready for the kids
that would come back from school. But we'd take it as a matter
of course."

A GOOD FRONTIER COOK   "My mother never cooked in her life
until she came out here. From the time they got married until they
came out here, they lived in London, England, where the stores
were just around the corner. So she had never cooked anything, I
don't think, unless she fried a fish or something like that. So when
she came to bake bread, she had a devil of a time. She didn't have
any knowledge of how to make bread; she knew there was something about yeast which you treasured very carefully and took to
bed with you in a little crock with a sock around it to keep it from

freezing. And then she would just have to mix this flour and stuff up and do whatever you had to do and trust to luck, and luck wasn't very good most of the time. But after five or six years of that, she was a good frontier cook, and we had good bread, and all that sort of thing."

THE RED BLANKET   "There was an isolated farm in Saskatchewan and no neighbours nearby at all. The husband was away much of the time working here and there, trying to scrape up enough money to make ends meet and his wife was alone, totally alone, for weeks at a time. She saw no one. She had no one to talk to. Loneliness was driving her out of her mind. She just couldn't stand much more of it.

One day, at this time, she did some washing and put it on a line in the yard. When it was dry, she brought it all in except a red blanket that was still wet. She left it on the line and a wind came up and from the window of the shack they lived in she saw the blanket flapping and moving on the line. It almost seemed there was someone walking around in the yard, something alive out there. It fascinated her. She clutched at what was a straw of hope. And every day when there was any kind of a wind blowing across the prairie, she would put the red blanket on the clothesline where she could see it flapping from the window. She began to imagine there was a person out there, another human being. It was as if she was less lonely.

That red blanket in the wind was the only thing that saved her sanity."

NEST-EGGS   "Where we lived at one time there was a woman that became a very good friend of ours, that was quite a character. She drove a horse and buggy, and on the way to town one day the horse got frightened of something and ran away. And she was thrown off and her leg was broken, badly broken.

They got her home and got the doctor. The doctor set her leg and told her that she would be at least three months in bed, and she was not to get out. There wasn't a thing that she could do but just stay there.

So she said: 'Well, there isn't a damn bit of use me lying here doing nothing.' So she got her son to bring her a basket of eggs. And she lined herself all around with eggs. And in twenty-eight days she hatched out twenty-one chickens.''

LOAFING AROUND THE HOUSE ALL DAY ''It was very very difficult. I spent, I think, half of my time running back and forth to the outhouse with children. If you have two or three children, they're small and they have to go to the toilet so often and I felt that very hard work. I also felt it very hard work trying to fire a wood furnace. The wood was always much too heavy for me, and I felt all these things, such as washing, such a burden because you'd have so many diapers to wash and the water was hard, and another thing you had to heat it on a wood stove and it took so long to get ready, let alone do the washing. And the children would be away to school, and before the washing would be completed, they would be back home for lunch. I used to think I would have got more done if they hadn't come home for lunch, if I could have sent their lunch with them, I think I would have got more work done, because they just seemed to get nicely finished up in one meal and there would be another. And the same thing, they would be back at four o'clock again before I would have many things done, and the days were very long and sometimes very wearisome, and especially if they got sick.''

HIGH ON THE LADDER ''We had an invasion of skunks one year. They nested under the back kitchen and we would tie a trap to a post and usually each morning we'd get a young skunk. My husband would haul them away—as long as you kept a skunk moving, he couldn't spray. So each morning, this was a ritual, he hauled away a young skunk.

However, they got into our ice well which was a hole built by the side of the house, probably ten, twelve, fifteen feet deep, and a pair of them had got in there, fighting. They'd fought and killed one another, and the smell nearly drove us out of the house. I complained bitterly about this, but my husband went off to the field in the morning and he left us with it.

So the girl that was working for me and I decided we would do something about it. We got all rigged up with old clothes because we would smell so badly; we put bandana hankies across our noses so the smell wouldn't send us too far, and I got a rope on a pail and I went down a ladder into this well.

The idea was that I was to put the skunks into this pail and she'd wait till I got up, and then she would pull the pail up. However, when I put the skunks in the pail she got excited, and as I climbed up she pulled the pail up, so I came up with my nose practically in the pail of skunks all the way up, and that I can still smell."

A HOPELESS SITUATION FOR HER   "There was a woman who was quite cultured. She was German. She could play classical piano, and this is how we came to know her, my mother arranged for me to take piano lessons from her. And one day when I came in she was crying and my mother was trying to comfort her. At the time I didn't realize what it was all about, but in thinking back, it must have been a terrible situation for a cultured woman like that coming from Europe, becoming a drudge on the farm and no way out, married to a man who had no thought beyond using her as a labourer on the farm, as far as I could tell. It was a hopeless situation for her, and there wasn't much comfort my mother could give her because what could she do? She didn't have money or any way of making a living there. I think there must have been many, many women like her on the prairies that suffered terrible ordeals of that nature."

TEN

Entertainment

The Country Spirit . . . Nothing Like a Country Auction . . . Everybody
Would Sing . . . A Thumping Trump . . . The Phantom Farmer . . . Every-
body Had a Ball . . . Homebrew with Bite . . . The Magic of These Books . . .
An Exciting Spectator Sport . . . Winter Violin . . . Mischief for Idle Feet . . .
We Had a Radio . . . A Week's Papers . . . A Powerful Thirst . . . Involved in
the Church . . . Good Medicine . . . Two Practical Jokers

F arm work is hard, it has always been physically very
demanding. But the people I talked to made it clear that in the
more settled areas of the country the grinding work was compensated for by home-made fun and entertainment. Some women told
me their fathers played the fiddle for the family every night, except
on rare occasions when he was just too tired. Men now in their
prime remember haying all day in the fierce sun and going
off eagerly to take part in a ball game that night. If nothing else,
one member of the family might read aloud from the "Family
Herald" at night, and there would be games and frolicking with
the children.

None of it was spectatorial. They entertained themselves —
everyone pitched into the fun with gusto. At dances and box
socials, the babies were placed carefully at the side of the room and
slept peacefully through all the hullabaloo. On the prairies, in
little red schoolhouses, a blizzard might trap everyone, and it
could be the next day or the day after before everybody got home.

It seems to me that, very often, it was a natural, happy world.
Where people got the energy for all the social activities that went
on after a solid day's hard work, I don't understand.

THE COUNTRY SPIRIT "In those days when we worked the horses, we had time to relax; every Wednesday afternoon, regardless of how busy you were, in the summertime we'd have picnics out in the country, and you'd take Wednesday afternoon off and go and play ball, and as long as your neighbour went, you were willing to go too. And in the wintertime, the country spirit was much different than it is now. We had house parties every Friday night. We'd take turns going from one house to the other, and we'd play cards and dance later on, and make our own ice cream and have lots of fun, and we never had a nickel to spend, but we had better times then, I'm sure, than the young people do now."

NOTHING LIKE A COUNTRY AUCTION "The farm sale is the sale that I probably like most to conduct. As I say I like to conduct all sales, but at the country auction sale, especially a century farm, if it's announced a century-farm auction sale, there's always a certain amount of goodies been around there that have been in the family for a good many years. Now you get the enthusiast bettor there, the collector, and as you're looking over your audience, studying them, their smiles, their frowns, they're eager to get at things and they're shoving to make sure they get in. And the church groups there with their homemade pies and tea biscuits and good cream for your coffee, and just the general good nature of the whole community, there's just nothing like it. It just makes you feel good, and, as an auctioneer, you're just in your prime at one of these sales."

EVERYBODY WOULD SING "In the big living room was a piano, and my grandmother played the piano, and my grandfather played the harmonica, and my uncles played the guitar, and we used to sing and have these great little parties. Oh, the neighbours would drop in and everybody would sit around and they'd sing, and my mother and father would be there and we'd have a great time."

A THUMPING TRUMP "There was no electricity in our home at this time, there was a lamp set on the table, and they were playing cards around the table. And I can still remember seeing Dad, when

Mrs. Bernard had a good card, she had the Ace or Jack of Hearts coming in to her and she would be going to take that trick, and she'd raise her right hand in the air with a card in it, and I can still see Dad reaching for the lamp to hold it off the table. She brought the card down, hit the table so hard, it jumped the globe off the lamp and it broke. This is the way we grew up. We had our own entertainment, as it were."

THE PHANTOM FARMER   "We had in the years gone by a world-professional speed-skating champion. Of course Saint John in those days was really noted for its speed skaters, in fact they were famous out of all proportion to the size of the city. But some of these skaters were from the farms from the St. John and the Kennebacasis rivers, and the world champion at the time of this story was Hughie McCormick.

Hughie had just returned from having won the world's professional speed-skating title in Norway, and he came home with the belt which indicated his championship. And he was skating this night on the river and practising as he did every night. In the part where he was skating, there were farms coming right down to the river all along the shore, and out of one of these farms, apparently, a skater stepped onto the ice. I don't know precisely at what point it was, but Hughie heard him in the distance behind him and he paid little attention at the time.

But slowly the stranger came nearer and nearer, and Hughie had to step up his pace. He was going, I suppose, at a leisurely pace . . . well, like a three-mile race at first . . . but as the skater began closing in on him, he was on a real sprint, and Hughie set off like he was in contention for the world title. Still he heard the flash of blades at his heels, and slowly the figure passed by and into the distance. And Hughie always referred to him as the Phantom Farmer, but in any case, ever after, when anyone patted Hughie on the back and said: 'Hughie, you are the greatest skater in the world.' Hughie would laugh to himself and think: 'Yes, but there's some young unknown farm boy up on the Kennebacasis who could really show me how to skate.'"

EVERYBODY HAD A BALL   "When we were kids at school, as soon as the bell would go, we'd start in, and whoever said one first, one and two would be at bat, three was the catcher, and four was the pitcher. Number five would be on the base and so the rest would be scouters, and in their turn they'd have to come in, six would come after five, and so on.

Every spring, everybody had a ball made for them. My mother used to make them. You'd take a cork—you know what a cork is— you used to take that and yarn; we would take and ravel old socks or something like that. You ravel them and you'd wind the yarn all around the cork as big as you wanted. And then you'd take shoes. In those days they wore high shoes, you know higher shoes, where the bottom would be gone but the sides of the shoe would still be in good shape, so you'd go to work and you'd cut two round pieces for the ends and then you'd take one strip around the centre, and Mother did that, you see, she had that down to a science, she could do beautiful work, she was a beautiful sewer anyway, and then she would cover it with that leather, and that kept it from getting wet. If they didn't have the leather on it, they'd soon get wet.

You'd bounce the ball as you'd stand, and you'd hit it on the floor, and if it bounced back to the ceiling and down again, the ball was all right."

HOMEBREW WITH BITE   "We were drinking a fair amount of that homebrew that particular summer, and I don't know, I think you sort of get immune to the stuff. But we used to sit down at suppertime and we'd get going during harvest and drink a twenty-six, and gosh, the only thing I can remember is the next day I'd wake up and for some reason my front teeth would be particularly sore — you'd think that the nerves were right at the tips of your teeth. I'm not sure exactly why, but there was something good about that particular homebrew."

THE MAGIC OF THESE BOOKS   "We had a party line and we got a call from Mrs. Reid, one of our neighbours. She said that her boys were past the *Boy's Own Annual* and *Chums* stage and would I like their copies of all those various books? Well would I? Golly, I was enthralled. I picked up half a dozen of these annuals—*Boy's Own*, *Chums*, *Chatterbox*. You know this provided me with a wealth of exciting, clean, well-written stories of British school life and adventures of young people all over the world.

In addition, by the way, it provided instructions for almost anything you could think of. I was poring over them at every conceivable opportunity. I would do what jobs I had to do on the farm and then go back to the magic of these books, and I must say that they were an absolute magic to me.

Now perhaps I took all these instructions too seriously, because I recall one of the features, I think it was in *Chums*, was a series of lessons on swimming. Now we had no water at all for swimming in our immediate area, but the writer of these articles in the *Chums Annual* said this was absolutely no barrier to learning, and the reader would lie on his stomach on a bench and practise the various strokes daily, and at the first opportunity he had to enter the water, and I'm quoting this because I remember it so well: 'He would find to his delight that he could swim.'

I would lie on the bench on my stomach, lay flat along the bench, and of course this put my hands free and my legs free so I could kick and do all the various strokes that they mentioned in there. Now, after weeks of practising on the bench and on dry land, I went on a family Sunday picnic where there was a pond, and I could hardly wait to show off my newly-acquired skill. Buster Crabbe was just nothing compared with me — I was sure that was going to be the situation. So, full of confidence, I jumped into the pond. Immediately my nose and my throat filled with water, and I was in an absolutely choking panic. Fortunately, my father pulled me out, waterlogged, half-drowned, and rather discouraged. Now it was at this point in my life that I learned that one has to practise in the medium, and I've always held that pretty close to me ever since. I learned to swim subsequently, but that was years later, and actually I think I really acquired a mental block because of this experience, because I swim about as well as I sing, and that is very, very poorly."

AN EXCITING SPECTATOR SPORT "One Saturday a plane came over and landed in my dad's hayfield, and it was there all day, and he took off Sunday afternoon. There was a good many people came with horse and buggy, and cars, to see the plane. They had heard about it being down on the ground. Sunday afternoon, he took off from our hayfield, and as he took off, he didn't clear the trees enough, and he caught the undercarriage of the plane, and he tipped over, and landed on one of the cars that was there to see him. He damaged the plane a little bit and damaged the car, but at least there was no one hurt."

WINTER VIOLIN "My dad had his violin, and it was used constantly. I can't remember going to sleep at night without my dad playing the violin for us to go to sleep. And he played for dances — all winter long he would play.

Now in the summer he couldn't, because when he was out working in the field with horses all day, he came in too tired to play that arm out playing for a dance all night. He used to play pieces like 'Over the Waves' and 'Merry Widow Waltz', 'Red Wing' for a two-step, and 'Marching Through Georgia' for a four-step, 'Clementine' for a three-step."

MISCHIEF FOR IDLE FEET "I often heard that the older ministers, and even some of the old Scottish people — they had a very very strong feeling against dancing and card-playing. And I never forgot my father telling a story of an old minister who was in the town, who was quite against card-playing and dancing. And he met my father in the blacksmith's shop in the morning when he was after delivering his milk to the factory. They were talking about some party or something. And he says: 'Oh,' he says, 'You were dancing were you?'

And my father said: 'Sure, I was dancing.'

And he says: 'Did you think it was a sin?'

My father said: 'No, I didn't think it was no sin.'

'Well,' the minister says. He says, 'If you didn't think so,' he says, 'it was no sin to you.'

So that's one of the ways of looking at it."

WE HAD A RADIO "We had a radio, I think maybe it was a Philco, I can't remember for sure, but I know it had quite an impressive console, at least I thought it was. In those days you had to tune in the stations, and we had three big, round, three-inch walnut knobs that you twirled tuning to get the station to come in, and there was a lot of interference, squawk, crackle, whistles, just at the most interesting and exciting part of the play, and the thing would start to fade out on you. My brother and I used to like to listen to *The Shadow* and all these scary radio plays.

I remember one night listening when my folks were away and the two of us were in the house all by ourselves, and it was a really grisly play, and of course your imagination really was put to work on these radio plays, and I could just see this horrible face hanging in the window that was described on the play, and I was afraid to go into the kitchen, afraid to go outside, afraid to go even to the outhouse through the trees.

It is really unbelievable to think that we could sit there in our house on the prairie and actually hear the voice of a man like Byrd, down in the Antarctica — that was unbelievably far away, and we really couldn't believe that we were listening to that man. It was a whole new dimension brought into our lives by the radio. On the farm we felt quite isolated, but now the world was coming in to us."

A WEEK'S PAPERS "One thing the *Family Herald* had was old pictures. It seems that every year they sent out a picture and I don't think any home was without these pictures. 'Awakening' was one of them, and 'Welcome Home', a lady welcomed home that collie dog, that's a picture that's seen in all the old homes in the large gilt frame. There was several big pictures that you can see now in old homes, old pictures that were the premium from the *Family Herald*.

But the family had their *Family Herald* and the *Country Guide* and of course the Eaton's catalogue, which served all kinds of purposes. And then there was newspapers. But you'd get a week's papers at a time because you only received your mail once a week, so that that wasn't so good.

Everybody had their church magazines, which were read far

better than they are now because there's too much going on now. You don't sit down and read a church magazine when you get home—you're away in the car."

A POWERFUL THIRST "After a wood bee, it was common to have a keg of beer, and sometimes a few bottles of liquor. Heard my dad tell us a story about an old lady down in the Betty Settlement in Howlett. That they had a wood bee there, on her husband's place, and they had a keg of beer, and this lady was particularly fond of it, and they knew that they'd have to put it someplace where she couldn't get it or they wouldn't have any supper.

So the fellow tied a rope around this keg of beer and pulled it up to the peak of the barn—the rafters—so she couldn't get it down. So she went to the house and got the rifle and the washtub. Drilled a hole in the bottom of the keg and put the washtub beneath it and caught the beer. When the men came up from the bush she was laying beside it so tight she couldn't walk. She shot a hole in the beer keg . . . necessity is the mother of invention."

INVOLVED IN THE CHURCH "My aunt was a great person. She belonged to the Gleaners and she would make all the different seasonal pies for the different events that would happen at the church. The Gleaners were a group of women that met once or twice a month, and they would quilt and they would sew and they would do things for the church and raise money to make outfits for the choir. So much a part of your life was involved in the church, in a loving way. It wasn't that you felt you had to go to church. It was just that your life was involved around your church.

We were Anglicans, but that doesn't make any difference. In a small town years ago there was so much of your life was involved in the church."

GOOD MEDICINE "In prohibition time I guess my dad pulled himself out of debt selling moonshine . . . bush whiskey. They used wheat, a sack of sugar and Fleischmann's yeast and a barrel of water and let her start to work and then two weeks later you'd cook it, put it in jugs and age it a little bit, mix it down, dilute it — it's better whiskey than you can buy anytime.

I hid it in a fence line one time when I had a man working for me and I told him to build a calf feeder there and I showed him where to put it, and here if he didn't move it over about ten feet and he drove the crowbar right through a jug of my whiskey. So that was the end of that. But I never told him about it.

The cops never caught us. I remember my dad telling he had it hid in a wheat bin way up on top and he had the bin full and they were going to chop it open. And he told them if they broke it open, they'd have to shovel it back in, so they left it alone.

My dad never sold it in small lots. His best customer was the local druggist. He didn't peddle it; he put it in medicines. Those medicines were pretty popular, let me tell you."

TWO PRACTICAL JOKERS "He was always a practical joker, my grandfather. One of the things he liked to do at threshing time, he would offer the men a seat and then he would move the chair out and the fellow would sit down on the floor, one of his favourite little farmer jokes. And my younger brother, who was also a practical joker and much like my grandfather, he wasn't very old, about six or seven, but just old enough to move the chair. So he said to my grandfather one time: 'Here, have a seat.'

And my grandfather fell for it and went to sit down and my young brother had moved the chair, and my grandfather toppled onto the floor. Anybody else, I think, would have been in a rage, but he just got up, laughed and said: 'Well, he's a chip off the old block.'"

ELEVEN

Plain Hard Work

Like a Galley Slave . . . Washing the Cream Separator . . . Apples Don't Just Grow on Trees . . . Pick and Shovel . . . The Business of Shearing . . . Forty Acres of Tomatoes . . . To Make It Interesting . . . Lots of Things I Hated . . . Very Few Words . . . The Politics of Ploughing . . . You Were Busy . . . No Handouts

Plain, hard work is what farming has always been. Picking stones from a field and getting them on the stone boat and to the side of the field. Every year, a new crop of stones surfacing and staring you in the face. Women going out in the morning to the milk separator so there'd be cream and the precious weekly cream cheque. The tedious job of cleaning all the parts of the separator that otherwise would be gucked with a sticky mess the next day. Working in a country elevator day and night during harvest-time until every bone ached and you scarcely could remember your own name. Digging wells, down and down and down, and still no water. Endless stories of back-breaking work and, too often, after it was done: nothing. Failure. Start all over again.

Farming is twenty-five per cent common sense and experience, thirty-five per cent good luck, and thirty-five per cent bad luck, and the other five per cent is anybody's guess. And it is, always, one hundred per cent hard work.

LIKE A GALLEY SLAVE "It was all work, entirely different to what it is now. We'd be up by six, sometimes by five in the morning, and you had to get the cows, you had to milk the cows, and we had sixty-five sheep at one time, and oh, four horses and a lot of cattle.

You see the work now is so different to what it used to be. Butter was eighteen cents a pound and eggs ten cents a dozen, and you worked like a galley slave all the time. That was our life at that time and then you are raising your family along with all this other work. I have worked in the fields. I have done everything on the farm, I think, except plough. I couldn't plough, but I've worked other machinery, the threshing machine. I love farm life, and I've gone out when it was moonlight and the children were at their lessons, and I've gone out and helped stook the grain. Oh yes, I was strong and I think it was hard work that made me strong.

People took pride in work on the farm. Now so many people, they don't know how to work at all. Children aren't brought up to work like they used to be. Often when the children were small, and we had a hired man, I'd sit up and be mending till probably two o'clock in the morning, and then I'd still get up at six o'clock in the morning. That was our life. I'm eighty-four now, but I couldn't have suffered very much."

WASHING THE CREAM SEPARATOR "The whole job used to take me about twenty minutes to do properly. I would use the big bowl of the separator; I would pour the hot water into the big bowl and then I would wash all the pieces in the big bowl and then finish off by washing out the bowl itself and dumping the water into a pail, reassembling it all, putting it back. And in the summertime, when there were a lot of flies around, I used to just keep a clean tea towel up there at the barn to cover it over with.

You can't use soap or detergent to wash the separator because it would just jell in there, get mucky and thick and it would just be hopeless. So what you used for washing the separator was just really as hot water as your hands could stand. If I got out around 9:30 I was usually finished washing it about ten. It doesn't seem like too long, I guess, but it was a chore I hated. I never knew of anybody that enjoyed washing a separator. I think it would take a lot of imagination to find any pleasure in that job.

I was glad we didn't have the separator at the house because there's always a sort of a milky smell from it and you would notice it when you went in a farm home, if they had the separator in their back kitchen. It was what I would call a farm smell, but having it at the barn was fine. I'd much rather walk to the barn and clean the separator than have the separator at the house."

APPLES DON'T JUST GROW ON TREES   "To grow fruit, why it's the initial planting and the waiting for the trees to come into bearing that are the big drawbacks, and in the meantime, you try to eke out a living by various means.

We were told there was a market for tobacco, so we planted tobacco one year and had a barn built to flue-cure the tobacco and we got it all stowed away and were flue-curing it, and the company that was going to buy the tobacco didn't materialize so we had a lot of tobacco that was no good. We kept it for two or three years, then eventually somebody came and said they'd take it off our hands at a very minimum price.

Another year, why, we tried growing potatoes. Well, we harvested the potatoes, they were a fair crop, and we put them in the basement, but when the time came to sell them, why, we couldn't get fifty cents a sack, which didn't pay for putting them in the basement or taking them out. Another way of trying to make ends meet when you were waiting for your fruit to come in was to go into the bush and saw wood. So we cut cordwood for the school at about three-fifty to four dollars a cord stacked in the schoolyard. That kept us busy in the winter and kept us eating, that, and the hope that it would only be two more years before we would have fruit to sell. It's really ten years before you get a paying crop of the old-type trees.

While I was waiting for my orchard to come in, I had a team of horses and in those days why all the work was done with horses and I hired myself out to other people that had orchards bearing and I dragged the spray machine and the cultivator, and I hauled their apples with the team of horses, about a sixteen-hour day. This

omestead of a Prosperous Farmer, near Edmonton, Alta.

108031

Threshing Outfit crossing Prairie, Western Canada

Canadian Harvesting Scene —Threshing

Canadian Harvesting Scene : Threshing

Harvesting, Western Canada

Carrying Grain to the Elevators, Saskatchewan, Canada

Shipping wheat, Granum, Alberta

5 elevators. one built in J avig. Capacity . 200,000 bushels. Wheat shipments of last season 750,000 bushels.

Cowboys, Calgary, Alberta,
On Line Can. Pac. Rly.

Cowboy and Horses, near Macleod, Alberta

M 222 Cow Boys at Dinner. Round up series

M 1052 Cow Boy
on a "bucking" bronco

BRANDING A STEER.

What are His Chances in Western Canada?

brought in a little money and kept us going in the meantime. We just had to do it. There was no alternative. If you wanted to make your orchard go and you wanted to eat in the meantime, why you had to do these things.

We planted fifteen acres, fifty trees to the acre, so you see seven hundred and fifty trees. And you bought these trees from a nursery and at that time I think they cost about fifty cents each. Today they cost three dollars. The small trees were a problem because in the wintertime the mice worked under the snow and they would chew the bark off all the way around, which means that you had a tree that wouldn't grow, so you had to replace it. Today we put wire mesh around the trees, and that keeps the mice away from them when they're small. Besides the mice, there's the mole that works underground. It doesn't eat the tree, but it eats all the roots off it and then you still haven't got a tree. They were worse than the mice and harder to catch because you had to poison them underground. They didn't come up above the ground at all. The mice we poisoned or put these metal bands around the trees, and the moles, why we would poke a hole to their runway and drop some poisoned grain down in them.

You could easily tell when a mole had been at a tree because the tree just fell over a good many times, and it's strange how they knew the direction of the row, because they would go right down the row, not take one tree, but take two or three trees in the row. They ate the roots off, and that was the end of the tree. Sometimes if they didn't completely eat all the roots, why, the tree would shrivel up during the summer. We didn't lose a great many trees, but it was always ten or twenty-five, something like that, which always meant more work and more expense to replace them. And then when the trees got a little older, there were diseases, such as collar rot, where the tree went bad at the base where it entered the ground. Some varieties were more susceptible than others, and they were more trouble than the mice and the moles, because when the tree got this disease it was ten, twelve years old, just starting to have fruit on it. So you had to start all over again where that tree was.

Later on we had other disasters, you might say. The McIntosh, one of our chief varieties, why, if we had a good windstorm in

September when they were just about ready to pick, why, you would find half of them on the ground. But today, you aren't troubled with this, because you have chemicals that you spray ten days or two weeks prior to picking, and that makes the apple stay on.

There were other disasters, like the frost of January 1950. We were more vulnerable here than in the southern part of the Okanagan Valley. The weather was quite normal until the middle of January, when the thermometer fell rapidly to about thirty degrees below zero with a strong wind blowing, and this continued for about two weeks. A storm such as this had never hit the Okanagan in the history of the valley before, and you didn't know . . . you were hoping that it would give up, and you didn't know what the damage would be at all. It was a matter of the wood of the tree freezing and becoming loosened from the cambium layer, so it was practically like girdling the tree of the bark. We thought there might be a remedy. We tried nailing it back onto the stump again, but this didn't work.

With a lot of the trees, we didn't realize they were injured, we were hoping they weren't injured, so that we didn't really find out the extent of the damage for three years, because some trees that survived, they had leaves but they wouldn't produce fruit, and we eventually had to take them out. This was worse for some varieties than others. I got particularly badly hit by having Yellow Newton apples and Delicious apples. They were more susceptible than the McIntosh. My orchard was fifty per cent Yellow Newtons, which were a dead loss. They were gone for sure, and the Delicious, they partly survived, but I would have been much further ahead to have chopped them all down right then, because they never did come again to producing good crops. And this disaster, when it was finally totalled up, we had lost two thousand trees out of our orchard of four thousand. It isn't a case of just planting a new tree. It's like clearing virgin ground of big trees, because these trees were twenty years old and they took a lot of pulling out. A team of horses couldn't pull them out, you had to get a tractor to pull them out. And then you had the brush and the wood to get rid of, and a hole to dig for the new tree, and new earth to put in the hole where you took the old tree out.

The wood did have a little advantage when you got it sawed up into burnable lengths, because we all burned wood in those days. We didn't have electric stoves and things, the power didn't come into really extensive use here till much later. We just had to keep on going and think of other means to keep you going in the meantime. In my case, why, I had a spray machine, a truck, and a tractor, and I went to work for other people with my machinery to tide me over till the new trees would come back again. But it was a matter of about five years before you got the whole orchard rejuvenated."

PICK AND SHOVEL   "In the digging of a well, a shovel, a pick was the instruments of punishment and to elevate the dirt; first you would go down about six to seven feet and shovel it out by hand, throw it out the bank and another man would scoop it away. After you got over seven feet deep, then you had what we call a windlass, and it was a frame with a shaft through it and a crank on the end of the shaft that you could turn. A rope was wrapped around and around it tied to a pail, a good-sized pail, and lowered down. And the man on the surface, we would crank up the pail of dirt as you filled it, and while we was cranking up, you'd dig out, you'd get ready either pick or shovel, another bucket ready for him when it came down again. In the wells I've dug, I've dug wells to the depth of twenty feet, which was the water level in our particular area, and it would take me two good days to dig that with a helper. At the first six feet it was quite easy because you shovelled it out. From then on it had to be hoisted out with this windlass."

THE BUSINESS OF SHEARING   "We started out shearing in the spring around the twenty-fourth of May, and we'd finish probably by the middle of June. It lasts about three weeks or a month at the most, depending on the weather. If we had a lot of rainy weather we'd have to wait, of course, till it was dry, and we couldn't go steady every day—a back wouldn't stand it.
    Shearing is not an easy job, it's a back breaking job, and when I'm talking about shearing, I'm not doing it with hand shears, the way the old timers really did it. At that time they had a shear that was similar to a scissors but much bigger, and that was terrible because

on a sheep with good tight wool, it was a job to shove that shear in through the wool.

I remember the first time I saw an old neighbour shearing sheep, and I was pretty young. He had the sheep up on a platform and had their feet tied, and he was whittling away with his old hand shears, and the poor sheep would be there half the day, and you know, it was terrible . . . and many cuts too.

The rig we were using had a three-inch-head power clippers and was about three inches wide. So if we got sheep that were fairly fat and in good shape, we could really take it off in about three minutes or a little better.

There's a right and a wrong way to do it, and if you are standing almost level with the ground on a platform, you'd set the sheep up between your knees on their rump and you start shearing right by the neck, and you'd shear the brisket down and take the wool off the belly and run one streak out on the one leg, and then you'd go up the neck and work it from that side. When it's done, then you spin it around and finish it on the other side from the inside up to the backbone all the way around. And when they're through, the fleece should lie on the table there with the inside out and clean, ready to roll up and be tied.

So you needed at least one man to wrangle the sheep and one man to tie the fleece where two are shearing . . . I mean clean of outside straw and dirt, you know. We never washed the sheep before we sheared them. And the wool wouldn't be washed until it was ready to be processed. We always sold the wool with the grease in. Sheep will shear out from six to fifteen pounds apiece, depending on the breed, the size of the sheep, but we had crossbreeds that would shear twelve pounds year in, year out.

It is rather a shock sometimes earlier in the season for a sheep to be shorn. If it suddenly turned cold, you know, and you've got a cold rain or something, they'd usually hustle away to shelter somewhere. We had bush pasture, so they were pretty well protected there, or they'd even go inside the shed.

The sheep are not too happy about being shorn, but if you don't try to shear them when they're too full, bring them in and let them starve for a while, they're not so uncomfortable sitting up on their rump, so they'll not bother too much. I've shorn some big bucks that would weigh two hundred pounds, and they were an armful all right to handle.

Not very often did a sheep get away. I was pretty powerful in those days and I always had them sitting between my knees and I had one hand on one of the legs somewhere and there's different holds you can hold a sheep so that you have a pretty good advantage over it. Sheep won't bite. I've never known one to deliberately bite you, but they do kick a bit, but that's all in the business of shearing.''

FORTY ACRES OF TOMATOES   "We planted tomatoes by hand. Today you put in a machine, you can do ten, fifteen acres a day, but we dug the holes by hand with a hoe, a crew went ahead and dug the holes. We had to haul water in barrels from the creek in Vernon here and take it out there and a bucket of water would maybe do eight holes. We would hand-plant all these tomatoes and it took, I think six thousand plants to an acre, and we grew, at that time, about forty acres of tomatoes, so that's quite a bit of planting. So it used to take us, with a big crew, it used to take us about three weeks, in order to plant all our vegetables.''

TO MAKE IT INTERESTING   "Farming is hard work. You get tired but it's not nerve-tiring, it's physical. The next morning you're ready for it again.

A farmer has to be everything. He has to be a mechanic; he has to be a vet; he has to know about crops and anything that goes wrong, he has to do it himself. You know, you can't go run to a store, run to Victoria to get everything you wanted in the early days. You had to be able to do everything, mend, carpenter, anything that went wrong, you had to do. The mowers used to break down, you know. You'd break a blade and you had to do something to get it going. The hayrake would lose a shaft. You'd go into the bush and cut a pole and wire it on and finish raking your hay before it got rained on. There were always emergencies arising to make it interesting.''

LOTS OF THINGS I HATED   "You see the washings, we're on a side hill, the washing the soil down lets more rocks work up. And when you're on a flat bit of ground, the frost seems to heave them up. No matter how many times you plough in, you're always in rock, in Yarmouth especially. In Nova Scotia, the subsections, like up in the Valley, they don't have these rocks to contend with, their land is more heavy loam and deeper soil. I hated it, but still at the same time we had to put up with it. Lots of things I hated.

We'd have to have two or three yoke of oxen on a road machine, you know, to clear out the ditches, and then grade the roads in the spring of the year. We'd put our teams on there and then lots of times we'd have to gravel a piece of road that was worn out, we'd go to a gravel pit and haul gravel to dump on there. It was a tax, a road tax. You had to work out so much and then when you had worked over that, they'd pay you.''

VERY FEW WORDS   "Back in those days, the bulk of our population consisted of farmers, and farmers as a lot were probably not the best educated, and they were very taciturn by nature. They didn't talk a lot. And today we have a world of words and paper, very little work. And in those days, there was a lot of hard work and very few words. And the only paper could be found in certain areas . . .

But I have seen farmers work for a whole day and never speak to each other, and not because they were mad at each other. And I think this was a distinctive mark of farming and of men who knew what had to be done, how to do it, when to do it, and how to co-operate with each other. And I practise this myself to this day.''

THE POLITICS OF PLOUGHING   "I liked it — it was hard work and sometimes I thought it would be nice to have a farm. But I don't think I'd want to work it on that basis, where there was absolutely no spare time whatsoever. Every morning at daybreak he'd be banging on my wall — there was just a wall separating us, in the farmhouse — and he was a bachelor knocking on the wall to wake me up before daylight.

The things that I can remember most about the farm is that he had a walking gang-plough, and some of the fields were pretty stony, and several months of frost heave brings the rocks up, and at least once a day I'd get the handles of the plough in the ribs. When it hits a rock it springs up and you've got the plough in your ribs, either that or it throws you right up and off your feet.

Another thing about this particular farm, we had a pair of horses, and they're pretty conscious of their politics down there, and one of them was called Tory and the other one was Whig. He was born Tory and he'd say: 'Clk, clk, clk, come on Tory.' And the other one being Whig, he'd say: 'Get up Whig, you old slut.'"

YOU WERE BUSY "When I first started, the average elevator would hold about thirty thousand bushels. The average train would have about fifty cars, so a train could empty not only one elevator, but an elevator and a half. It usually took an hour to load a boxcar, you had to put the doors in it and line it with paper on account of leakage. And it took an hour, provided you were moving: you had to be moving and moving fast to do it in an hour. I can well remember one time during the harvest time when I started the elevator engine at five o'clock on Monday morning because there was a train came in with empty boxcars, and I didn't stop it until the following Tuesday at eleven o'clock. I hadn't had my clothes off nor had I been to bed for exactly eight days. So you were busy. And in that time, I handled a hundred thousand bushel of grain.

Well, in order to handle a hundred thousand bushel of grain in an elevator that held thirty thousand, I had to be putting it out as fast as I was taking it in. I'd take it in all day and load boxcars all night. The coffee pot was on the stove all the time, and I chewed off the end of a loaf of bread and a hunk of baloney.

When the farms would see the smoke from the train, they'd start loading up and heading for town, and by the time the cars were spotted there'd be somebody there wanting to get unloaded. And we would unload them. There was a continual stream. They would haul day and night if you'd let them. And sometimes they would, regardless. So long as they knew you were there, they'd keep coming."

NO HANDOUTS "Getting down to working in tobacco and getting down between them rows they're usually planted thirty inches apart, and they look endless when you start from one end to the other. The beauty part about it was, it all had a little bit of bearing of making men out of them. They started there when they were young, and I've had numerous ones, and we have the grown married couples that come and visit us and they all said it was a little backbone of hard work, that when it come to study, they knew how to do it. It had been their life—hard work.

Working in the tobacco is hard, there's no question about it, and it's a young man's job. Now myself, I wouldn't want to do it at my age now, and I'm not old and I'm not young, but I mean it is a young man's job, and what it boils down to is perseverance. And for that age of students that worked in tobacco—sixteen, seventeen, eighteen, and college students at nineteen and older—this was a fast buck for them. I think when we finished there in 1967, my last crop I grew, I think we were paying eighteen dollars a day and their board. And they made their day as long as they wanted to. If they shuffled at seven o'clock in the morning, they could be in at two o'clock in the afternoon.

There was quite a few of them that didn't stay with us, but I just don't think they had it in them anyways. Maybe the boys, let's put it that way, and I've primed day in and day out and we've had fellows that primed with us day in and day out, year in and year out, come back year after year. But the fellow who didn't have too much ambition, too much desire, he was looking for something easy, he liked the handouts. And there was no handouts there."

TWELVE

When I Was a Kid

A farm is a paradise on earth for kids. Farm kids have always been able to play in the barn with the kittens in the loft, hunt gophers, watch clouds, chase butterflies, make rafts and tree-houses, get lost, tease dogs, gorge themselves on berries, and help Dad in the fields when they wanted to. Even an only child could be enormously inventive and create a whole delightful world for himself or herself. Farm kids have always had it made. As I talked to men and women well past the traditional fourscore-and-ten, they would bubble with joy as they told about their farm child-hoods. So, too, would teenagers who'd just come off the farm a few months before I talked to them.

Even indoors, there was a great world to explore. The frost patterns on the upstairs bedroom windows were to be wondered at and studied. You could always romp with Grandma and Grandpa and get them to tell stories, and there were numberless games known and others to be invented.

No wonder farm people grew up happy and with a sense of fun. And maybe all that running around and expenditure of energy was an adequate preparation for the demands of farm work they would have to face up to as adults.

A LITTLE BIT LONELY   "When I was a kid growing up on the farm, I sort of envied the kids in town who could run right across the street and there was somebody you could play with and this sort of thing. Now I'm really glad I grew up on the farm. Whether I would want to live on it now or not is something I haven't really thought about too much.

When you live on the farm, you know, it's relatively isolated compared to the kids who live in town. And unless you get your parents to drive in, or you want to walk however far it is into town, or ride your bicycle, you've got to stay pretty much by yourself. And you go to school and you hear your friends talking amongst each other about how they got together on such-and-such an evening, and you weren't there because of course you couldn't go that distance. And it's a little bit lonely that way.

Other than that, there are some really terrific times, you know. I think growing up on the farm gives people a quiet type of strength that maybe people growing up in the city don't really have. I remember being lonely by myself, and I didn't really want to talk to anybody, so I'd just go sit in an isolated spot, call my dog, and just sit there and rub its ears.

Or else, we had some trees behind our house, and if you wanted to get away, you could just walk along this little path nobody else knew was there. And pretty soon the trees opened up and there was a big space and there were a few wild strawberries growing here and there. And you could just sit out there among the trees and really be by yourself and nobody could bug you 'cause they didn't know where you were."

PLACES TO PLAY   "In the back was a beautiful big barn, of course it's still there, and I used to spend a lot of time in the barn. I can remember when my uncle was milking the cows, he used to squirt it at the cat, and he used to squirt it into my mouth, and it was really something that I wish the children could do. I spent a lot of time in the barn, because the cows were in there and I used to play amongst the cows and the horses. And upstairs in the hayloft, oh, I don't know how my mother used to put up with the hay I used to get on me. But I used to jump in the hay and play in the hay, and when they were putting it in, jump out into the pile.

And beside the barn was a manure pile, and I used to play on top of the manure pile. Now if my children did that I'd go right... I don't know what, but I'm sure I wouldn't allow that. But the manure pile was really something to play on. When you're children, imagine the places that you'll play.

VERY EMBARRASSED "Well, boys are always fascinated with machinery, and when I was young, before I started to school, I used to go out with my father in the spring and he was using horses at that time to plant the grain, and he used to fill up the box with grain and I would ride on the drill for a while, and then when the box got partly down he would put me inside the box and close the lid and I would go to sleep in there until he got to the other end.

During this time one day I had a bit of an accident. I was riding along on the drill beside Dad and had my hand underneath and I got my little finger caught in the gears, and it got squashed. Fortunately, I pulled it out and it didn't do too much damage but it still shows today, and I was very embarrassed about this. I didn't say anything to Dad because it wasn't the kind of thing I should have been doing, putting my hand down there anyway, and so I shut up, didn't say anything to him, just left and went back to the house and kind of washed it off myself. Mother was out in the garden picking raspberries at the time, so I just kind of wrapped it up and put my hand in my pocket and went and picked raspberries for a while. And it came time to go to bed at night and Mum was wondering why I wouldn't take my hand out of my pocket, and she finally encouraged me to do this and take it out, and here she found my squashed little finger. It still isn't normal today — it's a little bit shorter."

WORKING WITH YOUR PARENTS "A beautiful thing about being part of a farm was that you could work with your dad. And that was, I think, a wonderful experience for all of us, girls included. We were not always kept in the house but we worked with our father and our mother. And that was a special experience.

My grandfather built for us a playhouse out of willow. Imagine that! He had the time to do that."

A SLIPPERY SPOT   "One winter I was taking the piano, and each Saturday I had to get into Peterborough for lessons, which is a drive of thirteen, fourteen miles. My brother usually took me and I can remember one morning we started off; we were in the sleigh, at the very back of it, and father had it all fixed up with bricks and all the rest of it because it was twenty below zero when we left home, cold, clear, but a beautiful morning.

My brother and I were sitting there quite comfortably, but when we got into the town, I guess he forgot that there would be slippery spots. We went around a corner and the sleigh slewed, hit a track, and he just went out like *that*. He shot right out of the seat, taking everything with him in the way of covers. He landed sitting in the road. The horses were well trained and he yelled and they stopped. But I don't think I ever laughed harder at anything."

LILAC HOUSES   "I had one sister that was two years older than I, and although we loved each other very dearly and were very close, many times coming home from school, something would trigger us and she would throw her schoolbag at me and I'd throw mine at her and half the time the stuff would roll out in the lane in the mud. We'd get home and my mother would say, 'What happened to you two, you look like you've been in a mud fight?' and be very cross with us. But apart from that, if we'd get mad around the house, we'd chase each other up and through the barns and the drive shed and all around through the lilacs. Our lilac bushes were so thick that we had houses in them and during the summer months, that's the way we used to amuse ourselves. We used to play house in the lilacs, and we'd have different rooms, all through these lilac bushes. We didn't have to have play houses—they were our play houses."

A LITTLE SCORCH MARK   "I can remember an incident that happened on a farm when I was very small, I think I would be five or six. I was in the bedroom this day playing and I noticed a match on the dresser. So my mother had very lace-like curtains on the windows, and I thought I would just light this match and just put a little scorch mark on the curtains. I remember striking the match and slowly putting the match up to our curtain, and instead of a scorch mark, it just went 'Poof', and the whole thing was on fire and I came out into the kitchen and told my mother that I thought she should go into the bedroom. As soon as she hit the door, she just yelled and jerked the curtains off the rod, down on the floor, and tramped them out with her feet. She said: 'Now you go to the field and tell your father what happened.'

So I had to walk back two fields; my father was hoeing mangels on a very hot day. So I told him what happened, and he said: 'You get back to the house and bring the strap back to the field.'

So I very slowly walked to the house, told my mother what my father had said. She said: 'Well, here's the strap, you get back to the field.'

So I carried that heavy, darn thing all the way back, and when I got there he used it on me and then I had to carry it back to the house again."

COYOTES WERE PART OF OUR LIVES   "The coyotes are beautiful. Really they are. Of course they howl; it just seemed to be part of our lives, just like the noise of the frogs in the spring and the fall were so much a part of our lives. We took them for granted. Now when I go there and hear the coyotes again, I appreciate them much more than I did. So many of these things, you see, were part of our lives. We don't think about cars when we're in the city, nor did we think about coyotes when we were in the country. They were just there.

We were very secure. Somehow, in spite of the fact that our parents were living in this frontier country, and far away from doctors, and living on their own wits most of the time, we still were very secure. And so we knew the coyotes weren't going to hurt us. They weren't going to come to the house. We knew they were frightened of us because we had walked by them and seen them run from us."

A COYOTE IN THE BASEMENT   "I remember coyotes were after our sheep and so we had set traps: each day the men had traps set to catch them. And one day they caught one and hit it on the head and brought it home, and of course you skinned them because you got a few dollars for the coyote hide. So they hung it up in our large basement to skin it the next day. And my dad and my uncle, off they went to a grain meeting.

Well, before the night was up, the coyote came to, and it started to howl. It was hanging by its hind legs in the basement. And my mother started the Delco lights that we had for our home lighting plant, started that going to make a noise, but that didn't cover it, and we had the record player, the old gramophone going as hard as we could, but it howled above that, and my brother and I—we were about six or seven years old at the time—we howled louder than the coyote. We were sure the coyote was going to come upstairs, even though my mother showed us she locked the basement door with the little key, but that didn't help. We were sure it would eat its way through the basement, and she took us down to show us how it was hanging by its legs and couldn't get away, but it didn't satisfy us at all. And we just howled our heads off all night. We sure didn't go to sleep."

EGGS FOR CANDY   "We would walk to the post office where they kept candy and peanuts and stuff of that sort, and my mother would give us a dozen eggs to buy anything we liked when we would get to the store. And we'd start off with our little basket with a dozen eggs in and we'd walk two miles to the corner store. And candy was only ten cents a pound then and everything was so cheap, and usually the storekeeper was sorry for us walking two miles, so we'd have an extra handful of candy in our basket. We were very small children then, sister Mina and I were eight and ten years old. It would happen once in a month perhaps. If we were good children, we were given the dozen of eggs, and we'd have a handful of coppers.

The candy was called mixed candy. It was pink and white and licorice and stuff like that mixed in it, and we had it in a little paper bag, and of course we opened the bag on the way home to eat the candy . . . oh dear . . . . We would bring some of the candy home to treat the older people, and tell them all about the trip we had."

RAFTING IN THE PIGPEN   "Out on the farm one time—it was in early spring, after the snow had melted—it had rained quite a bit, and the pigpen out there had quite a bit of water in it. We decided to go rafting. So we built ourselves rafts and we went rafting in the pigpen.

And we had a real great time. And all the pigs, who, I'm sure, must have thought that we were crazy or something, they kind of stayed away from us. But once in a while there'd be a mother sow or something out there, and she'd kind of give us the dirty eye. Or if we were trying to hit for the fence before she got to us, well . . . . We used to play king-of-the-castle on the raft and fight. And if you lost, you ended up in the mud and the water. And we were about, oh, I'd say about eight, nine, in around there. We used to have a jolly good time. Mothers must have had a terrible time in those days."

LOCKED WINDOWS   "I remember we lived through the Lindbergh kidnapping, and we went to bed many nights after that . . . oh, months . . . that we wouldn't open our windows. Our windows were locked tight—if you remember, the little Lindbergh child was kidnapped through a window. All you had was the radio as a medium for news in those days, and the radio was full of this Lindbergh kidnapping, and here we were, young girls on the farm with our windows barred. Even though we were in Ontario on a farm outside Unionville, and we liked fresh air, we were afraid to open our windows in case that would happen to us."

GREAT NEWFOUNDLAND CHASES   "When I was a little girl growing up in Newfoundland, my Uncle Will had a pig. One day somehow or other this pig got out of its pen and started running around everywhere. It ran up harbour and all the kids chased it. We chased it and we chased it and I don't know who got more tired—us kids or the pig. Anyway, we finally caught the pig and got it back to my uncle's, and whenever my family get together, we always laugh and joke about the day the pig ran away.

Another time, when my brother was twelve or thirteen, he wanted to kill one of our chickens for Sunday dinner, just like my father used to. So he asked if he could chop the head off the chicken with the axe. My father said that was okay. So Junior got the axe and he got the chicken and he took a swipe at it and he didn't do a very good job because the chicken's head was only half chopped off and the poor chicken ran all over the potato garden with its head hanging and us kids running after it. Finally the chicken flopped and that was it. I remember that day."

BEFORE I WENT TO SCHOOL   "We grew semi-ripe tomatoes, there was no canning in those days, strictly semi-ripe tomatoes, green peppers, corn, squash, and things like that, and we took them to the packing house. As a matter of fact, in those days, we packed everything ourselves out there and took them to the packing house, and I can tell you the returns were terrible.

Before I went to school though, I had to get up every other morning, I would say till the end of June or so, and pick cucumbers; because cucumbers were not to be picked when it was hot. They had to be picked in the cool of the morning or the cool of the evening or else they'd wilt, and I would have to pick these darn things before I went to school and of course, in strawberry season, we had a little patch of strawberries, the same thing, I had to pick those in the morning before I went to school. But I can remember one year that Dad had shipped something like fourteen hundred crates of cucumbers and we finally got a return from the Vernon Fruit Union telling us that we owed them seventy dollars, and so you can see that there was no money in farming in some commodities. We didn't make any great sums of money, but we lived off the land to a point. At that time, we went back to pigs, for our own use, we had a cow, we had chickens, and we managed to get by somehow or other."

A SORE EAR   "We were playing hide and seek when we were children, my sisters and some other people, and they was hiding in the barn, so we got in there looking for them and couldn't find them. So I figured maybe they were buried in the hay, so I got the pitchfork out and started looking, drove it through my sister's ear.

I was scared to go home that night. But when it got dark I went home, and I just got a severe talking to. It put a hole in her ear — it just left her ear sore for a while — and it healed up all right after that."

TRYING TO DRAIN THE WHOLE COUNTRY "The other thing we used to do was dig ditches. I don't know, but I think I dug more ditches in my lifetime than most other kids. Whenever it would rain I'd be out there with a shovel and a hoe and trying to drain the whole country of water by digging ditches. That used to be a lot of fun. You'd get out with your rubbers and there'd be a big puddle of water close to the ditch, so you'd take your shovel and you'd start digging through the headlands or through the sod and try and drain this water off the field and off the yard and off the Red River Valley."

DEVELOPING CUSTOMERS "Crows are known as predators on other birds who destroy insects. Consequently, the municipality where we lived paid a bounty of four to five cents for a blown crow's egg — you know, you puncture each end of the egg and you blow right through it — and we got five cents for each crow's foot we turned in.

Now my brother was two years younger than myself, and I suspect that I would be about ten years of age when we had a financial crisis in our young lives. We could see us going to the local picnic with no spending money at all, and that was a tragedy.

So we held a financial conference, you know, like the boss man said: 'We've got to increase our earnings, our dividends; how are we going to do it?'

Well, obviously the first thing was to stop raiding crow's nests and stop taking their eggs. Now that sounds as if we're being a bit dumb. We're not. We could make more money if we left the eggs alone and let them hatch, then we could bring in crow's feet, which paid us twice as much money as the eggs. We'd let them hatch and then we would get the young crows before they could fly and we dispatched them and removed both their feet and turned them in. They were worth a lot more money than the eggs — it was just a matter of waiting for your customer to develop."

SUNSETS "You never see a kid lying out on the pavement in the middle of the city staring up at the clouds going by, you know. But we used to do that — lie out on the lawn in front of the house and watch the clouds go by and pick different pictures out of them. Or at evening we would go into our parents' bedroom — and their window faced west. And we would look out and, especially in the spring if there had been a lot of water, and there'd be water all over the fields, with a few trees just silhouetted against it and we'd see the most beautiful Saskatchewan sunsets, there's nothing to beat them. You know, there really isn't."

BIOLOGICAL WARFARE "There used to be a family just across the road, and we'd fight with them continuously, all the time. Now we used to have a pretty good knack for digging up good weapons and all this. We would go out and raid the turkey nests, gather up all the turkey eggs, and then we'd hide them and let them rot. And then when we got into a fight with the neighbours, we'd throw these rotten eggs.

Their mother never liked the stink or the mess that all these rotten eggs made. Matter of fact, she didn't like us fighting with her kids. But we'd usually get bawled out once or twice, and well, we'd let them alone for a while. And then we'd start up again. But those rotten eggs were very effective. They worked really well."

THIRTEEN FIRES "There's one night I'll never forget. Any time there was a bad thunderstorm, Father roused us and we were dressed and ready for any emergency that might arise. On this particular night—I wasn't nervous of thunderstorms, my sister was, so I was the one that was stationed at a window to watch our barn—and during the night there were thirteen buildings burning across the lake, it was the south side of the lake, and we could see thirteen buildings. One was a barn about half a mile from us; it was burned. It was after haying time, so they lost a lot of their feed, their winter's food. The beauty of that storm and the terror . . . the two of them together. I just never forgot it."

A PLEASANT EVENING CHAT "One evening when we were going to bed, and running around upstairs for a little while instead of settling down as we should have, we played hide-and-go-seek. And as you perhaps recall, there were stovepipes running from the stoves downstairs to the chimney upstairs. And in that way we got the maximum amount of heat from the stoves down below. So we were playing hide-and-go-seek. We were kids about in the eight- or ten-year age bracket, and just having fun. And one of us upset the chamber pot. Well, the contents ran down along the stovepipe, and in the room below sat my aunt and uncle and their company, having a pleasant evening chat.

Things really started to happen after that. There was a fine cleanup job to be done, and the rest of the conversation ended in another room."

RESPONSIBILITY "We had a dairy farm in the Fraser Valley. Although we weren't isolated from the community, as a lot of farms are, we used to be very involved in the farm. It was a family farm, and all the family did a lot of work. So as a boy I wasn't too involved in a lot of community activity such as little-league baseball and Boy Scouts, like a lot of my school chums were. I seemed to spend most of my time, after school and on weekends, working with my father and my brothers on the farm.

But looking back now, I really appreciate the opportunity that I had to be involved in the farm, and the responsibility that I had at such a young age. Both my brothers and myself were quite young when my parents would go away for the weekend and leave us in charge of the farm, and milking the cows. And though at the time we felt very deprived and very hard done by, and had to do a lot of work, looking back on it now, I really appreciate having that responsibility."

YOU CAN'T SMILE AT PEOPLE   "The city had no bearing on me at all. I couldn't wait to get back to the things that were real. The fun that we had—it was really lovely. I guess in those days the city was a bustling place, just too noisy and too full of bad things for us. And when I came to Toronto when I was sixteen, I went up and down Yonge Street smiling and saying hello to everybody, because that's the way I'd been brought up. And I soon found out when I had people following me home. My mother said:

'You're just not in the country any more. You're in the city; you can't smile at people and say hello to them and pass the time of day.'

I soon didn't. I had to learn not to. So you see, even though you're bubbling over with personality and that tremendous cultural background, you have to change with the scenery. You have to change with the environment. You have to curtail all that or soften it or put a brake on it. And this is unfortunate."

THIRTEEN

Accidents, Illness, and Death

No Hurt to It, at First . . . A Very Good Smack . . . A Sick House . . . Silo
Dangers . . . Quicksand . . . Down the Well . . . Such a Noise in My Head . . .
Torn Clothes or Broken Bones . . . A Very Tragic Event . . . The Cutting
Box . . . Good for Man or Beast . . . Dr. McKenzie . . . Turkeys for the
Doctor . . . The Way to Go . . . Grandpa's Bell

A t times the farm was, and is, a veritable casualty ward.
It's not that accidents happen regularly, but when they
do, with heavy machinery involved, or big dangerous animals,
they can be spectacular and disastrous. I ran into any number of
farmers who had had altercations with various kinds of saws or
machines and come off second-best. They were cheerful about it,
and they'd learned to get along with a few fingers missing on one
hand, or even with an arm gone.

Farmers are philosophical about these events. Nature has taught
them that you have your ups and downs, and there isn't any point
in complaining about bad luck. So the most that happens is that
there's a little quiet muttering on a damp day when the stub of
a finger aches like the devil. But the next day the sun's out and it's
all forgotten.

NO HURT TO IT, AT FIRST   "Way back about thirty, forty years ago, I was down to the neighbour's on Good Friday helping him get his wood buzz-sawed for the following winter, and there wasn't too many grown men on the gang, and I was pushing the saw and a bunch of boys were handing up the stuff, and they were good boys. They were doing all right, but there was some small stuff and they kept putting that on and it came to the end of that small stuff, and one piece dragged down with the saw and threw my hand against the saw and took off a finger, and it happened very quick. It happened so sudden that I didn't know whether I was cut or not. I noticed that, and when I pulled my mitt off, why I could see that two fingers in my left hand were pretty well cut up. But they weren't bleeding bad and no pain whatever, which is understandable, because when you get a severe cut like that, a quick thing, the body somehow or other sort of anaesthetizes the thing so that you don't feel it for a time. It's after a while.

This thing happened at about a quarter to twelve, and Mr. Howell where I was cutting, he took me up to the doctor at the village, and he dressed my finger. The whole front of my middle finger was just a pulp, and the doctor held that up and picked the sawdust and stuff out of it. I had no feeling in that at all. I couldn't feel anything, and he bandaged it up and put some stuff on it. The feeling started coming into it at three o'clock — it took that length of time for that feeling to come back.

I would think it was three or four years before it was back to really normal, but I could . . . amazingly I could milk a cow within a week's time. I could milk a cow and I don't know how I did, but I managed somehow or other. But I had to carry it in a sling for a few weeks and it seemed that everything I did, like if I was handling a box or a rail or a board or anything like that, it would always come and hit my hand, and it seemed that every time I was around a horse it would be sure to throw its head or switch its tail or something and hit that bum hand of mine, and it seemed from morn till night that hand was always getting in the road of something or other. It did cause me a lot of pain eventually, but right at the start, when it happened, there was no hurt to it."

A VERY GOOD SMACK "I can remember sitting when I was very small on my grandfather's knee, oh, talking and telling stories; and he had a very badly damaged thumb. He and his brother were fencing one day, and my grandfather was holding the post, and Uncle Richie hit him with a very good smack with a big wooden mallet and badly damaged his thumb. And it was always of great interest to me as a small child to look at this thumb that had a big knobby, horny nail on it."

A SICK HOUSE "We were sawing wood with a buzz saw and my father was throwing away blocks and the man that was feeding the saw, he slipped and shoved Father right into the saw. His lower arm was cut into the bone, a straight cut, and his upper arm was lacerated, and then he was cut below the shoulder just the width of a ten-cent piece away from his lung.

And he laid for three hours. The roads was bad and the doctor had to come out with a horse and buggy. So he come out and he took a hundred and ten stitches to close all these wounds. Nobody could understand how he didn't bleed more than he did. He didn't bleed. There may have been a tourniquet put on it, I don't know, but the neighbour and my uncle held a coal-oil lamp for the doctor to sew up these wounds and dress them, and he laid right there on a bed in the front room.

And shortly after he done that, my grandmother fell down the cellar steps and dislocated her shoulder, and my brother and I both had the flu, so we had a sick house for a while."

SILO DANGERS "We have a silo behind the barn, and when you open the silo, you have to clean the top of it off of what we call spoilage and throw it down before you can get to your good silage. So this was in the winter time, and I was throwing out spoilage. There's a feed room at the bottom of the silo with a chute up the side, and I did not realize I was throwing out so much spoilage until I was finished and went to come down the chute, and I got halfway down the chute and I found the chute was full of silage—the feed room was full, the chute was full, and I was trapped, I had no way out.

'Now this was about two o'clock in the afternoon and my wife was working at the hospital; there was nobody at home, and it was a cold winter's day. So I climbed through the top of the chute, took the top door out, and got up on the edge of the silo. The wind was blowing, it was cold, and I was fifty feet in the air on a six-inch ledge. I had to hang on with my hands and crawl around that six-inch wall to the outside ladder and get down that way. But I sure made sure, the next time I was throwing out spoilage, that I only threw half as much out, that I didn't go through that episode again.

You can get gas poisoning from silage after it is filled very quickly—the next day there's an odourless gas that you can't smell or see. I remember going up into the silo one time. I got part way up the chute and I knew something was wrong, and I slowly backed down, and by the time I got down I was very dizzy and nearly collapsed. I remember going out and sitting on the feed manger for ten or fifteen minutes to get some fresh air, and I eventually came to the house. But every year we hear tell of one or two people getting killed by silo gas."

QUICKSAND "In our district the big problem was shortage of water, the closest spring was seven miles. So my father was very anxious to get a well. And the first one that was put down was with what was called a boring machine, that made a very wide hole. And two Frenchmen came to do the work.

They came to a place where there was rock across that needed to be blasted. So they put down a charge of dynamite at night, and then the next morning the younger boy went down with a crowbar to tap around down there and see how much of the rock had been broken. Previous to this they had gone through thirty feet of quicksand, and that all tumbled in on him. And that boy that was up on the ground nearly went insane to think that he had let his younger brother go down there.

Some of the men came there and started digging to try and get this sand out. And one of the bachelors said that he would go down at the last through this last ten feet of the quicksand. Because if it fell in on him, there wasn't any family left. But thank goodness the man got out without any injury and brought the body out.

But that was a real tragedy, and my sister and I were just petrified with the idea that there was a body there. So we ran down to the neighbour's so we would be away when they brought the corpse out of the well."

DOWN THE WELL "The workmen were out picking stones and rocks out in the field and they asked me to go and get some water, so I had this bottle, and I had taken a wire and tied it around the neck, and I'd moved some of the two-by-fours off the top of the covered well. This was a twenty-five-foot well and the water level would be about six feet below me when I leaned over and put the bottle down into the water, and unfortunately I lost my grip and fell into the well.

I was four and a half years old and I feel I remember all this, but people have been telling me the story. Now because I was weighing, what . . .forty pounds at that age, I don't know how many feet I went down, but I felt as if I went right down to the bottom and came up again.

I went down once, up, down and up, and every time I'd come up I would scream and shout. Meanwhile I lost my shoes and my socks, and as I came up I really was panicky and I was swallowing an awful lot of water. I was panicking so much and kicking so much, my momentum brought my body to the top of the water. But I wouldn't stay. I would panic and I would scream and shout and I'd go down again. And I was scratching rocks—it was made out of rock all inside and beautifully built—and I'm grabbing rocks and I'm trying everything.

Finally this man, he heard me screaming; he ran for the shed where the well was and I hear somebody shouting in French, hold on or do something and I just held, and this chap — I'd like to remember everything, but I've been told the story that he threw about four two-by-fours to one side and he jumped right into the well and just grabbed me immediately. I was just screaming and shouting. I just lost complete control and I didn't know what was happening. It was kind of cold water—I appreciated the cold water when I was down at the farmhouse drinking it, instead of being in it.

And the workmen came running as well and they got me out. I'm told by the workmen that the doctor came to the house — he was summoned immediately and ran to the house. What they told me is they held me with my head upside down, and a lot of the water came out that way, and with burping and coughing and whatever. But I was told that I was very close to losing my life. And I think they lost interest in their thirst. I don't think anybody drank any water that day."

SUCH A NOISE IN MY HEAD "One day we had a terrific storm and there was this awful crash and I had metal hair curlers in my hair, and I always say that's what struck the curler, because I've got one ear that's damaged, and I always blamed that for it. It hit the phone and balls of fire flew out, and it came out through the dining room and split the sumach tree in front of the window in half. I figured I was in the direct line of it, and when it bounced off the phone, I just felt as though my head had burst, I had such a noise in my head."

TORN CLOTHES OR BROKEN BONES "We used to have a pump house where we had a big steam-cooled or water-cooled engine with a gasoline engine. A big large gasoline washing machine.

And my mother was washing clothes this one day and as she was washing she caught her dress in this pump jack. And she was just about headed to be sitting right on top of this pump jack, and she would have had a lot of broken bones and I don't know what else, she was screaming while this thing was pulling her into the pump jack. And just as she was pretty near right on top of it, my dad fortunately was there to grab hold of her and pull her out. But in the process she lost pretty near her whole dress, and she walked up to the house looking pretty embarrassed. I can still remember her going to the house with very few clothes left on.

Humorous after it was all finished, but at the time it was pretty scary. And she could have been seriously hurt."

A VERY TRAGIC EVENT "A farmer near the town of Domain had a hired man, and he put him on to do field work with a one-way discer. This was about the middle of the summer and the farmer was making summer fallow, and the farmer went to Winnipeg for the day with his family and, when he came back, he thought he saw something unusual out in the field—the tractor didn't appear to be going around the field in the square fashion which most of the fields are shaped out there, but it seemed to be going around in circles. And so, upon investigating, he found out that the driver of the tractor was not there, and he proceeded to look further and found that the hired man had fallen off the tractor and underneath the discer—and at that point the tractor's wheels were turned, and so the tractor was just going around in circles, and kept going over the hired man for several hours that day.

They virtually had to pick up little pieces of him at the end of the day when they finally stopped the tractor — it was a very tragic event."

THE CUTTING BOX "One item that I can remember home on the farm isn't pleasant to remember but it certainly sticks in my mind. We always used to prepare feed for the cattle in the fall with the cutting box — this was a community-owned machine and was owned by about five or six different people and would make its rounds to cut up the clover, oats, and hay, and so on, and make a big pile of feed in the winter.

We had a fellow working for us at that time and he was feeding the machine and he wasn't quite accustomed to it, and he fed it a little too heavy. The machine was driven by a tractor with a belt, and he got off the load to stand on the machine to get it working again and it started to move—it had a reversing mechanism in it. He got it reversed and then he slipped and fell, and he fell feet first into the feeder. He got one leg free but the other leg got caught and, before he could reach the reversing mechanism, it had chopped off his leg about halfway to his knee. But he regained consciousness long enough to shut the machine off and reverse the mechanism and take him out of the machinery.

He got an artificial foot after that and, after a period of adjustment, he worked on farms for a long time after."

GOOD FOR MAN OR BEAST "There was an old man used to come occasionally, usually about twice a year; he sold medicines. One in particular I remember was called Schmidt Oil. And it was a remedy that was used for almost everything. You could take a few drops orally, or you could rub it on an injury or a sore. It was used, I believe, for man or beast.

He was an old man. He travelled around with a horse and buggy. And when he came, I remember, at least to my aunt's home, he would arrive late in the day. He'd stay for supper. He'd sit and talk in the lamplight in the evening and end up staying for the night, sleeping on the couch downstairs because these itinerant characters were never allowed to sleep upstairs in the beds of the families.

Goose grease was a popular remedy. You rubbed it on your chest if you had a cold. You greased your boots with it. And turpentine, a few drops of turpentine on sugar you took for a cold. I recall my cousin almost choked on it one time — the taste was horrible and I guess he was concentrating on the turpentine instead of on the sugar."

DR. McKENZIE "For many years our home was the only place around Black River with a telephone, and if people needed a doctor, they had to come there. You would hear the knock at the door at night and somebody was sick. Well now they would have to phone and the doctor would have to perhaps drive ten or fifteen miles with horse and sleigh to get to that sick person.

I remember that Dr. McKenzie lived in Loggieville, and one time he had to go to Kouchibouguac. He drove to our house and left his horse there and my father took him to Bonnie Flanagan's Halfway House, and he left his horse there and Mr. Flanagan took him to Kouchibouguac. They came back around five o'clock in the morning, snowing. I remember coming downstairs, a very little girl, the lamp on the table, and my mother was getting the breakfast for my father and the doctor. And she said: 'I suppose you didn't get much for that trip, Doctor.' He said: 'No, that was a God-bless-you job.' Then my brother took him to Loggieville, and he said he slept most of the way in the sleigh."

TURKEYS FOR THE DOCTOR   "This Dr. Simpson was a very respected doctor in those days and he was paid in the fall. This bill I have tells of Dad settling the bill with eight tree tops, four trees, so many bushels of wheat, and so many turkeys, and balanced by cash, thirty-five dollars paid in full, marked by Dr. Simpson."

THE WAY TO GO   "My great-grandfather lived right here in Chegoggin and he come into the house one morning and had his poultry and he brought corn meal in to scald it. He emptied his water out of the teakettle and started to stir it, and then he fell right dead on the floor. He was getting along in his seventies.

And then when I was working on some logs, hauling them out, my father said: 'You're going to the woods, I'll help the boys get some potatoes planted.' And he went to the field and was just driving along with the horses. My brother had a hold of the horse that covered the seed, and my father just stumbled and he never spoke.

And then my brother, I built three greenhouses for him, he was on his way down to the greenhouses. He was only sixty-nine, and he was on his way down there and he stumbled and fell. We called an ambulance, got him to the hospital, but he only lived a few hours.

I want to keep my boots on—that's the way I want to go. I don't want to die in a hospital. I've been there two or three times, and I didn't like it."

GRANDPA'S BELL   "While we were still on the homestead, my grandma and grandpa lived near us. They lived just across the garden from us, and they were very old, both of them in their late seventies. And because there were no phones and no way of keeping track, they strung a wire between grandma's house and my bedroom—it came in through my bedroom window. And there was a bell on the end of it. So if anything went wrong over at Grandma's, they would ring that bell. And I always got the news first, because it was in my bedroom.

And the bell did ring one day. It was in the middle of the day. We all heard it. And because Grandpa had been sick, we sort of knew what it might be. And my mom rushed over. But she told me to stay with the little kids because I was the oldest, so I stayed behind. And I remember that the potatoes boiled over, and the whole house smelled of burnt potatoes. And of course my grandpa died of a heart attack shortly after the bell had rung."

FOURTEEN

Special Events

Halloween Trouble . . .A Halloween Mystery . . .On the Wires . . .And John Spoke Up . . . The Week of the Fair . . .Hand-Knit Drawers . . .Ukrainian New Year . . .Auctions . . . The Day the Mountie Came . . . The Manure Spreader . . .Every Vote Counts . . . Berry-Picking Expeditions . . .Christmas Shopping by Catalogue . . . The Christmas Parcel . . .An All-Night Session . . .A Toboggan for Christmas

Halloween used to be a great time for pranks in rural Canada. Nowadays mailboxes are still taken off posts, but certainly not as many privies are upset as in the old days. The old-time pranks were ritualistic: young bucks were supposed to raise hell on Halloween, and raise hell they did.

The pranks were sheer devilment, often involving a great deal of silent effort, but very seldom was a person hurt or property damaged. It was accepted that this was the night for letting off steam, and the farmer who found his buggy perched precariously on his barn roof tried to laugh at what had happened, along with everyone else. After all, as many farmers pointed out, the perpetrators of the prank were usually the same lads that worked hard for you or your neighbours the rest of the year, so this was their night to howl, and it would be a poor sport indeed who would complain.

I heard very little about New Year celebrations, and the big event at Christmas was not the day itself but the school concert that preceded Christmas. Many, many people joyously recalled the Christmas school concerts, mainly because of the unplanned hilarity: kids would stumble around the stage forgetting lines in the Christmas play, costumes would be any old way, Santa Claus would be sweating in his makeup and suit, and there was a great

deal of spontaneous laughter. Christmas concerts in country
schools may be a little slicker these days, but they still generate the
same kind of nonsense and laughter.

HALLOWEEN TROUBLE   "Many times I got into trouble on Halloween. Of course the standard procedure was upsetting privies. If
you're smart, you move it ahead four feet, and then wait for the
results, which are nearly inevitable because it's so dark.

I can remember one Halloween my chum and I moved eleven
cords of wood and stacked it on a chap's verandah, and then we lay
across his lane in the long grass on a very beautiful warm night,
strangely enough, until this chap came back home. And when he
came home here was eleven cords of wood to move before he could
get in his door. And we laughed so hard, he heard us, and he
jumped the fence and chased us for half a mile. I think I would have
made it if I wasn't laughing so much, but he caught us and we spent
all the next day moving the eleven cords of wood back."

A HALLOWEEN MYSTERY   "On Halloween, I don't know who
did it, I wasn't one of the pranksters on this occasion, but when we
got up in the morning, my dad's wagon was up on top of the barn.
How they got it up there, nobody knows. There was no damage
done. The wagon was completely all assembled together and everything, but to get it down, it all had to be taken in pieces to be
brought down, and who put it up we never did find out. We never
heard no sound; we never heard nothing about them out there."

ON THE WIRES   "Many a time, on Halloween, boys upset the
outhouse. Once we found it away up on the telephone wires. They
got it up. They used to put the sleighs up there too. Oh, there was
fun in those days, too."

AND JOHN SPOKE UP   "Talking about the old horse-and-buggy days and Halloween pranks, that's one of the things I can remember. A bunch of boys one night, they got the buggy out of a neighbour's driving shed. They brought it up to the driving shed, and he had one of these low driving sheds where there was a part built down on it, and it was only about six feet from the ground. So this bunch of boys, they started to push the buggy up on planks onto this building, and the owner was in bed, supposed to be sleeping, but he wasn't sleeping; so he sneaked down and he got in with these boys and helped them to put it up. And they put it up right on top of the house, right crossways of the house, and they came down and turned around and pulled the plank away and they said:

'Boy, I wonder what John is going to say when he finds that.' And John spoke up and he said:

'Well, boys, I helped you put it up, how be you help me take it down?'

So they had to help him take it down."

THE WEEK OF THE FAIR   "The Beeton Fair was always the last week in September or no later than I think the fifth or sixth of October. When I was fifteen I was taught how to do pickles and bake cakes and what have you, and then as I grew older, I went on the Fair Board and exhibited at the Fair, and I've exhibited now for about forty years.

For about six months before the Fair, I would lie at night wondering now how would I show that, or what would I show and how would I decorate it. Once you start to exhibit, it sort of gets into your blood—you just can't get out of it. One night I was lying thinking of what I would do different, and I thought:

'Well this year I'm going to try putting a glaze on my fruit cake, and decorate it differently.' I did the fruit cake about two months ahead with nuts in the centre and cherries around the edge, sort of decorated it a bit differently. I made homemade bread and buns, tea biscuits, cookies, and we churned our own butter, and in those days we picked our chickens, and there was a class for dressed chickens, not cooked. The first is raw and later we had to cook

them. And fancy cookies and salads and pickles, jams, jellies . . .
I've had as many as fifty-three entries.

I've worked till six o'clock and gone to bed and the alarm would
go off at half past six and I'd get back up again and go at it. I'd work
all night at it, and my husband used to stay up till maybe three
o'clock because he knew I was nervous staying up at night, decorat-
ing and icing cakes and that, and then he'd go up to bed and I'd
have maybe sheets to press or pillowcases to press and I'd get so
tired I'd go up about six o'clock and get into bed and maybe just get
in there half an hour and the alarm would go off and I'd roll over
and say: 'Damn, get up and go back and get started to finish.'

I'd start first thing Monday morning and bake right through all
night Tuesday for to get things ready for the Fair, because you're
supposed to have it all in fresh. The entries would be all in Tuesday
at twelve o'clock, so you had to get up good and early in the
morning, and if you worked all day Monday you didn't get time for
your afternoon sleep, and to get everything all ready you'd have to
work right through all night. Some of the things, like your pickles
and your jams and your jellies, as the season came in and you were
doing them as they came along, you were preparing them, but your
general baking had to be done fresh for the Fair. Butter and stuff
like that all had to be done in a day. When I knew they were in there
judging cakes and pies and that, I was always very curious, I could
hardly wait till they got all finished and we could go and have a
peek and see how many prizes we got. I won several trophies that
I've got yet, and I prize those very much, but I'm quitting now—I'm
too old. I've had thirty-nine entries in and got thirty-six prizes.

Once it was all over and you got home from the Fair, you didn't
have time to go to bed and sleep all afternoon; you have to catch up
on all the work you've missed at home, because you got nothing
done the week of the Fair at home.''

HAND-KNIT DRAWERS   "There was chunks of fancy work and
knitting and all that stuff come from a woman who lived away
above Fredericton, an old Mrs. McKay. And she had the most
remarkable display of stuff, you see, a display of knitting that you
wouldn't see at any Fair today.

I'll bet you there was twelve or fifteen pairs of hand-knit drawers, men's drawers, hanging up there. And quite a joke among some of the women, because they come along looking at these drawers hanging there, and whoever knit them hadn't left the front open, you know."

UKRAINIAN NEW YEAR "In our area just outside of Selkirk most of the community was of Ukrainian descent, and we had one unusual tradition which I think is kind of unique in some respects. Every January seventh, which was Ukrainian New Year's, all the children would get together early in the morning. We'd get up at four or five in the morning, depending on what the weather was like. And we'd get on our winterized bicycles and we'd take off.

The whole purpose of the matter was to go around to all the neighbouring farmers and wish them a Happy New Year, and also, to some degree, ensure that they have a good crop that year. We'd take a little bag of wheat — we'd go to the granary and get a little bag of wheat — and we'd take a bag of wheat and go to each house, and we'd knock on the door and we'd wake up the people. And they'd come out and we'd walk in the house and we'd take a handful of the wheat and we'd walk throughout the whole house, spreading wheat all over the floor, and saying a little Ukrainian verse which basically meant that we wished them a Happy New Year and a good crop in that particular year. And in turn the people would give us money for coming around.

I can remember when I was about thirteen was the last time—we were sort of the last ones that went around and did this, and I think that was pretty well the end of it. I wonder if it's still conducted anywhere in Canada."

AUCTIONS "We bought all the machinery for the farm at auctions, virtually all the machinery second-hand, and after looking into what one should pay and how it should work, and the neighbours here and the kids of neighbours helped me decide what to bid on, and we discussed price. I went to a lot of these auctions and they're very sad. In most cases, it's because someone has gotten too old to work anymore and can't handle it, or someone has died.

There was an auction where a fellow, a tractor had rolled over on him, and at that particular one the machinery was all so bad that in fact neighbours were buying it when they didn't need it — and that's a very powerful spirit, but it's sad and I can't go there and have a good time.

I'm impressed by the auctioneers, and I've been to enough of them to see fellows working different situations, and I admire the style and I'm intrigued by the personality. There's a certain excitement, especially when people are spending four thousand to five thousand dollars for a piece of farm machinery, and in most cases that four thousand to five thousand dollars is a much larger investment for them than for a lot of other people I know in our lives outside of this community. But I think a third to a half of them were sales as a result of some kind of tragedy or failure. It was not a happy event. The family people sitting around watching you traipse into the living room and carrying away stuff that had been in the family a long time, picking over things. One auction in particular, a fellow's tractor sold for a good two thousand dollars less than it was worth, simply because of the turnout and who was there, and that man certainly wasn't having a good time."

THE DAY THE MOUNTIE CAME   "In the early days in our district, one of the highlights was the day that the Mountie came. Once a month he came through from Swift Current. And to see that scarlet tunic up on a hill—this man on this beautiful horse—and the country was flat, so you could see for quite a distance. He came to the post office. He stopped at the stopping houses where people got meals. He stopped at the schools to check and see if any of the people were sick, if any of the homesteaders were in need in any way. And when he came to the school, we children had to stand at attention until he got off the horse, then we stood at ease.

He spoke to the teacher, and of course we knew that he was the Queen's representative. And then when he was through having the interview with the teacher, we went to the flagpole and took down the flag. And believe me in those days you didn't put the flag up and let the wind tear it to pieces. It was put up on the pole in the morning, taken off at night, and folded. We would fold the flag and then he dismissed school for the day.

So we were always glad if he left an hour or two before three-thirty."

THE MANURE SPREADER   "In one of the Saskatchewan elections, it was decided we should have a debate between the leaders of the political parties, and the invitation had come from people in a rural community close to Chaplin, west of Moose Jaw. And it was to be held outside, in June. The Liberal leader was Mr. Walter Tucker, but he had some other engagement and didn't turn up. So the only person turned up was Mr. Rupert Ramsay, who was the leader of the Conservative Party. And it was particularly appropriate because he had been a professor in the Department of Agriculture in the university prior to going into politics, so he was a good person to talk to farmers.

And we went out to the farm where they were to have this, a nice little bluff, and the people had arranged their cars so they could sit in them, and a few of them had got benches and were sitting on benches, and we were all ready to start, and they were going to put up a platform. And so the farmer rolled out the manure spreader and we were to stand on this manure spreader and the chairman, who was a reeve in the municipality, introduced me, and I remembered Mitch Hepburn's old story. So I thought this was a great time for me to steal his story, so I started out my speech by saying:

'Mr. Chairman, this is the first time in my life, you know, that I've ever stood on a Liberal platform.' (I didn't want to say Conservative, because that might hurt Rupert's feelings, and he was a very nice fellow, a gentle sort of chap.)

And there was a big farmer sitting on a plank just in front of me and, with a voice you could hear to the far end of the crowd, he said:

'All right, Tommy, it's got a full load, you can throw the lever.'

I learned then that you've got to be very careful with trying to be funny with an audience and figure you've got somebody with a good wit in it. So that's my experience about addressing farmers in the farmyard."

EVERY VOTE COUNTS   "At that time the polls opened at nine o'clock in the morning and closed at five at night. Into this community there'd been a new family moved in, and at the day of the voting nobody was sure what his politics were. The Conservatives didn't know and the Liberals, they didn't know. So it was about fifteen minutes to five when they saw this man walking up the road. So my wife's grandfather, Henry Lyon, walked down the road a piece to meet this fellow and to find out what his politics were. Apparently he was a Conservative, so Henry got into an argument with him and kept the argument going until after the polls closed, so the fellow never did get voting."

BERRY-PICKING EXPEDITIONS   "We used to go on saskatoon-berry-picking expeditions. Everybody, all the family, the grandparents and the uncles, we all used to go out to where the saskatoon berries were, which was close to a salt-water slough. It used to be all dried up and it would be all crackly with the salt in the salt-water slough. And the saskatoon berry bushes were, I can remember them being, handy to these places.

The saskatoon-berry bushes were not quite as high as raspberry bushes, but they were a good height for picking. And the berries are purple, and the flavour of a saskatoon berry, you wouldn't believe, and my grandmother preserved them in sugar like in bottles, and she made saskatoon-berry pies by the dozen, and just the thought of saskatoon berries—I'd just love to be able to get home to pick some saskatoon berries.

We'd pick all day in pails, probably a lard pail or a great big peanut-butter pail or jam pail that we had, and we'd pick them . . . oh, lookit, you'd spend all day out there because we took our lunch with us, and it was a sort of family picnic while we were picking these saskatoon berries."

CHRISTMAS SHOPPING BY CATALOGUE   "Christmas was terribly important to us. But half the fun was in getting the catalogue out about the end of November and trying to find gifts for everyone in the family with the two dollars or whatever that you had. And then you'd send off these orders—you made them out so carefully, and they had to be secret. And then you'd send them off and then wait to see what would come back.

And of course what came back was usually substitutes. So that really you had two surprises: (a) to see if the stuff would really come; and (b) to see what it would really be like after waiting all that time. And then we would keep it secret, under our beds and so on, and get it all wrapped up for Christmas."

THE CHRISTMAS PARCEL "When Christmas rolled around I'd had a lovely letter from home saying that there was a parcel on the way. And I knew that would be good. So a neighbour and I hitched up our little jumper — we called them jumpers, they looked like outside toilets, you know—and put it with a team. And we set off with a lot of rugs and robes: it was very, very cold. But we had a footwarmer, so we were really very cosy. Of course we started to laugh because she'd come from London, and we thought of ourselves going down Picadilly in this outfit.

And then we get to the store, which was five miles away, to get this parcel. The store was a little tiny post office called St. Lina. And then we had a little look around St. Lina, bought a few things, and got the precious Christmas parcel.

As we were coming home, we stopped at another neighbour's and we thought we'd say hi to them because we were trying to make a date for Christmas Day so that we could all be together. Well, I tied the team up to a railing outside their place, went in to have tea, came out — fortunately didn't stay very very late — to find smoke coming out of the cutter. And what happened was: as we'd got out of the cutter, we'd tripped this footwarmer, and the charcoal had set fire to all the things in the cutter. We were just very lucky that the team didn't run away. It hadn't got to the team — it was just coming out of the cutter. So our precious Christmas parcel was burned, though it wasn't burned totally. We were able to cut off an inch of burnt cake and rescue a little. But that was heart-breaking."

ALL-NIGHT SESSION "A big event was the Christmas concert. And the teacher would let you start about a month ahead of the date for the concert to rehearse for this. And we also had all the bachelors that came from the Old Countries and had sung in choirs. They would come and sing 'In the Shade of the Old Apple Tree', or 'When Father Papers the Parlour', or something like this. There was lunch served after the concert. Of course Santa Claus always came first, and all the children were given a little bag of candy. And it was our Sunday School superintendent and his wife who took care of that. She was a seamstress, so she sent to Eaton's and got this mosquito netting in green and red, and made the little bags. And every child was given one of those.

And then the lunch began. Now they made the coffee in a boiler, and they made tea in great big pots. The ladies brought huge sandwiches — not these dainty little things they serve now. And it was either ham or mostly canned salmon, that's the two things that they would have.

And then the ladies would deck up their cakes. Three-layer cakes with lots of icing and what have you. And it was a really wonderful lunch.

Then the children—the little children—were put to sleep on the desks. The school desks were put on two boards so they could lift a whole bunch of them and put them back near the wall. So they put those back. The children were bedded down—the ones that went to sleep. And then it was time for them to bring out the violins and the mouth organ, and if somebody had a banjo or a guitar they brought it out. And we danced until the early hours of the morning.

If a blizzard came up, you stayed until daylight. Or if it still continued, you stayed there, because there were so very few landmarks that people could get lost and wander and go in circles and be frozen. So many and many a night in the Penkill school, which was very close — our first school, very close to the post office — it was an all-night session. They danced, and then when they got tired dancing, somebody would tell about their experiences, somebody would get up and recite a poem or something. There's where we drew on the talent from the Old Country. A lot of those bachelors brought wonderful talent along with them."

A TOBOGGAN FOR CHRISTMAS "My dad had four brothers and they had a number of kids. And at Christmastime everybody got together and we had a big supper on Christmas Eve, and we would have a lot of traditional Norwegian food.

And after, the big thing I really enjoyed was that we would get the old half-ton truck out, and one great big toboggan that one of my uncles had built, and we used to hook this toboggan up to the truck. It would pull us usually from my grandpa's farm to my dad's farm, which was about four and a half miles, on the road. And this was really an exciting experience for me every year.

The time I remember most was when my aunt bought me a toboggan for Christmas. And I insisted this toboggan had to be hooked up behind the truck as well as the big toboggan. And I was riding on this toboggan, for four and a half miles. Well, to say the least the toboggan wasn't that strong of a thing for this kind of treatment and after four and a half miles of travelling at about fifteen, twenty miles an hour — to me it was about sixty — there wasn't much left of my toboggan.

But I really had a tremendous evening. I can remember there was probably twenty or thirty of us, and people getting lost when we got out in the field making circles, and there was people all over in the snow. It was just a tremendous time."

FIFTEEN

Coo-Boss!

Cows Have Personalities . . . The Chihuahua Cow-Chaser . . . Such Good Friends . . . Little Squirt . . . A Wonderful Memory . . . Cattle on the Ice . . . Cow and Calf . . . Cows are Smarter . . . Robbing the Dead . . . Guernseys Are Lovely Cows . . . Riding the Cow . . . The Herd Boy . . . We Refused Twenty Thousand Dollars . . . A Working Dog . . . Blue Cow, Chocolate Dessert . . . Your Turn to Name the Calf . . . Coo-Boss! . . . Bringing in the Cows, City-Style . . . Friends . . . Never Trust a Bull . . . Tony the Bull

I found farmers ambivalent about cows. Many of them pointed out that cows aren't as stupid as most city people think they are. But whereas they could never say enough in praise of horses, there were very few farmers who carried on much about cows. One small, wiry, breezy old farmer-fisherman in the Maritimes was the exception. He thought cows were brighter than people and he loved to lie down in the grass and just watch his cows. That was Steve Churchill near Yarmouth, Nova Scotia, and he was a live-wire if I ever met one. I think he was over eighty, but he could talk faster than a circus barker and he was very, very funny.

I have a vague feeling cows have not had their due for all they have done for mankind, but if farmers themselves won't take up the cudgels on their behalf, then I'm not about to do so.

Let's just say I think there's a certain affection shown in that charming call when you hear it sounding across the meadow . . . "coo-boss . . . coo-boss . . . coo-boss . . ."

COWS HAVE PERSONALITIES "Cows have personalities. There's always one who is the boss of the herd, and she won't stand any nonsense from any of the other cows. She goes to the drinking trough first, while the other cows stand back and she has her fill. And then some of them are very gentle, will let you pet them, and some are really cranky. They don't want to be petted. Apparently they make friends with one another. When a cow is left to herself to calve, she'll take a friend with her to where she's going to have her calf. And if they get a grudge against a cow, she'll fight to the end. I saw one chase another around the field about half a dozen times, galloping after her. We had to go and separate them.

And apparently the cows know their names. I have a friend who bought some of my Jerseys and I went to visit them, and they have loafing stalls, and we were standing at the bar. I was looking at the Jerseys and she said: 'Come on, Joan.' and Joan came up to us, and then she said: 'Come on, Myrtle.' Myrtle leaves the herd and comes over. So they know their names."

THE CHIHUAHUA COW-CHASER "I recall we had a little chihuahua dog. It was just a little tiny thing—it wasn't more than about six inches high.

And we used to use this little dog, believe it or not, for chasing cows. We had a purebred Aberdeen Angus operation. And as always, you have to go get the cows to bring them home in the evenings.

This little dog would get lost in the grass that would be, I'd say, a foot high. And if you ever saw something funny, it was just hilarious, because these cows would just be running all over the place. You'd hear a yip-yip-yip all the way along, and these cows would just be running all over. But the thing was, you'd never see what was really chasing these cows, because this dog was just buried among the grass. It was just hilarious."

SUCH GOOD FRIENDS "I can recall having a great attachment for a calf that my father had given to me, and he and I became such good friends that I thought there was a great trust there. And in the spring I asked my dad to let me take him out on the halter, on a rope.

And he said: 'Yes, that's quite all right, only don't let him get away.' So I took him out, and if you've ever seen a year-old steer that's been in the barn all winter, when he first smells that spring air—he took off. Father said don't let go of him, so I hung on, and of course he took me off my feet and I slipped through the barnyard, and I was a mess, out at the other side until we landed at a fence and everybody stopped. Father said: 'My good sakes, why didn't you let go of him?' And I said: 'You told me not to let go of him, so I hung on!'"

LITTLE SQUIRT   "My earliest recollection is walking from the house to the barn. I was all of four years of age. I stood in the doorway of the barn looking into the semi-dark interior, which smelled of newly-cut hay, cows, and fresh milk. I could barely make out the figure of my mother with a milking pail between her knees, sitting close against the side of a cow, but I could hear the sound of the milk stream hitting the sides of the pail.

Suddenly I was struck right between the eyes and was blinded. I let out a cry and turned to run back to the house. My mother had directed a spray of milk right at me, hitting me on the face exactly where she wanted it to land. It was a long time before I ventured in the direction of the barn again at milking time."

A WONDERFUL MEMORY   "Cows are not dumb in any way. I think they're a lot smarter than a lot of people. They've got a wonderful memory. Now if you didn't feed your cows in the winter, say you started to feed them on the first of March, and you turned those cows out in the fall. Well maybe a day or two before the first of March, those cows would be looking for their feed. They've got a built-in calendar, and they've got a prodigious memory. I've seen a bunch of cows there with eighteen inches of snow, and one old cow got in the lead and I wondered why they didn't go in a straight line, and when the snow went away, this packed line of snow where they had walked was right on top of a very faint cow trail. They couldn't have felt it with their feet. She knew exactly where that trail was."

CATTLE ON THE ICE "There's a lot of strange things that happen on the farm. One thing that stands out was the bad accident my next-door neighbour had. His farm, like my own, has the Saugeen River running through it. And this was in the dead of winter, a very cold time. His cattle got out and got down on the ice, and he came running in to tell us they were in trouble, and I'll never forget seeing those lovely cattle swimming with their heads up above the ice. They had crashed through.

And we were down there, several of us neighbours; we chopped channels through the ice — it was ten, twelve inches thick — and were dragging these poor brutes out. My neighbour lost eight head that went down. They had just ventured out on the ice, and they broke thorugh. And we were soaking wet because it went over your boot tops and you were trying to get ropes and chains around their necks, so you were soaked to the shoulders. It was a pretty chilly time, it was twenty below zero, and I was chilled through and through that night. We only managed to get one out, and it died almost as we got it out."

COW AND CALF "We'd just put our last penny to buying a cow, and that night a thunderstorm came up and I was pregnant myself this time, and so was the cow. It was going to be a toss-up who got their babies first.

But a thunderstorm came up and struck the cow down and killed her. So that was our money gone: cow and calf. We had no milk whatsoever. We had to send over to one of the neighbours, and they kept us in milk."

COWS ARE SMARTER "I think cows have got more intelligence than human beings as a rule. I love cows and I was milking when I was six, seven years old. My father worked away with his oxen and I had to do the farm chores, milk the cows, and I loved cows. I love to feed them. I love to lay down and watch them eat. I've had them kick me when they had sore tits or something when I was milking — we used to have to milk by hand in those days — and I'd just get up and put a rope on her leg so she couldn't get her foot ahead to strike me.

If I bought a cow from a man, I named the cow for his wife. I was in the milk business and I'd go out and buy cows from my neighbours, and if the neighbour's wife's name was Bessie, I called the cow Bessie. He didn't mind, thought it was a joke. There was a lot of Marys and we put an initial by the Mary . . . Mary E, or Mary D, Mary C.

To sit down and milk twenty cows after I'd worked hard all day, I would go to the barn tired, but I'd get my pail underneath those cows and milk—it rested me. I liked it all."

ROBBING THE DEAD   "One of our neighbours was always getting into trouble. He just didn't know how to feed stock, at all. And he came over one day to our shack and he said: 'Daisy is dying.' And so we had to go and help him. Well, when we got there, it was the last piece of cattle that he had that belonged to the Soldier's Settlement Board, all the rest had died. So he wanted to save this at all costs.

So, it had given birth to a little calf, and the cow couldn't get up. So we had to go over and take our precious feed with us to feed this wretched cow. And Harry said: 'Now Bake's no good. He'll never be able to handle this job. So you take your orders from me: we've got to get that cow under cover.'

The barn had no roof and it was high up with manure. So there was only one place to put it, we had to put it in Bake's shack. He'd been of the Guards . . . the Queen's Guards, and he didn't know a thing about homesteading. So it was a tiny little shack, we had to move the kitchen cabinet. And Harry said: 'Now we'll get this cow's head headed for the doorway with a rope round it. And we'll put the rope through a window. I'll drive the team and you give me the orders.'

So, the cow was sliding nicely on the snow, headed for the doorway, when Bake said: 'Stop.'

And so I said: 'What's the matter?'

And he ran into the house and he fetched out a little tin mug. I said: 'What's this for?'

He said: 'I want to find out if she's dry.'

So Harry came and he said: 'What's the holdup here?'

I said: 'Bake's milking the cow.'

He said: 'For heaven's sake he's robbing the dead.'

So we finally got over this episode and we got the cow into his shack. Now the big decision was: which way we'd have the cow's head . . . to the head of his bed head, or the other end. Well, he chose the head of the cow. He said it was pretty horrible. Daisy was breathing on him all night, and when she mooed it was just terrible."

GUERNSEYS ARE LOVELY COWS   "Guernseys are lovely cows. They've got a good form, a good shape, a lovely colour. And generally, if you have to beef them, you get a good lot of beef.

Our neighbour up here, he imported the Guernseys here, the first one, and he was a very clear-headed man. He used to go to Toronto to the Summer Fair and then again to the Winter Fair, and there was three millionaires there in Toronto growing Guernseys, breeding them, and he would win all of the prizes. And they'd come down there and they'd buy some animals from him to take up there, and he did well there."

RIDING THE COW   "I used to have to clean the manure out and give the cows a fresh bed, and I used to have to give them their hay and water them every night, but I enjoyed doing it because I love cows. I love animals, particularly I love horses, but my father never ever bought my sister and me a horse, so we used to ride the cow.

So one would get on the cow's back and the other one would twist the cow's tail to make it go, because the cow was kind of reluctant to move. It would trot a ways while you were twisting its tail, because I suppose it hurt, you know. I suppose I was about nine years old and my sister would be seven. I suppose we used to jump up to get on it, but I know that when a few years later my father sold the cow, when they beefed it, you know, they told us the cow had a broken back."

THE HERD BOY   "When I was a kid around here, there weren't too many people in High River, I suppose maybe a thousand people or something like that, and a lot of people had their own milk cows, and in the summer, one of the boys who was through school would take these cows, would gather them up in the morning after they had been milked bright and early, and then herd them down by some open water where there was grass for the day, and then take them back at night. The people would shut them up in their stable and milk them again, and then they would go out the next morning.

And some of them were a little too cheap to pay the herd boy, so they would take them out themselves. And the herd boy would go around in the night and pull the picket pins and let these cows get out, and they would go into the first garden, and the next day there would be an awful squabble and somebody would get punched on the nose, and the fellow would probably send his cow out on the herd after that.''

WE REFUSED TWENTY THOUSAND DOLLARS "We had a bit of pasture and Rob and I bought this heifer from Howard Gurney for four hundred dollars. And Rob took her up there to Toronto, she won in the milking contest, she was first in her class. She was first in the best Guernsey, and then she got the first for the best female on the ground. The judge was from Wisconsin and he judged cattle from Halifax to Vancouver and he said he never saw the likes of that heifer. There was three millionaires there and they chased Rob all over the fairground; when he was loading her they kept outbidding one another for that heifer. They offered him twenty thousand dollars, they was going to keep that cow there, but Rob said: 'No, nothing doing.'

He brought her home. The next year we was going back again and Howard said: 'You'll have to have your cattle tested,' so that was all right, send the vet in.

And do you know, we lost five or six cows and one of them was Moss Rose, this cow that we refused twenty thousand dollars for. We paid four hundred dollars for her and we got a hundred dollars compensation for her. And that's all we got out of it. The most of the cattle, they'd give us a certificate and allow us to sell the meat, but he said: 'That cow is so far gone, we can't. You'll have to bury her.'

But we buried the whole business. I said: 'I'm not going to sell diseased meat.' We just ploughed a big trench, quartered and skinned them, threw them in there, and buried them. But that's what a licking we took then. The cow had TB. And this took place near our farm at Yarmouth, Nova Scotia.''

A WORKING DOG ''And in those days my dad could let the cows out on the roadside to eat the grass, and they would go just a certain distance. And this one day a fellow came and was talking to my father, and he said to him:

'How much do you want for the dog?'

My dad said: 'Oh, seventy-five dollars.'

And the fellow said: 'Seventy-five dollars — no dog is ever worth that.'

But my dad said: 'He is to me, he's worth a hired man.'

And he said: 'Why, can he work?'

'Oh,' Dad said: 'I think so.'

And the fellow said: 'No dog is worth seventy-five dollars.'

'Well,' Dad said, 'that's all right; he's worth seventy-five dollars to me, maybe not to you.'

The fellow said: 'How do I know he's a working dog?'

'Well,' Dad said, 'it's just about time for the cows, Jack, go fetch the cows.'

And the dog went and he brought them all back, but one. Dad said: 'Jack, you're missing a cow, where is she?'

And the dog just looked at my dad and he turned around and he went and he cut through a field and he found that cow and brought her home.

And the fellow said: 'Here's your seventy-five dollars.'

Dad said: 'No, two hundred dollars wouldn't buy that dog.' And we had that dog till he died. He lived till he was about seventeen years old, and one night he died by the barnyard gate.''

BLUE COW, CHOCOLATE DESSERT ''We called this cow the Blue Cow because it was definitely a blue colour. A very mischievous cow it was, it was quite a character. One time Mother put a dessert out on the back porch to freeze, chocolate pudding, chocolate dessert, and the next thing we knew the blue cow had climbed the steps and eaten this chocolate dessert ... the only cow in Canada, probably, that liked desserts."

YOUR TURN TO NAME THE CALF   "The barn was a major entertainment place, I believe, because you had the horses, I mean you had the animals. There was always babies, whether they were little pigs or little calves — they were all kept in and around the barn, and they were always special. My father always announced the arrival of something at the breakfast table. He would say 'It's your turn to name the calf' whether it were a calf or a colt. We always had two or three colts in the summertime, my father was interested in horses and had good horses.

I remember when it was my turn to name the calf, I called her 'Nellie', I haven't any idea why 'Nellie'."

COO-BOSS!   "I was glad when evening come and the children were in bed, and probably my husband would be out ploughing, or maybe they still hadn't come home from threshing from a neighbour's, and I could sit out on the front lawn and watch the sun setting. Also, I loved the morning, to get up and walk for those cows when the sun was coming up and the dew on the grass.

There were times when the children or I would have to go for the cows, probably six o'clock in the morning, if the men were working at some other project, probably seeding, or maybe up in the barn taking off a load of hay. And I remember the kids going sometimes on bare feet, and they would get a cow up and stand where she had been laying to get their feet warm. We would walk back a lane to the field they would be in, and have a dog along with us, though the dog never worked very well for me. I would usually have to call and sometimes round up each one separately, get them all into the lane, and then it was easy from there to the barn. I would go back the lane calling 'Coo-Coo-Coo boss!' hoping they would come, but usually I would end up rounding them up in the field. And one way that worked quite well getting them up, if it were raining and I carried an umbrella, they were terrified of that umbrella, and they would come on the run.

Getting cows in the morning, that was always a problem. They never seemed to want to come in the morning. They would come for the night milking, but not for the morning, and I would be sent or some of the children of the family would be sent out for to bring the cows in. This is quite usual. But I used to take a horse.

You'd grab a horse, just whatever horse was real handy. You didn't use a saddle. You got him up beside the water trough so that you could make a leap and get on his back. You used a rope instead of a bridle. You didn't use a bit; you trusted the horse, and so you went back and the idea of this of course was to keep out of the wet grass. In those days we all went barefoot, and of course your feet got pretty cold. So this stopped your pant legs from getting all wet and your feet soaking wet and you saved your shoes or your bare feet from getting cold, and it was a good way to round up cattle. You could round them up with a horse a lot faster than you could on foot."

BRINGING IN THE COWS, CITY-STYLE "We had a cousin from London, Ontario, who frequently visited us or spent the summer holidays with us. On one occasion my father sent him for the cows in the evening, and there seemed to be a long delay before he arrived. My dad went out to look for him, and he was walking back and forth across the roof of the barn, one side of which faced the gangway and the other side reeled off down to the manure pile. But anyway, we were afraid to call for fear he would fall, but finally my dad asked him what he was doing up there, and he said: 'I'm just looking to find what field they're in before I go.' My dad just said: 'You'd better come on down and we'll get the cows later.' He didn't want any accident to happen."

FRIENDS "Another incident that was interesting was when two young animals, a colt coming two years old and a heifer coming two years old, made a friendship. A friendship grew up between those two. They went away to the corner by themselves. They tore around the pasture land together. What one did, the other did. And you have to see this to enjoy it, as I did."

NEVER TRUST A BULL "I certainly wouldn't trust a bull, because we used to have two, a purebred Jersey and purebred Ayrshire, and I wouldn't have trusted either one of them. We used to have a long chain, not a heavy chain but a medium-sized length of chain about three feet long, in the ring in their nose, and if they took after you, of course, they put their head down and then they stepped on the chain and it sort of slowed them up a bit.

I remember one day the Jersey bull put me into the water trough and there I stayed until he kind of gave up the idea of having a battle with me. I was there a fair while, and the hired man came around the corner of the barn and grabbed the pitchfork and chased the bull."

TONY THE BULL "Now we had a bull. His name was Tony and my father had raised him from a calf, and bulls are supposed to be very, very fierce, and I guess perhaps there were times when Tony was fierce and bad tempered, but to my brother and me he was a friend. We used to ride him, and we had Tony so well trained that, when we wanted to ride him, we would come and lead him up to a water trough, and we would use this as a stepping stone and we would get on top of his back, and we would ride all over the yard. And if we wanted to steer Tony, we would reach out and grab one of his horns and pull it, and that turned his head that way, and Tony would go that way. He, of course, was a pet of ours; we used to give him little treats, and one of the things he loved most of all was a rubdown, and Tony used to almost purr when we rubbed him down.

And one day, I had been up in the haymow and just come down, and my father was in town with our dog, and a strange dog had come into the yard and had cornered my mother, and the dog was really giving her the business. He was a wild, fierce dog; you could see he was going to attack her. So I turned quickly to run back and get a pitchfork to help her, and there was a snort behind me and here come Tony just like an express train and he put his head down, got his horns underneath the dog and he flipped him up in the air, and the dog landed about ten feet away, right on his back. He got up and evidently wasn't injured, he certainly wasn't too injured to do yai, yai, yai and take off through the fence where Tony couldn't follow him.

By this time, Tony was thoroughly roused and he was snorting and stamping there at the fence, so Mother and I went up and stroked him and patted him, and then eventually we got him back into the stable. So I gave him some chopped oats, which he dearly loved, and a rubdown, and I don't think the wild dog stopped running until he got to Saskatoon."

SIXTEEN

If It Wasn't for My Neighbours...

Neighbours . . . The Colour of the Horses . . . Help at a Fire . . . Too Heavy for Six Men . . . Sharing Food . . . I Had to Keep Going . . . Two Inches of Land . . . Farm Forum . . . A Great Help . . . The Peeping Tom . . . Indian Neighbours . . . Not a Registered Nurse . . . The Beef Ring . . . Just Married . . . Rather a Moody Fellow . . . A Little Boy Lost

I t isn't good fences that make good neighbours, it's good neighbours. Right down to this day, farm families have always been ready to help each other out when necessary, whether in a barn-raising or in a time of tragedy. You never know when you'll need help yourself, of course, so it isn't entirely altruism. On the other hand, people love socializing on the farm, they love news and gossip (they have a good, healthy curiosity about their neighbour's business), so that neighbours aren't only a necessity, they are also a delight. I must admit that some farmers can be as pig-headed as anyone on this earth, and if they think they have been scorned or insulted or cheated by a neighbour, they take a long time to get over it. The wrong can actually have happened, or it can just be imagined: it really doesn't make much difference.

I've lived in cities and I've lived just about as long in the country and it's my belief that neighbourliness is a creative force. I don't think city people understand what being a good neighbour means. The strange indifference that exists in the city, or that frantic desire to be left alone, is totally alien to the farm. Neighbours in the country are almost an extension of the family.

NEIGHBOURS "We lost our barn by fire in 1955, and if it wasn't for my neighbours, I don't think we'd be farming today. It was the day of the Highland Games and we lost the entire crop. Then one neighbour gave us forty tons of hay, a gift. They collected around $2800, a gift, and then when we were building the new barn, they came day after day and helped us, gratis too.

We have an old saying on the farm: 'You can get along without your relatives, but you can't get along without your neighbours.'"

THE COLOUR OF THE HORSES "I went onto a homestead sixty-five miles from Maple Creek when there wasn't a thing, there wasn't a telephone or a road. As a matter of fact, when we went onto the homestead, we had to find the corner post to find out where the road would be so we could put a house in the right place.

We had neighbours, and when we went to visit we didn't only go for a day, we stayed a day or two. If you saw somebody coming across the prairie, you figured they were coming to your place. Well, if it's getting near mealtime, Mother would put another piece of meat and another potato or so in the pot, and dinner was ready when he got there. We figured out who it was by the colour of the horses. And we had a good visit.

Nowadays you go to visit somebody, you go to look at TV or something like that."

HELP AT A FIRE "My first experience in life was a fire. My parents were living with our grandparents. It was on a Sunday afternoon; Aunt Mary and Uncle Mike O'Reilley and their families were invited, and dinner was just over when somebody said: 'There's a fire.'

It started in a chimney, in the back kitchen, and it spread rapidly and destroyed the house. Of course, they lived down by the Kerry Creek, which was practically a mile off the road, and naturally no neighbours could see anything in time to be of much help. However there were quite a few people there.

I had two brothers, and my brother and I were put over in the turnip patch with the baby carriage, and we were to stay there and keep an eye on the baby. And I can remember people yelling and the flames shooting up and the house roof going in, and I remember somebody coming out the front door with the parlour table. It's strange how you remember those things. Everybody was excited, yes, people were yelling, you know, do this and do that, and I can remember people going helter-skelter. You know, at those fires, people do more damage half the time than they do good. They destroy things really, they bring things out and toss them, glass and buffets and things like that. Then lots of times they'd be smashed because they'd carry them out carefully, then they'd drop them. They'd get so excited."

TOO HEAVY FOR SIX MEN   "In 1956, just as we were preparing for harvest, and I was working under the one-ton truck, I observed an orange glow in the building that I was in and I went outside and saw that the barn was on fire. At the same time Dad was rushing from the house—he had just completed the milking for the Sunday evening — and the barn was well in flames and we couldn't get anything out of it at all. The building next to it was only about five feet away, and before we really knew what was happening, there was people coming from all directions, and the yard was full of cars. Within a matter of a very short time, the barn was completely destroyed.

One of the most interesting things about this was that we had a very heavy old-time grain crusher in the building which was next to the barn, and four men came in, and I don't remember who they were, but they were neighbours, and they carried that thresher out of the building, away from the building, so it wouldn't be destroyed — and when we went to move it afterwards, six of us couldn't move it."

SHARING FOOD   "Certain times, in the fall of the year especially, the farmer's wife had need for extra quantities of meat, either for visitors, or in some cases where the threshing gang got stalled because of rain.

I recall one time that my father had a threshing outfit that required thirty-six men to operate it, and quite a heavy rain, and we had this threshing gang for three weeks, and although the neighbours went home, the help which came from Ontario on the harvest trains usually lived in cabooses, and they stayed at our place, about twenty of them, for three weeks. At that time arrangements were made between the farmers' wives. They would throw in their share of food for this week because they didn't need it. Then they would get the share later on. But on this particular occasion, I remember my father killed an extra beef and three pigs, all of which was consumed in this three-week period by the men."

I HAD TO KEEP GOING "One day when I was a very young girl, about fifteen, living on a small farm in Saskatchewan, I was staying at home because my mother was ill, and because my father was blind and couldn't look after her. He had had an accident years before — he had had a runaway with the team, and the horse had stepped on his shoulder and broke it. And he hadn't really had it set properly, and they think possibly it had severed the optic nerve. And since then he had gradually gone blind until, at this time, he was completely blind.

My mother had a cold and a bad fever, and it was very very cold outside, and we were not in a position to get in contact with a doctor or relatives. We had no phone, and the roads were pretty well blocked. It really was a wicked night: the wind was blowing and the snow was blowing across the roads so you could hardly see ahead of you. It was a real blizzard on the bald prairie. Unless you've lived there you wouldn't realize what it was like.

My mother was real sick through the day, and we should have done something; but on account of the weather we hadn't. But towards evening she got worse, and I realized something had to be done. And the only thing I could do was go for my brothers, who were a mile and a half away, across the fields, with no road. And don't forget, again, I was only fifteen.

I was very frightened, even of the dark, and it was so cold, and in that part of the country we had coyotes, and we heard them continuously through the night. I had heard that they would attack a person if they were very hungry. I also had heard that they were afraid of fire, and would stay away if you had a light with you. So the only thing I could do was light the lantern and take it with me.

I bundled all up because I knew that it was so cold that I must keep warm in case I got lost. And I lit my lantern and took extra matches in my pocket so I could relight it if it went out. And I was on my way.

It was a pitch black out, although there was a bit of moon, but lots of clouds. I knew all the landmarks and the bushes and that between our place and my brothers', but on account of the storm it was very hard to see. Occasionally you couldn't see anything in front of you, and the snow was so deep that I had to crawl through snowbanks at one time or another.

During one of these times, when I was crawling through the snowbank, my lantern went out. I just panicked, you know, I was just scairt to death. I tried frantically to light it, and of course the wind blew the matches out. I heard the coyotes and I had to keep going. There was no other way, regardless.

I struggled on. My chest was aching with fatigue and with breathing the real cold air. And at that time I didn't know it, but my nose was bleeding. It never entered my mind that I wouldn't make it, but I didn't know when. Finally, after what seemed like hours and hours, I saw the light in my brothers' house, and hurried on — frightened them to death when I stumbled up their porch, like. I don't know how long it took me to get there, but it seemed hours and hours.

I couldn't talk at all when I got there, and they didn't know what was wrong, but they figured it was serious. They got a paper and pencil, and I shakily wrote down, Mother was sick. So they harnessed the horses, and we took off, as fast as we could, in a sleigh. My two brothers, my sister-in-law, and myself.

It didn't take long, although we had to go around by what they used as a road. And when we got there, Mother was no worse, but so bad that they knew she had to have a doctor. They rigged up a homemade stretcher, put her in the sleigh, and took her to the nearby station, which was two miles away, Cheviot. And luckily it wasn't too long till train time. Took her to Saskatoon, where they immediately admitted her to the hospital. She had pleurisy and was near pneumonia. If we hadn't got her in that night, it possibly would have been the end of her, because we had no way of looking after her at home.

My mother was in the hospital for quite some time — I think around two weeks. She did recover, and came back to the farm. By that time I had recovered my voice: for several days I couldn't speak above a whisper. It was quite an experience. I can remember it clearly. And the good thing of it was the family insisted that Mother and Father move to the city, where they had close neighbours and a phone."

TWO INCHES OF LAND   "Farmers generally speaking will try to stay away from courts of law. As a matter of fact, I would say that many of them don't trust a court of law; they think the law is probably obeyed, but justice is not done, and they try to stay away from litigation.

But don't try to take anything away from a farmer in the way of land that he legitimately thinks is his own—there you will have a fight on your hands, and most often it is over line fences and property. Whereas a farmer would make a man move a fence for two inches of land, he would turn around and give him a couple of acres of corn for nothing, because he needed it."

FARM FORUM   "I think we had farm forums in our area for about three years, and we discussed problems much the same as we do today. Anything that came on from Toronto, we discussed that, of course, but then later on we discussed 'What is Wrong with Farming?' Why are we not getting what we thought was our fair share of the profit that was going on? We thought other people were better off than we were. I wonder about that today. I don't think perhaps that they were any better off . . . we were any better off or they were any better off. I can't just put my finger on any one topic, but one of the ones they threw out was 'What Do You Gain from a Farm Forum?' And I remember some of our people saying:

'Well, at least we get to know our neighbours better anyway.'"

A GREAT HELP   "I feel that the Indians were really part of the pioneer days and they were a great help to everyone. But there was some amusing things, too. I can remember one man that came along one time, an Indian, and he had a long knife in his hand. He came up to the door and he said:

'I kill.'

What he meant was that he would butcher for any of us, of course. But it sent them all flying into the house and the doors locked and barred. But the poor man meant that he was the butcher of the district, and he would butcher for them, because he knew that most of them were rather greenhorns and didn't know how to butcher."

THE PEEPING TOM   "We live in an old house in the little hamlet of Thompsonville, Ontario, which nestles half-hidden in a tiny river valley, surrounded by farm country. Some time after the turn of the century, our house was rented by a farm labourer and his wife. She was young and quite attractive. The farm labourer used to work late sometimes at an adjoining farm, and one winter evening he was coming home in the dark through the snow, having had to do some extra work at the farm where he was employed, and as he trudged towards his house he noticed a man peering in the bedroom window. He shouted at the man, who ran away. The farmhand ran after him, and as he passed the bedroom window he noticed that his wife was undressing and getting ready for bed.

The farm labourer was furious and followed the tracks in the snow, which led only a short distance to the shack of an old recluse who lived a few hundred yards away. He burst into the old fellow's place and berated him for peeping at his wife. The old man was distraught and sobbing and said that he was very sorry and he had meant no harm, and he added: 'You have no idea how lonely I am.' The farm labourer told him never to do it again and went home, half mad and half sorry for the old recluse.

The next day someone was passing along the road and happened to glance in at the old fellow's place and saw what he thought was something suspicious. He knew the old fellow slightly so he knocked at the door. There was no answer, and since the door was unlocked he went inside.

The old man was dangling from a beam. He hanged himself some time that night."

INDIAN NEIGHBOURS "We lived about three miles away from the Indian reservation and the Indians used to go back and forth, and we were afraid of them at first, because not far from Frog Lake there is a monument where the massacre had taken place a few years before that, and we were afraid of the Indians. But later on we realized that they weren't hostile any more, and we weren't afraid of them. They used to stop in to get some bread and butter and eggs from us and the other neighbours, and they'd repay with fish or moccasins and beaded leather-goods, and they'd stop in to warm up in the wintertime, when they travelled back and forth.

And once in the wintertime a young Indian couple stopped and their baby was crying very hard, but by the time they unwrapped the baby, the baby had died of exposure. So then they drove away and we don't know what happened."

NOT A REGISTERED NURSE "The neighbour across the trail had been very, very good to us and she said: 'I have to go to Saskatoon to have my baby, and I can't afford it.'

Of course I said: 'Well, don't let that bother you, I'll look after you providing you ask the doctor out, because I'm not a registered nurse.'

So the time came, and first of all we'd only been out there two weeks when my little girl — she was three years old — took diphtheria. So we were quarantined. And then one day, Mr. Lawford—that was our neighbour—came running across. 'Quick, quick!' he said, 'Come quick!'

I said: 'Ooooh, hold on, man,' I said. 'Plenty of time.'

And he said: 'No, your barn's on fire.'

I said: 'The barn's on fire!? However did that barn get on fire? I haven't been down there with matches ...'

'No,' he said, 'I lit a straw pile and the wind blew the fire right across the prairie.'

They put the phone call through and of course all the farmers came up and ploughed a fireguard. The barn burned to the ground, and I lost several chickens, But anyway we got over that.

A little while after, he comes running over and he said: 'Come quick,' he says, 'the wife's taken sick.'

So that let us out of quarantine. We used to have to put an order up the top of the pasture if we wanted anything from the stores. And whoever saw that notice up there brought the stuff and put it down there. Then we put the money after. So this let us out of quarantine.

And I went over to Mrs. Lawford, and she was in labour. Of course it's a lot of difference in those days to these days. She'd got a few baby things, and I had to turn around and pop 'em all in the oven and scorch them to make sure that they were sterilized.

She phoned the doctor and he was seventeen miles out, horse and buggy. One doctor to cover a fifty-mile area. So I got her over it, and we had a lovely boy. We said if it was a boy, it was to be Victor. If it was a girl it was to be Victoria, because this happened on the twenty-fourth of May.

So it turned out a lovely boy, anyway, and the doctor came down — he'd been stuck in the mud. He had to cut across the prairie because the roads were under water. And he said: 'Where's Mrs. Lawford?'

I said: 'She's in bed, Doctor.'

He went in the bedroom, and of course her and the baby were in bed. He said: 'My goodness,' he says. 'What doctor did you have?'

And she said: 'Just Mrs. Jones.'

So he said: 'Well you're booked from now on.' And so from then on — I was out in Canada a good eleven months then — and I don't think I put a month in at home from then on. I was called all over, and within three years, I brought sixty-nine babies into the world.''

THE BEEF RING   ''Beef ring started because of the fact that it was so hard to keep meat. So as soon as the warm season started, people would then open up the beef ring, and this was formed with a butcher, and he was butcher, secretary, bookkeeper, and all, because he would know the weight of the meat as he cut it. And the meat had to be brought in one day, every man in the beef ring supplied one animal a year, and then the next evening, the butcher slaughtered it and washed it and skinned it and hung it up. Then the following morning he would cut it up into little pieces or sizes that were required, and it would be put into bins built on the wall of the ... it was a granary that was used, actually, I think, for a slaughter house. And each lady left a clean white flour-bag with her name on it in her bin, and he would slip in the pieces of meat. And by the end of the year, you had received your whole beef back a few pieces at a time each week.

So one thing that my uncle was always amused at, the women all claimed they kept track of every piece of meat they took home. At the end of the year, every woman had received five shanks, even though there was only four-legged animals came in each week. He said: 'Every woman claimed she got five shanks over the year. How in the world could they get five?'

There was always a complaint about that. If you were given a shank, you were then maybe cheated out of a roast. And of course there was suspicions sometimes that maybe a family that was having somebody special for Sunday dinner, if they looked into the bag and found all they had was a shank or something that wasn't just as tasty, maybe they did sometimes change. But I don't think that was done too often. I think it was just miscalculation."

JUST MARRIED   "I remember one time we had a neighbour there, he just got married and he was in his bedroom; it was quite mild, and we happened to be going by there and this couple was in bed, and the window was up. And they had several pullets, you know, roosters, they were roosting out in the lilac trees. So we got four or five of these and we shoved them in the window and run. We heard about that after."

RATHER A MOODY FELLOW   "There were some rather terrible things happened in our farm community. One thing I remember upset the whole community. A man who was a bachelor, rather a moody fellow, had a housekeeper with a little girl. The house-keeper was quite friendly with another family, and I don't know whether there was jealousy or what it was that happened. I believe they teased him, and he brooded on it, and one night when a storm was coming up, he went down and tried to burn out the people who had done the teasing.

He had a coal-oil can, he put a wick in and lit it and tossed it into their kitchen, and he went back to his house. First he knifed the woman, knifed the little girl, and then he shot himself. He had set his house on fire and, of course, he thought he was going to conceal all the evidence of what had happened, but because of the storm the rain put the fire out and they were able to reconstruct the crime.

I often wondered if he ever knew whether he had succeeded in burning out the other people. What happened, the husband, the father, heard the can rolling across the floor. He came out to investigate, jumped through the flames, got the fire extinguisher, and was able to put the fire out, and the house didn't suffer much damage. But you can imagine what excitement there was in the whole community, and the telephones and everybody calling."

A LITTLE BOY LOST   "About five years ago, a little boy was lost in this township, and the word got spread around that this wee chap, he was deaf, was lost from his home. It was right in the spring of the year, and everybody was busy, but you could see tractors sitting in the middle of the field — when the farmers got the word, they just shut down and away they went. The Amish Mennonite neighbours, there was horses tied in the fence corner, they were away, and all the night we searched for him, couldn't find him, and this was in a thick wooded part, lots of streams and lakes, small lakes, bog holes. There was a search on all night. I didn't know about it myself until the next morning, but I went immediately, and I think it was about five o'clock in the afternoon when he was found, and they were almost despairing of finding the boy alive, but he was found all right, pretty weak and tired.

And I'll never forget the ladies of the townships, this was Bentinck as well as Sullivan, providing lunch for us fellows, and hot tea or

A FAMILY ALBUM
The snapshots in this section were taken by a variety of farm families and
given to Allan Anderson for use in this book. From men at barn-raisings to
kids climbing haystacks, they cover a wide range of subjects, photographic
skills, and eras. They also catch some of the flavour of farm life.

coffee, and I don't think I ever was so tired as I was that night, tramping up and down through water and everything else. But it was really great when they found the wee fellow alive. He had gone approximately four miles from his home, and the sad part of it was, he couldn't hear us calling, and then, well, the confusion, there was about four hundred men out, and it wasn't much chance we had of him hearing anyway. One of the men just stumbled onto him and he was laying sleeping behind a log. They found a shoe a short time before and that gave a clue where he might be.

The police were out helping us too, but actually the rural farm people knew the rough wooded area; they did the actual walking and the police gave us lots of instructions how to stay so far apart, and that's a day I'll never forget, and what a relief for everybody when he was found alive, because everybody just had a horror of what they might find."

SEVENTEEN

Around the House

Those Big Houses Were a Necessity . . . Coming Down to Breakfast . . .
Tougher in Those Days . . . Hazards of the Outhouse . . . With the House on
Fire . . . The Catalogue . . . The Parlour Was for Company . . . Part of the
Family . . . Sandwiches . . . Parlour Visitors . . . A Coffin in the Parlour

In the old days farmhouses tended to be big and sprawling because the families were often large. To put it bluntly, the farmer
and his wife grew their own hired help. To put it another and
different way, they liked children: the family, with all its generations, made up a comfortable society, and even the hired girl was
part of the family group.

The use of a farmhouse was formalized. Upstairs were the bedrooms, where, before central heating, you got dressed in a rush in
the winter before you froze, as the water often did in the wash
basin. Downstairs, the kitchen was the centre of life. The preparation of food was only one of the functions that went on in the
kitchen. Here the family gathered and gossiped and snoozed, the
cat played in the big woodbox and the dog dozed under the table.

The parlour was a ceremonial room: for the minister or priest on
his rare visits, for relatives or friends from the city (but not for local
people when they dropped in). Sometimes the furniture was protected with dust covers and the blinds drawn. I've always thought
of farmhouse parlours as gloomy places and rather a waste of
space, but to the farm family it was a social necessity: that was the
way things were done. It was also a place of death. There the body
of a member of the family was decently displayed for mourners to
gather around and pay tribute in hushed tones.

You went from the kitchen to the summer kitchen, which was

usually just a porch, and then outside. A reasonable distance from the house, at the end of a well-worn path, was the outhouse, sometimes a one-holer or more likely a two-holer. I will never, never be able to understand how the old folks endured those winter trips to the outhouse. I will never, either, be able to fathom why rheumatism and a host of aches in the wrong place didn't result from exposure in the outhouse. However, there are certain mysteries that perhaps should be left unsolved, and certain questions that need not be asked.

All I can say is that people complained bitterly to me about going to the outhouse in the winter, but no one ever admitted to being the worse for it.

THOSE BIG HOUSES WERE A NECESSITY "The houses that were built in the late 1890s, some of the ones around Wawanesa are still standing. They were built of brick, and if you drive through this country today, you can see fifteen or twenty of those brick homes with ten or fifteen rooms in them; they are still standing.

These big houses were almost a necessity in those days, because the families were much larger than they are today, families of five or six children was not uncommon, a couple of hired men, two or three hired men, sometimes they boarded the schoolteacher, as we did at our place so many years, and even though we had seven bedrooms, they were all fully occupied. With the coming of the tractor and the machinery that took the place of the horses and the manpower, the hired man disappeared, the little schoolhouse disappeared, and with it the schoolteacher that taught in the rural schools, so there wasn't a need for the large, fine homes that they had in those days.

And so you find today the one-storey bungalow with two or three bedrooms has replaced most of these big homes as we had on the farm where I was born."

COMING DOWN TO BREAKFAST   "In the kitchen we had an
Eagle wood stove, and it had a water heater on the side of it, and a
big warming closet, and oh, the things that used to come out of that
warming closet when I got up in the morning, because before I got
up in the morning, my grandfather had got up and started the stove,
and everybody was practically halfway through their day's work by
the time I'd get up, and the house would be getting nice and warm,
though it was still ice-cold upstairs. And there was a woodbox
which the cat slept in, and of course it had to be filled all the time.

I remember getting up and coming down to this great, big, long
table, with bowls of honey and bowls of peanut butter and preserved fruit, especially blueberries in syrup, and you could have
this for your breakfast — a nice dish of blueberries or honey and
peanut butter; I mixed it all together, slopped it all together nice
and gooey, and I just loved that on my toast. And the table always
had the butter, which they churned themselves in a churn. I can
remember this big old churn sitting there.

There were two sort of kitchens, and the big range was in the first
kitchen, which wasn't as big. And the next kitchen was . . . oh, was
quite large, a big window and a great big table and all these chairs,
and there was a little sort of a nook over on the side where you
could go and sit there too, like the old-fashioned restaurant-nook
type thing. And then the next room was like a dining room. There
was a dining-room table, and my grandmother had all these great
big ferns—it was just like a jungle in there."

TOUGHER IN THOSE DAYS   "When I was home we had a
space-heater in the living room and that was the extent of our
heat . . . and the kitchen stove. And when you would get up in the
morning in the wintertime, you would break the ice in the water
pail to make coffee.

When we went to bed at night, of course, my mother had made
feather ticks, and I think you possibly could have slept outside
under these feather ticks. They were really, really warm and they
were about a foot thick, I think, and this is one of the ways you
kept warm. And of course before you went to bed, Father would
stoke the heater, would put a log of wood on, and this would
possibly last till maybe two in the morning. But, still, by the time

you did get up in the morning, the water was frozen in the pail, and the first thing you did was you lit a fire in the kitchen stove and then you went and you put a fire on in the heater, opened the door going upstairs so that it would warm up upstairs.

Mother was always the first one up in the morning, and of course you got out of bed, you got dressed. You didn't dare go downstairs, you'd probably freeze your feet on the steps going down, but you got dressed first and then you went down and you put the fire on. And you got dressed very fast.

The old outhouse was about forty or fifty feet north of the house, and of course in the wintertime, you'd have your coats on, your ski pants on, and you'd have to go. Your Eaton's catalogue was there, and if you were very fortunate and your mother did lots of canning in the summer, you had the wrappers from the peaches and the pears, which was a sight lot better than Eaton's catalogue. You weren't in there too long. You were in and out as quick as possible, because it was cold. I don't think we suffered from it because we were cold, but I think people were tougher in those days than they are now."

HAZARDS OF THE OUTHOUSE   "Well, I might tell you something about one of our neighbours. Their oldest daughter was nervous and she sort of had a nervous breakdown. Well, that was fine. My mother and father decided that after she had been in the hospital, they'd go up then and see the family. I would be about twelve then and I had to go to their outhouse. There was no inside toilets at this time, so I went out there in the dark of the night and no person with me, and all of a sudden when I got in, just ready to sit down on the toilet, oh, the awfullest noise arose, and feathers started flying around, and I got so scared I forgot what I went for, and here was a clucking hen with some chickens sitting in the outhouse. And you can imagine how frightened I would be when they had this woman had a nervous breakdown, and I felt sure that she had something to do with this. So I just went back into the house and I forgot about the whole thing what I went for. I just told the people in the house that I got a scare with this hen, and they just laughed.

Another thing, though, I can remember the smells of the out-houses. They really always smelt. You get used to that, I suppose. They smell very badly to me now when I'm not used to them, but at that time, I don't know that they really upset me so much. But they always had Eaton's catalogues, and they were always cold and often wet, and with squeaky noises always in the night. And if you took a lantern for to see your way, the lantern always had a peculiar smell of burning kerosene, a smell that I can hardly describe, but you could always smell that smell in the house. We used ashes, of course, for the smell for the house, and my mother would use Gillett's Lye, which would freshen it up for a while, but in a short time again, you would have this smell. I don't think any of them were any different.

Some outhouses were painted up quite nicely, and they would quite often have a half-moon on the doorway. Some of them had little ventilators like little birdhouses on the top. I think this was for ventilation and I think this likely helped. But I did hear of one outhouse, it was next door to us here, and anyway there was a lady there, and her little cousin came, and she had to get into the outhouse because she had to go to work. And he was outside and said he had to get in there, too. So she said come on in. He sat down on the other one; she jumped up and left and there was a crack in the seat and he got caught in it, in his seat, and he never forgot that as long as he lived.

I can remember one Halloween in Chesley. There was a woman, she was a very fat woman, and she was in this outhouse and she heard them out there, but she didn't want to let on she was in there, so she just kept nice and quiet. They didn't make any noise either. But they apparently had seen her going in, because one of them had a B-B gun and he just shot her in the seat. So I think that she got out of there pretty fast. They didn't need to turn the outhouse over. They really hurt her enough that way."

WITH THE HOUSE ON FIRE   "I can remember one time our kitchen caught fire, and Mother was on the way to the barn, going to feed her two cows. I was teaching school then and I heard the old fire bell ringing, you know, and I asked someone: 'I wonder where the fire is.'

'Down at George Campbell's.'

So I rushed home, and just as I rushed down there, Charlie Dixon — he ran a drugstore, though he was the Fire Chief in those days, volunteer service — he was there and he was telling my mother, 'Don't worry, Mrs. Campbell, we're going to take all your furniture out and we're going to get the fire out.'

And she said: 'Don't bother, Mr. Dixon, the fire is only in the kitchen. Just cut a hole in the roof and put the hose down and put it out.'

'But lookit here, we'll get your furniture out.'

'Don't worry about the house, what burns, put the fire out.'

He said: 'Well what are you going to do?'

'I'm going to the barn to feed my cows.'

With the house on fire!... They did what she wanted, they put a hole in the roof and it took all the plaster off the kitchen ceiling, and the water all ran inside around the piano. The fire was put out pretty fast, and Mr. Dixon announced again:

'We're going to get buckets, so now we're going to clean up for you.'

'No, no, Mr. Dixon, don't bother, you're a busy man. Joe, go get your father's big auger, and bore a couple of holes by the piano and one by the fireplace, and let the water run through to the basement."

THE CATALOGUE   "You sent to Eaton's for mostly everything in years gone by. You bought broadcloth for making quilts—that was a favourite pastime when we were younger. I had fourteen quilts when I was married. You'd buy broadcloth and you'd buy flannelette and your sheets would come out of the catalogue and boots and, oh, practically everything you'd wear you would get out of the catalogue.

When you finished looking at it in the house and it got worn and it was no longer any use, it went outside to the outhouse. Eaton's put out a summer and spring catalogue, and then they put out a sale catalogue, and you just loved to get those and read them all through and look them over. I've got one I'm going to keep for a souvenir. I think it's a darn shame it's all over and gone."

THE PARLOUR WAS FOR COMPANY "We used to board the schoolteacher — well, you have the biggest house, you take her, I don't want her. And so the teacher stayed at our place even in times when perhaps it wasn't most convenient. But the girls that were there were from a neighbouring area — we knew them and they were wonderful people to have. Sometimes it was even a cousin who was teaching there. I think she had the worst time of all because we knew her too well.

Schoolteachers had a bit of status anywhere, and if she offered to wipe the dishes, you thanked her for doing it, because she was never expected to do those things. She was expected perhaps to make her own bed and keep her room tidy, but in our particular case the schoolteacher was someone looked up to and, while she paid her board, she made herself one of the family, and youngsters obeyed her about as quickly as they did my father. But at the same time, she never butted in. Her room was her own. We knocked on the door if we wished to talk to her. If you went to call her at suppertime and she was in her room, you knocked on the door and told her supper was ready.

But most often they sat in the living room — dining room it was called then — because the parlour was kind of for company. It opened off the dining room and was another large room, and the two together made room for even a small country dance. Schoolteacher's board would have been fifteen or twenty dollars a month, because I know when I went away to school I was paying about the same, and that was five dollars a week from Sunday night to Friday.

The parlour in our place was where the piano was, and kids practised music lessons, and to keep an eye on them, of course, the double sliding doors between the parlour and the dining room would be open. It was also a place which one dusted practically every Saturday. That's one chore I do remember. And it had mahoghany furniture, which was beautiful, and I know where some of those chairs still are and are in use. It was opened every day to the rest of the house, because houses will heat better if you don't have a cold corner. So, in the winter the door was left a small way open into the dining room, and when the small fry were practising music lessons on the piano, the door was open wider to make sure that they stayed right at their chore.

The teacher usually had boyfriends, and usually the boyfriend came to take her home for the weekend, and as he was a farmer, he was working the rest of the week. He would bring her back Sunday evening, and if it was in reasonably early time, they came in and everybody visited together. My father was always very sociable. Boyfriends of teachers, or even my own as we grew up, were quite welcome to the place, sometimes so welcome that I wondered if I really did like them that much.

We could always manage to get a chance alone. We would usually take the car and go off somewhere; in the summer we would go down to the lake to go swimming. We had a lot of bush around our place—we could go for a walk, and it was very easy to disappear from the house.

I knew how to do that as a girl growing up. Right after dinner, you could avoid dish-washing by feigning something out the door, and once you got to the door you went past the car shed, you went past the little house beside the car shed, and on for a walk in the bush. And when you came back, you were horribly surprised that the dishes were all done."

PART OF THE FAMILY   "We always had a hired girl to help. My mother was really my stepmother and hadn't been that long on the farm, so maybe the girl had to help her or show her perhaps more than others. We had several Old Country girls who had come through assisted immigration and worked for a year or two years or longer and usually married some of the young men of the area and became just as proud Canadians as anyone else would be.

I remember one in particular. Barbara had not been on a farm before and was getting used to milking the cows and separating milk. We were going to town—the hired girl was like the rest, she went to town in the car the same as anybody else—and my father, seeing a neighbour had bought a new grain separator, remarked: 'Oh, Stanley's got a new separator.' Barbara looked over and said: 'He'd have to milk an awful lot of cows to make use of that.'

And when you think that a separator would be half the size of a bus, compared to the little one in the corner for the milk, you would understand the girl had not been on a farm before.

We never really had a great deal of trouble with the girls. But when we had some of the new-Canadian girls whose families from central Europe had moved into the edge of the Riding Mountain area, their fathers always regarded the girl's pay as partly his, maybe all his. And usually they made a trip down by wagon and team — sometimes in the earlier years it was even an ox team — to collect Mary's or Annie's wages. My father would always have to explain to him that some of the money had to go to the girl — they had to have some things themselves. This wasn't always very easily done, and one man in particular — and perhaps you couldn't blame him, because we had practically everything and anything that they would need on a farm — would perhaps lift a hammer or some small piece of harness. He always had a lot of hay in the bottom of the wagon box when he was down, and it was kind of an odd scene, for my brother would be quietly told: 'Have a little look through Mike's hay before he leaves. Don't say anything.' And the articles were retrieved, put back. Mike never said a word, neither did we.

The girl got up at the same time as the rest of us, my mother and father and the hired man, perhaps five o'clock in the summer, later in the winter — it seemed that that was awful cold and dark then. The men went out to feed the horses, the women got breakfast for the men, so that when the horses were fed they came in, had breakfast, time to sit a moment or two, then go out and take your team to the field. Then of course there was dishes, and butter to make, bread to make. Everything was produced on the farm.

Our house was a large house and, with the exception of the parlour, it was all gone through every day, after breakfast, between my mother and the girl, and sometimes one did one job and some the other. Dishes were washed, the separator was washed. Someone had milked at the time the early chores were done, and the vegetables got ready for dinner, and it was dinner at noon and supper at night — it wasn't much different from dinner either. Maybe you had fried potatoes instead of fresh-cooked ones, and cold meat. But there were desserts for each.

Beds were made, floors dusted, and these floors were linoleum floors and waxed, so they weren't that hard to scrub. It became kind of a farm as well as city fetish for the women to prove who had the shiniest wax floor. Usually after dinner and the dishes were done, clean towels put out at the sink where the men washed, and everything wiped up and tidied up, there was an hour or two that the girl could have to herself, though perhaps in a busy season of fruit picking or fruit canning she gave it up. But as I remember, she usually had a little bit of spare time before it was time to go milk the cows again and separate and have supper. And at our place, because there were children, we usually had two suppers, one just as we came home from school and another when the men came in after being a day in the fields, which would usually end up with supper at seven o'clock.

So the girl worked usually from shortly after five, when she got up, till when the dishes were done after the last supper at perhaps eight o'clock or a little after, with a little bit of spare time in between. And a real hurry on Saturday afternoon when you were going to town and she went with you, or any of the Fair days or anything else. The girl was part of the family and went with us, and my mother saw that she was just as well taken care of as we were. In fact for a long time we kept in touch with some of these girls as if they had been part of the family."

SANDWICHES "We have a black Lab puppy here; he's only three or four months old. We just got a hired man today and the hired man set his lunch down on the grass and I was on the tractor showing him how to run it. The dog came along and ate all his sandwiches, so we had to feed him in the house. I don't know, he didn't say too much, but the sandwiches didn't look as if they were that good anyway."

PARLOUR VISITORS "The parlour was a very select place. There was a parlour suite, and it was covered with tapestry or haircloth, I guess, and everything was dustcovered for selected visitors that would come, and they were ushered into the parlour. That was a small room in your home—the dining room was larger because they had lots of company and visitors who ate their meals there. The parlour was used for select visitors that came, and during the summer there were a lot of city people driving through the country, and they'd call in to your house. Well, you would entertain them in the parlour. They were people from the country that were educated in the high schools in Glengarry and went to Montreal, and they seemed to get into the right channel and made a lot of money, and then they would drive up to your house, and they were parlour visitors.

But your neighbours were entertained in the kitchen, and they ate in the dining room or the kitchen. When the minister came he was entertained in the parlour, because he was just able to call once or twice in the year, because he had so many churches to look after and small congregations. It was difficult, it was very difficult for him to get around to the people."

A COFFIN IN THE PARLOUR "The undertakers come and they take the body of the dead person, they take it away and I don't know what they do. They embalm it or whatever they do, and dress it, place it in the coffin and bring it back up. And in those days the houses had a parlour, they had that one room; if the minister came, they entertained him there, I guess, or anybody died or anybody was married. They used the parlour for something special. So I can see Mother's coffin today . . . I was only twelve, but I can remember so well, Mother was in her coffin there and just as beautiful as ever, except she couldn't speak to me.

There were crowds of people came. Mother was always kind to everybody. And we lived in a district that was a mixed district. There were French and there was Irish and Scotch and English, you know, it was mixed. And then south of us was a district that was French, and Mother was always so kind to those people. I can remember those men coming to see Mother and they would come out and they would be wiping their eyes. They were very fond of her.

Mother was in her coffin in the parlour for about two days, then they had a service at the church, and I can remember hearing them say there were over a hundred buggies in this funeral procession, one of the biggest ones that had been in that neighbourhood. She was very popular with everybody."

EIGHTEEN

Pigs, Skunks, and Other Wildlife

A Good Timekeeper . . . Our Pets Were Functional . . . Quick as Chain Lightning . . . Duck Snoop . . . Rammed . . . Little Chicks . . . Cats to Raise Foxes . . . A Foxy Salesman . . . Stinking Rich . . . Finger-Licking Good? . . . Pig Tails . . . Skunks under the Bed . . . My Pet Duck . . . The Mad Rooster . . . A Big Black Limousine . . . The Suicidal Chicken . . . On a Pig's Head . . . Rats on Fire . . . In the Pigpen . . . A Scape-goat? . . . After a Month . . . Bears on the Brain

There are always minor adventures galore around a farm-house. Anyone who has lived on a farm can come up easily with a clutch of stories about the smaller wildlife around the farm. We had a skunk under our old back porch for some days, and that is an occasion when one and all remember without fail to tread very lightly indeed. We had dogs that never, never learned that all porcupines had quills. I had one dog that was forever catching up with porcupines in the orchard, and at least six times I took that dog to the vet to have an average of fifty quills pulled out of its jaws.

I don't know why, but pigs on a farm often seemed to get in the way of human beings. People tripped over them or fell in their troughs. But pigs were essential to the farm: pork on the table was a necessity, and pigs for market were usually profitable, so pigs were tolerated. Turkeys are bad tempered and, in the old days, prone to disease, and it took a patient farm wife to raise a flock of turkeys for some extra income. Some farm wives were irritated by chickens, too, but I would guess most developed a kind of fond-ness for these hard-working birds. For myself, a sunny peaceful chicken house on a winter's morn is a most pleasant place to be: the quiet clucking of the hens, the warm feel of fresh-laid eggs, the sense of security.

A story I like, which I saved for this introduction, is about ducks. An editor and his wife live in Prince Edward County south of Belleville, Ontario, and they are trying to prove that a young couple can have a small farm and almost completely provide for themselves the necessities of life. She wanted to raise ducks, and she had three drakes but no duck, and she was looking around for a duck and phoning friends to see if any of them knew where she could buy a duck. One day she phoned a farmer friend who had that laconic response to situations typical of many farmers; when she had gone into her song-and-dance about the three drakes and no duck, there was a pause on the other end of the line and then the farmer said: "Don't make for a good layin' flock."

Ever since then, when things go a little haywire at our place here, one of us may mumble "Don't make for a good layin' flock" and we laugh a little and it helps.

A GOOD TIMEKEEPER   "We had lots of dogs, just farm dogs, you know. There was one dog, in the hot weather we would sleep out on the verandah on cots, and he would sleep with us, stay right beside us all night long, and at exactly the same hour every morning, he would nudge us — time to get up, not at six or five o'clock in the morning, but at the same time every morning.

That same dog would go to the field with the men when they'd be ploughing or working at the back of the farm, and sharp at eleven o'clock that dog would come home on Saturday morning. No other morning, Saturday morning because the butcher came. He brought us a roast of beef, and he always brought a bone for the dog, so this dog was always there to meet the butcher sharp at eleven o'clock, not ten minutes to eleven but at eleven."

OUR PETS WERE FUNCTIONAL   "Animals were a necessary part of our lives. Our dog was there to keep the bears away. And our cows were there to give us milk, and give us meat when necessary. My dad had pigs, none of us got particularly sentimental about the pigs because we had to feed the darn things and we had to clean out those stinky pens occasionally. So in our home anyway, our pets were functional. We didn't get attached to anything particularly."

QUICK AS CHAIN LIGHTNING   "I can remember one little experience that the Dad had with a boar. He was one of these big Yorkshires, and he was a dandy, too, a big one. And this hog would take after you if you were afoot. So the Dad, he decided one day that he was going to break him of this habit once and for all. So he got about a six- or eight-foot fir pole and sharpened it good and sharp with an axe. And this pig made a run for him, and the Dad, he made a drive at him with this thing to hit him in the head or the ear with this sharp pole. And he missed him. And the pig just grabbed the pole and bit it right off. Of course, needless to say the old man, he jumped the fence and run.

    If I remember right, I think he got rid of him right away. Because they're dangerous. They'd kill you just as quick as chain lightning. They've got these tusks that come out, and they have this upward motion. They just run alongside of you and throw their head up, and this tusk is about four inches sticking out of the side of their mouth, and they'd just cut you like a sabre. But that's the only one ever in my life that I saw that was mean."

DUCK SNOOP   "I enjoyed looking after the hens and hatching the chickens and ducks. But when it came to killing them for market, I left that to my husband. We used to have Muscovy ducks, and every night they used to fly up on our bedroom window-sill and perch. And when we used to wake up in the morning, there were the ducks staring at us through the window. Oh, I remember the Muscovy ducks on the bedroom window."

RAMMED   "We kept sheep at our place in a long pen about forty feet long and twenty-four feet wide, and in the morning in the spring it was invariable you'd have to go in and get a lamb and a mother out and take them over to the other barn where it was warmer. The procedure was to get a sack and wrap the lamb up in it and hold it to the mother and she'd follow.

Well, this morning I went in there and there was a pair of lambs, a pair of twins. I got them rolled up in the sack and I didn't take a careful look to see where the father was, and I was leaning over picking up these lambs and I was close to the wall, and it was a lumber wall, and the first thing I knew I was headed for the boards and I thought I'd broke my neck — the ram had drove me about four feet before I hit the boards. He got his ears cuffed for that . . . just my feelings hurt mostly."

LITTLE CHICKS "Mr. Wilson goes down to the hatchery and picks the pullets up one morning and brings them up and we have them then that afternoon. They're brought in cardboard boxes, little flat carton boxes. These are day-old chicks and they are brought in a cardboard box with a lid on it and I take the lid off, and out pop all the little chicks; and when they come to us they're darling little balls of fluff, you know. They're really cute little things and I have a pan of water there and some feed. And I take each little chick, pick it up, and dip its beak in the water so it will know where to get a drink, and then dip it in the feed, so it will know where the feed is, and from there they're pretty well on their own, and away they go. One lesson and one dip seems to do for most of them—they know where to look for the next one."

CATS TO RAISE FOXES "Back at Duck Lake, my father had a fox farm as well as a mink farm, and this fox farm was a big event in our area because we were the first in North Saskatchewan to have it. And I can always remember one thing about my father's fox ranch was we had to keep about thirty or forty cats in our home or back in our yard all the time, for the simple reason that when the foxes would whelp their kits in the spring, being very temperamental and very jumpy, they would come out of their boxes with the pup in its mouth, and we'd know right away that if we didn't get in there quick, she would eat the pups.

So we'd sneak in, grab the next three that were left — they generally came in fours — and we would take them and put them with one of the cats who had had kittens. These little kits would take the place of the regular kittens, the real kittens of the mother cat, and of course the mother cat would always be amazed . . . We'd always leave one kitten and two fox cubs with the cat, and in no time at all the fox cubs would outgrow the kittens, and the cat would never get over these little fox cubs pushing everything out of the road and trying to be fed."

A FOXY SALESMAN   "There was more lies told over the fox business than I think any other business on the face of the earth. Like one fellow was trying to sell a single fox, and it was red, but he told the prospective buyer: 'That fox's stepfather was the best silver black that you ever saw.'"

STINKING RICH   "All the big houses in Alberton, Prince Edward Island, were built between the years 1909 and 1915 or 1916 with fox money. The fox business was one of the most tricky businesses that a person could indulge in, because you never knew from one day to another what your losses were going to be, and in some years we were completely wiped out with distemper.

The stink of foxes was something beyond description, especially in the spring of the year during the mating season. If you got it on your clothes you might just as well go out and bury them. It's even worse than a skunk, I think. But you couldn't complain about it because that stink, it was a rich stink.

The people that went to church, if they didn't smell of fox stink, they weren't in the business. They made it a point to get some of that smell on their clothes to show they were in the fox business. Foxes were worth ten thousand to fifteen thousand dollars a pair.

And those foxes were temperamental! I don't suppose there's another animal on the face of the earth that is as temperamental as a fox, and if the least misfortune took place in the whelping season, the spring of the year, you could figure that you'd have a batch of pups killed or eaten. They would eat their young, and if we had a silver thaw or what we called a silver thaw, in reality it's

an ice storm, and when that ice commenced to fall off the trees —
most all ranches were in a grove or in a wood — and the noise of
the ice falling off the trees, then you could figure there'd be hundreds of pups killed, if you had a large ranch, and not only killed
but eaten."

FINGER-LICKING GOOD?   "This friend of ours was chopping
something one day and chopped the end of his finger off. And I
was working in the local hospital and in rushed Bob with this
finger that needed some attention. And the doctor said: 'Well,
really, if you'd brought the end of your finger in, we could have
sewn it on again.'

And he said: 'Well yes, I thought of that, but the goddam chickens ran off with it before I had the chance to get it.'"

PIG TAILS   "A neighbour of mine seemed to have a good deal of
difficulty getting pigs to fatten up and do well for him, as they
used to say in them times. In fact they just wouldn't grow for him,
and he was telling me about it this day, so I says: 'You know,
when a pig is doing well, he always has a curl in his tail.'

He says: 'I know that, but these fellows has got curls that are
lifting them right off of their feet.'"

SKUNKS UNDER THE BED   "We live in an old house, and the
front part of the house doesn't have a basement under it, and for a
number of winters we've had skunks living under the front part of
the house.

About fifteen years ago, we decided we were going to have a
furnace put in the house, and in order to do this the floorboards in
one of the bedrooms had to be taken up for the men to get down to
work. When they were digging under the house to put in the duct
work, they discovered that there was a little tunnel, and so we
presumed Mr. Skunk was living there.

Anyway they got all the duct work in, and got the furnace
installed and in good running order, and didn't have any mis-
haps. So they put the floorboards down in the room again, and as
it happened it was the bedroom where my father slept. So we had
to shift the furniture all back in and set the bed up again.

And the first night, in the middle of the night, there was an awful crash, and the next thing, all you could smell was skunk.

Well, we tore downstairs, and Dad's bed had fallen down, and startled him and I guess startled the skunk that was living underneath. Anyway, the poor skunk was so upset he just let off, and all you could smell was the fumes. And for days I had the clothes hanging out on the line to get the smell out. It was through the house, it was in our clothes, it was in everything. And every morning, I would take the clothes and hang them all out on the clothesline and bring them in again at night in case it was going to rain, and believe me that was a real task, hanging all these clothes out every day."

MY PET DUCK   "My sister and I and my brother each had a little duck when we were younger, and we raised them from the day they were old enough to leave their mother. We would put them in the pond every morning, and every evening we would go up and get them in, which was quite a job, because one of us would hold one end of a rope and one the other end and we would drag the rope across the pond and the ducks would be swimming ahead of it. But we'd get just near the edge and I guess the ducks would fly over the rope again and there we were, starting all over again, and so it was quite a job.

Then one day my mother thought they'd make a nice meal, and there was no way I wanted to eat my pet duck, but she decided that they were big enough now and they may as well pay us back for the money she had put into feeding them, I guess. So anyways they were to end up on our dinner table, and I swore that I'd never eat it.

After she had killed it, which I had no part of, plucked it and cleaned it and cooked it — well, it just didn't seem like a pet duck after it was all cooked, I guess. But it was good. It was delicious. When I think about it, it's awful, that I could love something so much and then turn around and eat it. But it was really good."

THE MAD ROOSTER   "We used to be on one side of the fence, and these roosters used to be around these rocks on the other side of the fence. And we used to bug them and throw rocks at them.

We really picked on this one rooster in particular, and we didn't realize we were doing anything wrong. But after a while this rooster just went kind of strange and he went mad, you know.

This one day I was with my grandpa and I walked to the machine shed to get something for him, and all of a sudden, this rooster come flyin' at me. The really scary part about it was that he didn't just come after me. I tripped and fell, and he got right on top of me practically, and he was starting to peck my eyes out. And I'll tell you, I finally got up and got away, I guess—but I don't exactly remember, I was so scared."

A BIG BLACK LIMOUSINE "We had a turkey gobbler that was a pet, and we'd had him for three years, and he was huge, had huge big wings that used to go zipping along the ground. We came up the lane from school this day and wondered who was in the driveway—we saw this big, black limousine parked outside. Now sometimes people would come out from Toronto—they'd be insurance people or they'd be somebody wanting to buy the farm, or there'd always be someone driving up to our place.

And this day we saw the turkey pecking away at the side of this beautiful black car, and there was a huge area, about three feet in diameter, where it had been pecking I guess for a good part of an hour, seeing his picture in this black car and picking the paint off, seeing himself and thinking it was another turkey. It had pecked away at the side until it had an expanse of almost a whole door cleared off, and it had turned this black beautiful paint into a metal door.

And my sister and I thought, now, whatever we do when we go into that house, we're not going to say anything about what happened or what we had seen, because you know that would be the end of our turkey and we'd had him for about three years and he was our pet, and we called him Gobbie. So we went into the house and this gentlemen was talking to my uncle and my mother, and we just went on about our business and didn't say anything. And that evening at dinnertime we couldn't contain ourselves and we told them what had happened, and obviously the man hadn't noticed because he probably got in on the other side to drive away. But he'd have no idea of what happened to the side of his car. And we used to think that was the biggest joke, and we talked about it for a long time."

THE SUICIDAL CHICKEN "Did I tell you about the chicken committing suicide? It was quite odd, as a matter of fact. The chicken committed suicide by managing to get itself inside the garbage can where we keep the feed, and it managed to close the top on itself, thereby smothering itself to death. I don't know how it got the top off in the first place, since it had a latch. But whoever went out to feed the chickens found this strangulated chicken in the feed bin. Then we told the kids to take it out and bury it, which they did, and the dog dug it up, and they went through this procedure several times, and they finally gave it a tree burial. They put it in a plastic garbage bag without telling us and went and hung it on the lot line, and then they went secretly every year or so to check on how it was becoming mummified."

ON A PIG'S HEAD "When I left teaching, and became a farmer's wife, all the boo-boos I made . . . it was terrible. Such as being midwife to a mamma pig.

I couldn't find the men that day, and I phoned to a lady up the road to try and find the children's father or the hired man, and she said to me: 'Oh, you'll be all right — just put a cold cloth on the pig's head.'

Now she was a farmer's wife, seasoned, and she knew better, but you see I didn't. So I did that.

The little wee piglets came all right. But the next time she had her family, she went off and hid someplace. I don't blame her."

RATS ON FIRE "We used to use heat lamps in the pig barns to keep the little pigs warm . . . and one of the heat lamps must have started the straw on fire; and the pig barn itself was just a poor type of building — it had straw in the walls for insulation and so forth — and it pretty well took off. The pig barn was attached to the granaries, and the granaries was sort of an L-shaped thing, and it had lots of rats. I don't know how many thousands of rats lived there, but this pig barn used to get so cold in the wintertime that the rats would line up on top of the old sows with the little pigs just to keep warm.

This fire did get away and it burnt down this complete L-shaped building. I can recall, I was only a kid of about six or eight at the time. One of the big highlights, of course, was watching the rats being on fire, running across the yard. It was quite a job for a bunch of us to make sure we killed these rats before they got into any of the other buildings, because their fur was on fire. They were just a sort of a fireball running across the yard in the darkness, and it was quite a job. We had shovels or forks or something and we would hit them as they were going by.

We lost all the buildings and we lost the sow and the pigs in that pen where the fire started. The other pigs, I believe my dad crawled into the smoke-filled building, opened up the pens, and got most of them out; and then of course once we got them out, the pig being a bright animal, they went back in again and we had to get them out the second time.

I think the rat population did decrease a great amount, in fact I don't think we've had any rats around the yard in any quantity since then, but that was a real rat fair right up until the time of the fire."

IN THE PIGPEN "I think feeding pigs was the worst part. Once I leaned over the partition because the pigs had hauled their trough away over and I had a pick and I was hauling that trough back, and the top partition gave and I went in. I had to take off all my clothes and then wash them, soak them, because you know what a pigpen is like, and I cried that time — I cried for madness, because I was so angry with what had happened. Nobody saw me, because I got to the house and got my clothes off, and got them soaking."

A SCAPE-GOAT? "My Dad had a few sheep at one time. And someone told him that if he had a goat with the sheep, the coyotes wouldn't bother him. And in that particular area there were quite a few coyotes, so he got a goat turned in with the sheep.

And one day, all of a sudden, here come the coyote chasing the sheep. And the goat beat the sheep to the barn."

AFTER A MONTH "We had a bad blizzard in the Claresholm district, and after the storm was over, the drifts were all over the fences and everything else. And I had an uncle that raised prize pigs, and he was missing an old sow and eleven pigs. And he couldn't find them anyplace.

And after a month, why, he saw some steam coming up out of a snowdrift. And he dug in there, and here was the old sow and her eleven pigs. And they were all alive and healthy. The old sow was as thin as a rake, but the little pigs were in pretty fair shape. Of course they had been nursing her, and she had nothing to eat other than snow."

BEARS ON THE BRAIN "We had quite an incident with a bear. A boy came through our quarter and he said: 'Mother has been worried about the bears coming for the children.'

Her husband had gone out and left her in the bush with the children. He'd gone out to make money. And we'd never been over there; it was a few miles back in the bush.

Harry said: 'That's ridiculous. There's no bears in this country at all.' Harry didn't think there was any truth in it at all.

And so about an hour or so later, this boy came back again. 'Will you come and help? Mother said the bear's taken the calf out of the corral and the cattle are very, very upset. And she's worried about the children tonight.'

Of course then we really had to go to see what was the trouble. Well, we got on our horses and our dog followed, and we had our guns. And we set off on this hunt. Well, we got to this little place, and Harry posted himself on the roof. We saw that what she said was true; the cattle were all very upset, and the blood was around where this bear had dragged the calf into the bush. We could see the trail. So he posted himself on the top of this barn, thinking the bear might come back again and he could get it.

It got dusk and the bear never showed up. Harry knew sitting out there in the dark was no good, so he said: 'We'd better go home.'

Well, the lady pleaded with us not to. She said: 'Don't leave me.' Well I looked at the place and I surely didn't want to spend the night there. She offered us her bed, which, I mean — poor soul — you can just imagine. So the bed was dreadful, of course. But there was a little tiny window over the bed, very low. And it had a little bit of cheesecloth to keep the flies out: there was no glass in it. And we went to bed, and our dog, Buster, stayed under the bed: I didn't want him to go away, you know.

We were tired out, but in the middle of the night I heard a funny little growl under the bed. And I thought: 'That's not natural.'

And I woke Harry up. I said: 'Harry! Get up, there. The bear's arrived.'

He said: 'Oh, you've got bears on the brain. Don't be silly. You're having a nightmare.' I used to have them regularly.

The dog still didn't settle, and I was very worried. But I listened to Harry — I listened to him a lot in those days, I don't so much now, but I did then. Well — we went to sleep again. In the morning we get up and they find the prints of the bear right under this cheesecloth with the claw marks on the wall just above our heads."

NINETEEN

New-Fangled Machines

These New-Fangled Machines . . . Not Like a Car . . . Thanks to Technology . . . A Common Life . . . Heavenly Light . . . One Way to Stop . . . The Best Tractor There Was . . . Grandpa and Machines . . . The Old Steam Threshers . . . The Tail End of Steam Threshing . . . Threshing Problems . . . Building Elevators . . . A Voice Out of the Wall . . . The Elevator Operator . . . Elevator Memories . . . When the Wind Was Blowing . . . Head and Ears into Debt

I haven't the slightest doubt that the greatest thing that ever happened to the farm was the coming of hydro. Farmers, and more particularly their wives, have tried to explain to me how miraculous it was, how they just couldn't believe it when the lights were first switched on. It wasn't that long ago. This farmhouse where I am now is plunk in the heart of Old Ontario, but there wasn't hydro here until 1941, only six years before I bought the place.

It's clear that hydro was an unmixed blessing. It made life on the farm much more tolerable and it most certainly eased the work load inside and outside the farmhouse. The arrival of huge, complex farm machines, however, had its bad side. More and more "new-fangled" machinery on the farm meant that work was speeded up, certainly, but it also constantly boosted the cost of farming. A certain amount of sharing of equipment helped, but many farmers simply wanted to own their own machinery. The increase of technology, furthermore, brought about a greater reliance of the farmer on the appliance dealers in the towns or on the outskirts of the towns, and that meant running back and forth for parts. Haywire couldn't fix everything. And the increase in costs put farming out of the reach of a young man who wanted to farm but simply couldn't afford it.

On the prairies the most important piece of farm machinery wasn't on the farm at all. The existence of nearby elevators was essential to the wheat farmer, and the relationship between the farmer and the elevator agent, and in turn between the elevator agent and the freight-train crew made up a fascinating triangle. Elevator operators worked fiendishly hard when they did work, and when they weren't busy at all they made a refined art of loafing. Some day I hope someone will write a detailed account of elevator operators and the world of the country elevator.

THESE NEW-FANGLED MACHINES "The horsemen that were raising horses and were breeding them for sale, they didn't like it at all when tractors first came in. They felt that they could get out on the land when the conditions weren't just right for tractors. Well, they might have had soil that worked when it was wetter, but most of the time soil has to be just right to work at any time, with any machine. And of course the tractor man, he used to point out that his motive power didn't need anything to eat while it was standing idle, and the horsemen, they even went as far as to figure out the cost of feeding a horse over winter. The horsemen felt that it wasn't fair to them, that they were being put out of business by these new-fangled machines that were coming in, like gas tractors, and they said gasoline at thirty cents a gallon, it wasn't economical, and the home-grown fuel for the horses was better, but they had to feed the horse over winter when they weren't even worked."

NOT LIKE A CAR "Buggies were well made. They were a lot different than the cars. Once you bought a buggy, with any reasonable care at all, it would do you your lifetime. You had to keep it oiled — naturally, you had to keep it oiled — and that would be probably every two hundred miles or something like that. But there was no problem with the buggies, they were well made and they gave you real good service. They would outlast any ordinary man: in fact there's buggies around that have outlasted three generations. They weren't like a car; they didn't smash up.

They were sure a cold thing to ride in. I can remember coming home from Clinton — I took my brother to high school up there — and I started out from Clinton with a horse and buggy on a cold, stormy day. There was a young lady that lived in the village of Brucefield; she asked if she could have a ride home, and I pitied that girl all the way home because she was so cold that she nearly froze. And I had a pair of mitts that I used to wear when it was cold, and I'd laid my gloves off, and she said: 'Can I please have your gloves to put over top of mine?'

She wanted to keep her hands warm. If I had been doing it now, I'd have warmed them for her, but I didn't know enough then. I was too young, I guess."

THANKS TO TECHNOLOGY   "That year, 1937, was the worst year of the Depression in the Hanley district, but you can rest assured that if you moved all of the conditions that you had in 1937 — the same amount of rainfall, the same amount of wind, all of those conditions — into 1975, that we wouldn't be sitting with empty bins. We wouldn't be sitting with relief cars coming in to hand you codfish and apples from Ontario and help from different places, because of our advanced technologies, the combines that we have today. If we had a five-bushel crop in the 1930s, we lost it all, because we didn't have equipment that would take it off. Now we have technology that we can farm the land so it won't blow away; with the difference in the wheat varieties we can get by with that same amount of rainfall, and if we do get an eight- or ten-bushel crop we get every bushel of it, where in 1937, with the threshing machines, with the binders, with the twine tie, we lost it, and so it's thanks to technology it's a different ball game."

A COMMON LIFE "After I came out of the hospital, I stayed in a place for quite a while with the hydro and all the facilities, but when I came back home again people thought: 'Well my gosh he'll get the hydro and telephone and everything in now.' But I changed back to the old way and I was awfully happy. I have the coal-oil lamp, I was always used to it and it's no change. If I go in and stay some place for a while, I don't just fall in love with the hydro. I go back and I live a common life.

I use the wood stove—I use all wood—I have a chain saw and I have two bushes and I have all kinds of wood and I cut my own wood and haul it and burn it, and it doesn't cost me anything, only labour."

HEAVENLY LIGHT "I'll tell you what it was like to have hydro. You could see in the house anywhere, and with two lights, one outside at the house and another one at the barn, you could see your way to go back and forth always. And to get up in a haymow and be able to see when you used to just have the light of the lantern down below in the barn — it was just like getting into heaven."

ONE WAY TO STOP "The first time I drove the tractor was in the spring operation. We were getting the land ready for seeding, and I was pulling a big discer. Of course this tractor was a new tractor, one of the bigger tractors in the area at the time, so it had a special thrill for me.

I went home very excited and told my mother, who was horrified at the fact my father let me on the tractor at that age. But in fact my father had started one of my older brothers off on a tractor in a very horrifying way as well. When he was about ten years old my father put him on an open-wheeled John Deere tractor with the hand clutch, and told him to take the tractor into town. The thing he didn't do was tell him how to stop the machine.

So as he was going into town, my brother, who was a little absent-minded, suddenly realized that he had to figure out how to stop this thing in a hurry. And he found the hand clutch, but he couldn't pull it back because he was a little too light and a little too small. So he ended up bouncing off a couple of trucks and finally into a car before the tractor came to a halt."

THE BEST TRACTOR THERE WAS   "I think that everybody had the best tractor there was, that was generally the idea. And those points were argued forth and back many times and often brought quite heated discussions, even to the point at times where the owners might take the tractors out on a trial with each other and they'd hitch them together and see which one was the strongest, which one would do the most, or which one would break the first —they'd give it a real test."

GRANDPA AND MACHINES   "Grandfather was really quite an old gentleman, a pretty hardened Swede from the coal mines. But he had arthritis quite bad, and to try and ease the pain, he used to soak his hands in hot wax. Because of this problem he used to have a lot of trouble sometimes, operating machinery — getting his legs going, especially if he'd been sitting for a while, when he'd get pretty stiff — and my father at one time put him on the tractor to do some cultivating. We had one of these small Allis-Chalmers tractors with the cultivator that was pulled behind. He got going out there one day, and he hadn't really left himself much room at the end to turn, and this particular time he came to the corner where he was going to turn around, and he just wasn't ready for it, and he went straight into the bush. And with that type of cultivator he had no way to back up. And here he was sitting in the bush there.

And so my father, as his habit was with Grandpa, came driving out there at this particular moment to check to see how Grandpa was doing. And here was my grandpa—he never wanted my dad to know that he'd made a mistake — here he was with a little pocketknife, trying to cut away this tree so he could get himself out of this predicament he was in.

I remember he had the same sort of situation happen with the half-ton truck. He was going to come around this corner and I don't know what happened — he got excited or something. But instead of hitting the brake, he got the gas pedal and drove us right into a big pile of rocks and made pretty good work of the oil pan on the truck."

THE OLD STEAM THRESHERS "The grain was fed into the machine and it threshed or cleaned the kernel from the heads of the grain, and after it was threshed, then the rear end of the machine had fans and knives and screens that would separate the grain from the chaff and straw. Therefore the machine is called by two different names, both a threshing machine or a grain separator. These steam machines, especially the big ones, they had to have two men hauling water, and a man hauling coal, and there was fourteen teams hauled bundles, and there was three spikers, and they pitched at the machine; four men fed the machine and one man rested with the team-master, and then the next load, the one that had been resting took his turn. Let's say fourteen teams, and there'd be an engineer and a fireman and two separator men and that's eighteen, and three spikers, twenty-one, and a bull cook, twenty-two, and cook cars and bunkhouses that went along with the machine. That would be twenty-three men at least . . . oh, there would be more than that, there would be twenty-five with the two field pitchers. They'd help load out in the field, load the racks out in the field when the team-master went out.

These outfits attracted visitors. Some days when they threshed, some days or all through the week, there would be carloads of people coming out there to watch them work. There was something about it that attracted them. In fact, nowadays with the combines the romance has gone out of threshing. No one looks forward to threshing any more. Of course where they didn't have the cook and the bunk cars, the housewife on the farm they were working on had to do the cooking, and I'm sure they're glad it's over with now."

THE TAIL END OF STEAM THRESHING "When I was about five years old, five or six, round in there, I just saw the tail end of steam threshing. We had a Waterloo outfit that came from Portage la Prairie and drove out to my grandmother's farm just north of Portage, and he threshed about five or six farms. And we used to sit on the side of the road — we knew the outfit was coming this day — and we'd sit and look down the road, and way off in the distance we'd see the smoke from the engine, and we'd see the outfit just coming up the road, and we'd sit there for about an hour, and finally it reached our place, and we'd see this big outfit turn in and drive out into the pasture and set up. And the speed of that outfit was one speed, and that was either stop or go, and about two miles an hour would be average."

THRESHING PROBLEMS "Usually in the harvest season, when the threshing season began, most outfits would start in the mornings about 6:30, and they'd run till . . . oh, some of them would run till 6:30 in the evening or even 7:30 . . . it sort of depended on what kind of a slave driver the boss was, I guess. But anyway they usually put in twelve or thirteen hours in their threshing, and there were times, of course, when they were running to a wet spell of weather, sometimes it would last even for two weeks, and the threshing would be laid up and the owner of the outfit then had to board the crew.

And that was quite a problem, because usually they would get rather uneasy and would want to move on to someplace else where they could find work, and usually quite a number of men always thought that it was possible to find some place else. The far pastures always looked greener. But anyway, if they did leave and then the weather cleared up and threshing was resumed again, then the owner had to look for a crew again, or a portion of a crew . . . whatever. And then again there were times when machines would break down, and then for the separator man, the tractor man, there was no rest; they worked day and night till the unit was back ready to thresh again. As the crew was standing around, they had to be fed and paid too, and it was quite a problem.

Various things could happen. They could break a shaft in a separator, or a fan blade go off the blower fan, or the grain pan in the separator would break, or belts break and so forth, castings break. There were quite a number of breakings that would happen. Usually there wasn't too much trouble with the tractors; steamers would probably give better service than the gas tractors in the early days.

I knew of a man who lived about ninety miles from his dealer, and one cool morning — they were threshing a little late this year —and one cool morning, when he started his tractor up—this was a gas tractor — the water pump was frozen and they turned the tractor over and this broke a casting on it. He had to drive ninety miles with horse and buggy and ford the Red Deer River, and he drove that ninety miles one way and got his part and drove the ninety miles back, and he did this in three days which was quite a record, he thought, and I guess it was, too, for a team at that time. He went continually till he got back, and his engineer put the part on after he got there, and in about three or four hours, the machine was ready to go again.

In those days there were a few dealers that carried parts in the small towns. Now those parts usually were carried only for the smaller tractors, where there were more of them. The bigger steam tractors and the bigger tractors, usually they had to go to the larger cities, maybe Calgary or Medicine Hat, Red Deer, Lethbridge, or wherever the closest point would be. As a rule, after an owner had a machine for a year or so, he generally got to know what part might be weak or need replacing every once in a while, and he carried a spare part or two to eliminate any lengthy breakdowns, so he had the part there and ready to put it in when he had the breakdown."

BUILDING ELEVATORS "The first elevators started off at about twenty, twenty-five thousand bushels, and they went from there on up until, when the Wheat Pool started, why, the largest elevator was forty thousand bushels. And they started building forty and sixty thousand bushels, which were built out of lumber. There are very few, if any, concrete elevators in Alberta.

They're built out of lumber — spruce mainly, and some fir and some cedar — and they're cribbed, one plank laid on top of another and spiked together, and there are many bins. The small elevators usually had twelve bins, three on each side and then overhead in the middle. But now they still have many bins because there's many grades of grain and different varieties of grain, such as wheat, oats, and barley. And now with the seeds, flax and rape seed and mustard, why, you have to have lots of bins."

A VOICE OUT OF THE WALL   "I can remember when my father was trying to get the telephone line put through. One elderly gentleman, he just refused to have the phone in that house. He wasn't going to have a voice come out of the wall. Well, the younger members of his family, his nephews, they did get it put into the house, but never as long as I remember, to his death, did he ever go near it. When it would ring he'd go way back to a corner. It just frightened him terribly to have a voice come out of a box in the wall."

THE ELEVATOR OPERATOR   "The country elevator operator, especially in the earlier times of this century, was quite an important person in the community. Sometimes he was a very important person in more ways than one, because he was the man the farmers held responsible for giving the farmer his grade of grain, weight of grain. They loaded the wagon, they weighed the wagon, dumped the grain and weighed the wagon again, and took off the difference, and that was his amount of grain that he had, the gross amount of grain he had on his wagon load. And then they took a sample and put it through a little cleaning machine and took out the dockage. So his grain might be docked two per cent, four per cent, or even ten per cent if it had a lot of oats and chaff in it. So this dockage was taken off the gross weight to determine the net weight of grain which he was paid for.

But sometimes the farmer thought he was being cheated, and in many cases they were. The elevator agent had to carry on the business of operating the elevator under the instructions of the owners of the company. He was the agent for the owner of the company and he was paid by them and worked for the company, not for the farmer. The farmers were very cognizant of this. Consequently, they didn't trust the agent altogether, insofar as the handling of his grain was concerned, and they would argue about it. But one of the privileges I suppose you'd call it, they got under the Manitoba Grain Act, was if they weren't satisfied with the grade, there was a series of tin boxes in the elevator the elevator agent had to carry. The farmer and the agent would take a sample of the load in the tin box and close it, put on a lock and key. The farmer kept the key and it was sent to Winnipeg and it was graded by a government inspector. That was the final grade — there was no argument after that. So he did have some protection under the Manitoba Grain Act.

There was some physical fisticuffs over the proper weight and grade of grain at various times. The farmer would get mad at one agent and obviously not be satisfied with his weight and dockage and take it to another elevator. They liked the idea of competition and two or more elevators in the town; they could go from one elevator to the other.

The country elevator agent was a source of news, of course. All the farmers wanted to know what their neighbour got or what grade of grain he got, that sort of thing, and he wasn't the gossip such as the town barber was, or the country storekeeper, I don't think, but insofar as the gossip of the grades of grain, he would know this sort of thing, he was the source of getting all this information back to the farmer. He was also, I would say, the barometer insofar as predicting or advising the farmer what the price of grain might do, although this was very difficult to do. At least the farmer felt that the agent knew more about it than he did, and to a great extent they took his advice on whether to sell today or tomorrow or the next day.

No doubt each agent had a few favourites, and when a few extra cars were coming in, these farmers were notified cars were going to be spotted, and if he wanted to load his grain he'd better come in and sign the car order-book and get his double bag or two of grain in the boxcar to hold it. Most farmers tried to get their grain in in the fall of the year if they could, before the snow came. It's a most disagreeable job loading up the grain in the wintertime and hauling it to town.

The country agent was usually a man who was born and brought up on a farm, but not always, and in most cases born and brought up in the community. The company tried to get, say, the eldest son of a prominent farmer, for instance, as their agent. They'd train him and send him up to be an assistant agent and then an agent in that community, because if John Jones is a very highly respected farmer, known for his honesty, etc., they thought his son would follow in his same boots, and the fact that John Jones's son Jimmy Jones was a manager of the elevator, that would help to draw in customers to the elevator, rather than some unknown person from far afield that they knew nothing about.

These are pretty hard-working men at certain times of the year. In the fall of the year, for instance, when the rush was on, many of them took in grain all day and weighed it, unloaded it, did the dockage and did the paper work, and during the night they loaded it out into boxcars, which had been spotted on the right of way during the day. Oh, there were times I suppose they never left the elevator for five or six days at a time. Their wife would bring them over their breakfast and their lunch and their supper, and sometimes she was able to stay and help them do some of the paper work, making out the cash tickets and so on. And some of the operators literally never took off their clothes, weeks at a time, with the rush of the harvest season.

In the wintertime things certainly slackened off a great deal, and there wasn't all that much to do in the elevator, and sometimes it got to be the meeting place of a few of the people in town who also didn't have very much to do in the wintertime, and they went there for their games of rummy or whist or poker as the case might be, and it got to be quite a favourite gathering place for a certain clientele of the people of the community, and a favourite place for tall stories. Like these.

One particular winter, it got so cold that it never got above forty below zero during the winter. So at Christmastime, this old bachelor, he was very careful with his money, he lit the lamp, and it was so cold the light froze right in the lampshade and it never thawed out till spring, so he had light twenty-four hours a day.

And the other thing that bothered them in those days was the chinook wind that came across the prairies often to Manitoba, although they weren't as common as they were out in Alberta. This chap one day was going to town with his load of grain when the chinook from the west kicked him. The temperature can go up from below zero to fifty above zero in a matter of minutes almost. And when the chinook hit, the snow just started to melt in front of him very quickly, and he had to look out and get his horses going; and he got his horses galloping and he was just able to keep his runners on the snow all the way to town, and behind him the black earth was showing up all the way down the road."

ELEVATOR MEMORIES   "I always feel like I'm home when I can see the elevators on the horizon, especially in the early morning. I've been a few different places where I couldn't see the elevators and I always felt homesick when I couldn't.

I experienced one fire in a country elevator. I'd been away on my holidays and came home. I was buying grain in Barons, Alberta, at that time, where there were ten elevators, and it had been a very dry summer. And just after we got home, there was a heavy thunderstorm with lots of lightning. There was a train switching in the yard and they saw the lightning strike my elevators. So they started to blow the whistle. They blew the whistle till they had everybody wakened up, and somehow or other in the process of getting dressed for to go to the fire, I put my leg down the sleeve of my jacket instead of my trouser leg. Now I had some fun getting my leg out of that, so by the time I got over there the elevator was well on fire.

I was living at the company dwelling at the time, about two blocks from the fire. The elevator was a complete loss. There was a lot of flax stored in the centre of it and flax is very inflammable, and if we'd have been standing there pouring oil on it, it couldn't have been any worse or hotter fire. But fortunately, it kept raining and the wind wasn't blowing and there was no other elevator lost, although there have been cases where every elevator on the line has been wiped out by fire."

WHEN THE WIND WAS BLOWING   "When the wind was blowing, you would often see ten or fifteen teams of horses with wagons lined up at the windmill waiting to have their grain crushed to take home to feed to their cattle and hogs. This wind-mill, which was situated on top of this large barn, was known in those days as a airomotor, but the common name became wind-mill, and there were hundreds and thousands of them to be seen across the prairies in later years.

It was quite unusual for it to be situated on top of the barn. Usually they were on sort of a steel tripod. There was sufficient wind most of the time to operate it for pumping water, which didn't take a great deal of power. But for crushing grain it took more power, and they had to have a wind running at oh . . . twenty, thirty knots an hour. And sometimes the farmers would line up to have their grain ground, and the wind would die, so they would just unhook the horses and take them home and leave the wagon there, and my father and the hired man would be crushing grain when the wind returned again that night, the next day or the day after.

At that time, the usual thing was to charge maybe one dollar a load or something like that, twenty-five bags of grain to do the grinding. It would probably take an hour to do it. It was fairly cheap at that time to have the grain ground that way, but in later years — before the so-called energy crisis that we are now in — the gasoline engine became common, and the tractor, of course, and the mill went out of style. Farmers switched over to motor power rather than wind power."

HEAD AND EARS INTO DEBT "This big machinery, big farms, and big operations, this means that the small man has not a chance in the wide world to ever get into business himself. If he does, he's either got to go head and ears into debt so far that he can make an awful lot of money one year, or he goes broke. Way back years ago, people would have one, two horses, a couple of cows, a couple of sheep, and a sow and a few hens, and that would be the full stock they'd have to start off on a farm. And you could go and work out for a couple of years, and you could own it. But now you couldn't start, if you worked out for twenty years, you couldn't earn enough to start farming. They have to get a big yield on this farming to make it pay today."

TWENTY

Keeping in Touch

*My Father's Store . . . The Little Store on Wheels . . . The Agent and the
Farmer . . . Signs of the Times . . . The Centre of a Farming Community . . .
Saturday Nights in Town . . . A Bad Line . . . Get Off the Line! . . . Very
Handy Mechanics . . . Just Saving Time . . . The Bucket Brigade . . . Tele-
phone Courtesy . . . Ringing Wrong Numbers . . . Heated Words*

F*armers still go to town once a week usually, sometimes twice
a week. It has always been a pleasure in the summer and an*
achievement in the winter. The youngsters might have a few pen-
nies for candy, and mother could poke around and fuss in the
general store and sometimes exasperate the storekeeper with her
fiddling about. Country stores were great places — full of goods of
all kinds and the most intriguing and delicious aromas. Jean
Isaacs of Cookstown, Ontario, gave me a most detailed and
charming account of her father's big general store and the wagons
that rumbled into town with their loads of humanity and of goods
to trade.

I remember Tottenham, the village near us, when it was a small
farm town. I remember the great long, heavy counters in the hardware store and the high open shelves stuffed with goods, some of
which hadn't been touched for years.

The farm town was the farm family's umbilical cord to the
outside world, and no wonder the family liked to come to town and
shop and chat and pass the time of day. It wasn't just a question of
buying supplies: it was first-class entertainment.

Equally fine entertainment was, and still is, provided by the
country phone, the party line, another umbilical link. We still have
a party line with nine people on it and I know exactly how farmers
and their wives feel about the telephone. The telephone is abso-

lutely essential in the country. The further you are from neigh-
bours, the more essential it is. Yet it is a cursed nuisance, too. Rural
phone lines aren't as busy as one might think, but they always seem
to be busy just when you have to make a call in a hurry. In this
entire book, if I have to make one criticism of farm wives it is this
(and this applies anywhere in the country): a woman, otherwise
tolerant and kind and wise, can be utterly ruthless about her right
to a nice, long, gossipy phone conversation with a friend, never
mind how many other people are trying to use the line.

However, the most important aspect of the rural phone line is
that it is a vital link in the courting procedure of the young, much
more so, I think, than in the city. Distances are too great for young
people to run around and visit all the time, so the phone is the glue
that binds. Pragmatic Ma Bell little realizes she is a prime agent of
romance in rural Canada.

MY FATHER'S STORE   "My dad had quite a large general store
in Duck Lake. He had a four-foot stove, which we'd put four-foot
wood in, and in the wintertime especially it was quite common on
a Saturday to have the Indians, some of the Métis, come in at nine
o'clock Saturday morning, and they'd all keep around the stove
getting warm, smoke their homemade tobacco as well as their
Ogden or whatever they bought, buy peanuts and oranges, and
stay there till nine o'clock at night, stay in the store.

The store would smell terrible with the odour of sweat, body
sweat, odour and that, but it didn't bother my father at all. And
nine or ten o'clock Saturday night, they'd get up and two or three
or four would be half looped from boozing it up — they'd buy
vanilla and lemon extract and then they'd get boozed up on that.

And my father's store was just the ordinary type of general store
which you'll never see again. Horse collars across the ceiling, and
whips and bridles and stockings on one side. You could go up and
grab a pair of stockings off a rack, blankets and hardware, and

groceries . . . the whole shebang, the most amazing store, and yet I can always remember those Indians sitting there in my father's store with their shawls wrapped around them, old squaws with their pipes and talking Cree, and my dad would talk to them. But that was their week's fun, these Indians would come into our store, my father's store."

THE LITTLE STORE ON WHEELS "In those days there were what we called peddling wagons. These were wagons with teams of horses and they carried just about everything that you needed, including bolts of cloth, shoes; and we didn't have too much money, so we used to trade the eggs that we produced on the farm for this produce. It was just amazing that little store on wheels, covered-wagon sort of thing, that used to come around. And that went on twenty years ago, maybe they've stopped that now. But it was one of the real features of country living in the old days — it was home-to-home delivery. There was hardly anything that you couldn't get on that wagon. The people who operated the wagons were store owners; they operated a store and then they loaded these things up every day. Everything was sold by bulk in those days, nothing like it is now, put in boxes. And we were always ready out by the wagon to get it, that I remember."

THE AGENT AND THE FARMER "Mr. Warman, he was an agent, and he and my father were very friendly, and one winter day Mr. Warman drove into the yard, and he had this organ on a sled where he had brought it over from Moncton to sell to Father. And Mother was getting dinner ready and we were coming home from school and we were thrilled and Dad, of course, he was playing the organ — one piece I remember was: 'Where, Oh, Where Is My Little Dog Gone?' And then Mr. Warman started talking to him:

'Now Dan, you should buy this organ for these children, because they need to have music in the home.'

And Father said: 'I haven't time to be bothered talking to you. Put your horse in the barn and come on in and have dinner anyway.'

So that is what happened, he came in and had dinner. So then after dinner, he went out after Father again.

Father said: 'Honest, I haven't the money to buy one. So I'll tell you what to do. Either take the organ and go now, or take this old mare and go.' So Mr. Warman decided he would take the mare.

And he said Dan Nickerson was the only one that ever got ahead of him in a trade, because the horse — she used to kick like anything — wasn't as valuable as the organ was. However we had the organ and had a lot of pleasure from it. He got rid of the mare because he sold it to some French family that lived up in Kent County, and it had lots of room there to kick all it liked."

SIGNS OF THE TIMES "I remember the billboard advertising. Tin signs nailed or painted onto the sides of barns, talking about Big Ben Chewing Tobacco, Dodds Kidney Pills, Zam-Buk Ointment. For variety, the travelling circus used to leave their occasional, very colourful, posters, showing glamorous trapeze artists, clowns, and equestrians, which provided colour in the community until the signs finally weathered into nothingness. Very occasionally you see a few of them, very faded, and quite often the tin has either been blown off or has been removed to make huts for children camping along the river. Most of the signs themselves that were painted have faded away."

THE CENTRE OF A FARMING COMMUNITY "As a child I lived with my parents in my father's grocery store. We had two rooms behind the store and the bedrooms and a big central hall that was used as, I suppose you could call it, a family room upstairs. The store was located on the main street of Cookstown, which is about fifty miles north of Toronto, and it was a big rambling place, a frame building; the store had the old-fashioned porch right out over the street, which covered the entrance to the store, and there was also a verandah upstairs that opened out from the living quarters.

Cookstown in the twenties was the centre of a farming community with a population of four or five hundred — in between there — which has since grown to approximately a thousand. The

store itself was a trading centre for farmers. They brought in butter, eggs, and things like this and traded them for groceries. And
most of the other groceries went on the bill until the farmer's crop
came in.

The door was centrally located and there were two rather large
windows, one on each side, and then there was a lean-to building
at the west side of the store, which was used in my early years as a
storage place for salt and barrels of flour and barrels of sugar and
hundred-pound bags of sugar, and at the back of that section my
father had vinegar barrels out in a little lean-to at the back, plus a
coal-oil tank which had a pump on the top of it, and if they
wanted a gallon of coal oil, they went out with their gallon can
and had it filled there.

The town was relatively quiet, although there were times, like
Saturday evening, which was the time for the farmers to come in
and socialize as well as buy their groceries and do their other
business in the town. But there was a fair amount of stir around
during the week with farmers coming in. They came into town
primarily to bring their chop in to be done at the mill. There was a
mill down in the northwest corner of the town, and of course
when they brought their grain in, they also came into the stores to
do their grocery shopping as well.

The wives sometimes would come with the men, and another
time they would send a list in with the men to do their shopping
for them. And another thing that was sold in the store were veterinary supplies like Royal Purple Kick ... whatever they used
when the chickens were sick, and calf meal and other medications
for sick animals were sold. There was a whole shelf full of Royal
Purple products in the store. They also sold block salt for the
cows. Actually, the stores were open every night of the week until
perhaps nine o'clock, and on Saturday night it would be eleven
before they got closed up.

The store was outfitted with long counters that had big drawers
in them, very large drawers that would hold as much as fifty
pounds of rolled oats in bulk, and also hold white sugar, brown
sugar, dried beans, raisins, rice, barley, all of the commodities that
you now buy in packages came in bulk, and the front of the
counter had little glass cases in front of each drawer that had a

sample of whatever was in behind it. And we kids used to get in on the act. We were put to work weighing up brown paper bags with four pounds of sugar for a quarter — I guess it was five pounds for a quarter in those day — and oatmeal in five- and ten-pound packages, and dates and raisins in one- and two-pound paper bags. The dates were wrapped in a heavy, waxed brown paper. They came in a big box and it was just a big solid mass of dates that had to be pried apart with the point of a knife and then put in a little block in this heavy wax paper. And then there was nutmeg, and the spices of course came in bulk as well, and things like cinnamon and sage and the herbs, well, they were all right there.

And coffee, although Dad didn't have a coffee grinder, but he did get coffee in bulk, and we also put that into brown paper bags. The store did have a supply of one-cent candy, and there was a candy case on the counter that was like a half circle, a roll-top almost. And the candy case had boxes of chocolate bars in it and penny candy in boxes, licorice, hoarhound, peppermints, sugar sticks, and the old hard candy.

The farm children used to come in with their mother, hanging on to her skirts if they were real little ones, and if they were allowed a treat, they used to be able to pick out their penny candy. And cookies of course came in bulk as well, biscuits of all kinds, and fancy cookies, and they were sold by the pound and they were put up in paper bags. They were lucky if they were allowed a nickel's worth of candy. It was more likely to be a cent. Some of the candies, like the black balls, they were two or three for a cent, and licorice ropes were a penny apiece.

Bread was delivered from Barrie in big wood crates with the lid that lifted up, and Dad always had one of those crates in the store, and it sat in front of the counter, beside the hot-air register. And this was where one of the clerks that Dad had hired used to spend a good part of the time, sitting on the bread box with her feet over the hot-air register.

I should tell you, too, about the hot-air register. In the winter-time that was the place where we pitched our wet mittens and wet red woollen leggings that we wore—it was before the days of ski-suits and this sort of thing, snow-suits. Red woollen leggings would get soaking wet and have balls of snow clinging to the wool, and when they were taken off, they were just pitched on top of the hot-air register, and the smell of wet wool permeated the air.

The farmers in the wintertime came in in big sleighs, and of course the kids were always hitching rides on the back of the sleighs. We weren't suppose to do it, but we did it anyway. Of course there were no cars in the wintertime. Anyone who did have a car just simply didn't drive it in the winter weather.

Of course in the summertime they came in buggies, and they came in big wagons, farm wagons, and they usually had bags of chop in the back of the wagons because they'd been to the mill. I think probably around 1920, I don't remember it, but I can just vaguely remember my father investing in a gas pump, and it was out on the street at the end of the lane.

Most of the farmers ran an account and paid it when their grain crop came off or when they sold some cattle, and the majority of them were certainly honest. Of course, during the Depression years they found it pretty difficult, and I know that my father had a good amount of money on the accounts that took a long time to collect, and of course some of it was never collected. There was a good proportion of it during the Depression years that was never paid. But the majority of farmers were certainly honest, and they traded things like butter and eggs and perhaps potatoes or vegetables, turnips, this sort of thing, for goods in the store.

The canned goods that were available certainly included peaches, pears, plums, peas, corn, salmon, pork and beans, spaghetti, tomatoes, pretty well the same thing, although probably the variety was much less. There wouldn't be as many grades of peas and corn, but the farmers didn't buy too much in the way of canned vegetables and fruit; it was more the town people that bought that, because most of the farmers raised their own food. The main things the farmers bought in the store would be flour in hundred-pound bags, sugar in hundred-pound bags; they bought oatmeal, raisins, dates, tea, coffee, salt, coal oil, certainly, and Dad also kept as I said the veterinary medicines; and they also bought things like rock salt and blocks of salt for the cows. And he also of course had barrels of vinegar in the basement. There would be cider vinegar and wine vinegar, and the people had their own gallon jugs, which they would bring in to be filled. And cheese was another thing that Dad bought in the big round cheese boxes, which held . . . oh, they must have held a hundred pounds anyway. We kids got pretty expert at cutting off a half-pound or a pound of cheese.

The stock in the store included some patent medicines of Castoria and Milk of Magnesia and Zam-Buk Ointment, Carter's Little Liver Pills, Mecca Ointment. These things were carried in the store even though there was a drugstore up the street. Zam-Buk was an ointment that you used as a general healing ointment, that you put on burns or a cut or a mosquito bite or almost anything.

Saturday night was a social night for the farmers who came in, and they would hang around until eleven o'clock, and they would stand in the store talking about the weather, the crops, local gossip, events that were going on in the town and in the surrounding community."

SATURDAY NIGHTS IN TOWN "I think Saturday night was the most popular night. The store was always open till the last person, the last customer was gone, no matter if it was midnight. And invariably the store in the small town would have the post office attached or the post office there, and the farmers would come for their mail and get their groceries and so on."

A BAD LINE "When the telephone system first came into the country, they had it in High River here, and the country was fenced up then, the country was almost all in barb-wire fences. They used the top wire of this fence as a telephone wire, and when it came to a road allowance, they put two high poles up and ran the wire up across the top, you see, so you could get under with the wagons and things like that. And two of the first country telephone systems were barb-wire fence. It was good enough in the dry weather, but when it rained it would sometimes short out."

GET OFF THE LINE!   "The telephones that we used to get along with, it seemed like a whole street could be on there. When you went to call up, you could hear the phones clicking down, and it'd get so you could hardly hear the person you were trying to talk to, with so many listening. So you'd say: 'Well, I wish some of you would get off the line so I could hear what they're telling me here.'

And sometimes they would. But there's some of them had the habit of having their rocking chair under the telephone, and they'd have the receiver down over their shoulder so it would be real handy — they didn't even have to get up to listen to it. So we were up against something in those days.

However, we could generally listen to the long ring, they put in a long ring when there was fire or anything like that, or anything unusual, central would tell us all what was going on. And there was one thing about those old phones, they were a very reasonable price. I think I remember we paid seven dollars a year for our phone . . . seven dollars for the whole year. That's much different from what it is nowadays.

We would have trouble with ice storms, where they'd load the wires and with about thirty or forty wires on one pole or one set of poles, and all loaded with ice; it made a tremendous weight. I've seen a whole stretch of poles up the road lying right down flat, and they'd have a gang come along and get the poles off the road so the traffic could move, and then they had a gang to get the poles up into place again, and it was a big job. It was surprising how quick they could get it going again."

VERY HANDY MECHANICS   "It seems that our telephone boys had led one wire a little bit over another one, and when there was lightning strike anywhere near it would catch on the line and then come along and blow out something in the telephone. One time it turned ours around in such a way that you didn't even have to lift a receiver to hear the other folks talking.

On a rural telephone there's usually several folks on the same line. This was one way of getting news around and if someone was ill — if a phone rang in the night somebody would come and

see — and if there was any illness or any reason for it, you would
have a neighbour there to help immediately. But this time when
the lightning struck, it apparently melted some piece in the phone
into another, and you didn't even take down the receiver to have
to listen, you could hear the other folks talking. You couldn't get
central, but we sure could hear anything else that was going
on nearby.

Now that didn't last long. It seems that somebody in the city
was looking for us on a long-distance call, and our boys are all
very handy mechanics, and because we waited a day or two for
the phone, somebody came in and jumped a wire somewhere, and
I called the operator to tell her the phone was out of order, and
she said:

'How's it out of order if you're talking?'

'Somebody opened it up and we just changed the wire and it's
all working for the time being, but I don't like the way it is.'

'Oh, they're not supposed to touch it.'

'You folks haven't been here, so it doesn't matter . . .'

'Well, I've been looking for you on a long-distance call.'

And then they fixed it.''

JUST SAVING TIME   "There was an awful lot of stories told, too,
about the odd things on the telephone. I think it's over twenty that
was on this one party line. Couple of old fellows talking on the
phone, and they said they'd call up their neighbour, mentioned
their neighbour's name. 'We'll call up Mac, over there.'

And so this Mac's grandfather was on the phone listening. He
says: 'You don't need to call Mac. He's out at the barn.'''

THE BUCKET BRIGADE   "Fire is always serious, but before we
had the fire department to call on, we all had what was known as
the rural line. There were twenty-two farmers on our line, and
everybody used what was known as the emergency ring, that is,
you cranked the old telephone, oh, give it a real long ring, and
everybody would go on, yes, yes, and you'd say where the fire

All of the photographs in this section—like the photograph of the farmhouse at dusk that appears on the cover—were taken by Peter D'Angelo, a young, Toronto-based photographer with a special interest in rural scenes. Despite his youth, his photographs have appeared in a wide variety of magazines, such as Maclean's, Chatelaine, and Saturday Night, and in several books on Canada.

was, and then everybody rushed there to help. Nearly all the farms had a cistern, a soft-water cistern, and they would get water out of there in a hurry. They all had a big lid; you'd dip pails right into the cistern and form a bucket brigade."

TELEPHONE COURTESY   "When I was a boy, I lived on a farm at Albert Head, and one of our neighbours was a Chinese farm worker named Romar, who used to work for various farmers in the district as they required him. He used to do a lot of work for these people named Weir, and sometimes, because of weather or other reasons, he wasn't sure whether he was to go or not, so he would come to our place to telephone them to see if he was required.

After one of us would put in the call, then we would hand the receiver to him, and when he heard a voice, he would say: 'Miser Wahr, Miser Wahr . . . ohhh . . . Missa Wahr, ohhh,' then he would go on talking. What he was saying was: 'Mr. Weir, Mr. Weir . . . oh, it's Mrs. Weir.' And when he discovered it was Mrs. Weir that was answering the telephone, he would immediately reach up and lift his hat off. If it was Mr. Weir that answered the phone, he wouldn't take his hat off."

RINGING WRONG NUMBERS   "I had the telephone in here for a long time, it was getting on my nerves. They used to start making wrong numbers, ringing wrong numbers whenever the dial system came in, and sometimes they'd be dialing numbers and they'd wake me up in the middle of the night—it would kind of scare me. I'd think that something had happened somewhere, some of my relations, when here when I got up and answered it, it was somebody wanted some other number. I used to be away and they'd be phoning . . . some stupid person phoning, ring the phone off the wall nearly and I'm not there. Then some of my neighbours would call up and say: 'I heard your phone ringing, your phone ringing and there's no answer and we wondered what happened.' It was just from one thing to another, and I got it cut off for a while. And when I got it cut off, it never seemed I missed it, so I just never got it hooked up again."

HEATED WORDS   "Breakdowns in harvest time and threshing time could be quite urgent affairs, and I can recall my grandfather came rushing in from the field one afternoon and he had to get on the phone right now and phone the town for a part. Now fortunately we were only three and a half miles from town, but do you think he could get on that phone? No, it was a party line, and a couple of the neighbour women were on the phone gassing and gabbing away, and he tried his darnedest to break in, and they wouldn't have anything to do with it. So finally, in desperation, him being Irish and quick-witted, he just got on the phone there and said: 'Mrs. Wishart, I smell your bed burning.'

And there was a screech on the other end and everybody hung up and he got on the line."

TWENTY-ONE

Ranching I

World Traders ... The Term 'Spread' ... Guns ... The Sundance Kid ...
Trailing Pigs and Yearlings ... Those Fellows All Got Churned ... A Wonderful Recovery ... The Frenchman's Mother ... Diplomacy ... Headed for
Boot Hill ... Fancy Saddles ... An Ear in His Mouth ... Not a Staid
Event ... Stampede ... Ranch Women ... A Master Rustler ...
Old Jack Morton

R emembering the Ranch   is really almost a separate section of
this book. Ranchers, particularly old-time ranchers, made
it very clear to me that they didn't want to be mixed in with
farmers. They weren't that polite about it, but that's what they
meant. There still is a strong belief among some foothills ranchers
that it is degrading to get down off a horse and get your hands dirty
mucking about in the earth. But this is a minority group of ranchers, because the old-timers are dying out fast, and only a few of
them still use horses in their roundups.

Ranchers are not just different than farmers, they are totally
different. They tend to be breezier, on occasion much wilder and
crazier, than farmers, they love to tell long and complicated and
funny stories, and they are great mimics. Many farmers have a dry
wit: if you take that wit, wring it out a dozen times or so, you will get
near to the wit of a rancher.

Ranchers vary greatly in size and appearance, but if I had to
describe a common type, I'd say picture a man who is neat and
sparsely-built and looks as if he has been sun-baked for fifty years.
I like farmers and I like ranchers, but there's one thing I'd say about
ranchers: they're a unique lot — there's no other group quite
like them.

WORLD TRADERS "The ranching people, the original ones, were very British and they were very Canadian and they didn't consider themselves isolated at all. They travelled back and forth to their own homes in Britain; they kept contact with their relatives and friends in Ontario and Quebec, and they didn't consider themselves in isolation.

They provided a product which had to be exported for many years for them to make a living; so they were really almost world traders. If they couldn't get their cattle shipped to Chicago, they went to Britain, and their whole attitude was very cosmopolitan, and they kept up their contact with their relatives and friends from where they came.

Another thing, they didn't come here and throw all their old traditions away, to come here and start anew. They came here to extend the traditions that they had already developed, and that is why you have some of these extreme stories about the tea sets and all that. But the whole thing was that they weren't ashamed of their past."

THE TERM 'SPREAD' "The word 'spread' is a term that is quite general, or used to be quite general in the ranching industry. It always is referred to with large ranches and how it came into being I don't know, but I've come across the word in quite early literature. There would be quite a number of spreads, 'cause in southern Alberta there were very many really large ranches with leases of a hundred thousand acres or so. I think, I'm not sure of this, but I think the term was used first in the American West and came up that way."

GUNS "These old American cowboys that came up, they all packed guns, and it was rather necessary because there were range stallions which would attack a person on a horse, and they could blaze away in front of the horse's face and pretty well stop him, or maybe have to shoot him. Those range stallions, they'd have a bunch of mares, you see, and if somebody came up on a gelding, they'd come right at you on the run. I've been chased by stallions. You get your rope down and swing your rope and beat him over the head, or if you've got a stock whip, you can get him with that, or get out of there. They'd come at you just like a bull, just as hard as they could, and they'd hit your horse, and if you stopped him, they'd hit your horse, grab him by the teeth, and maybe knock him down.

Guns was legal as long as they was packed in the open. You had them on a holster on your hip, you see, as long as it wasn't concealed. One man said he was going to kill the manager of one of the ranches, and the manager of the ranch was a Texan, and he was a gunman himself. And when this fellow came to shoot him, the Texan got his gun out and grazed his ribs on one side and grazed them on the other side with a couple of bullets, and that was the end of it. This was one of the few accounts I heard of gunfighting in the West here, in Alberta. It was down south here, south of High River."

THE SUNDANCE KID   "Another boy that came up to this country around about 1890 was a boy called Harry Longbow, and he worked here at High River when the railroad was going through in '93, breaking workhorses for the construction crew. And then he was a bronc rider, bucking-horse rider on the Bar U Ranch west of here. He was very well thought of. And afterwards when he went back to Montana, he became the notorious Sundance Kid. I've seen pictures of him and talked to people that knew him. He was a medium-height boy, very quiet, very well liked.

And he got into trouble in Calgary. He was bartending up there one winter. A lot of these old cowboys, when the roundup was over in the fall, they would get a job bartending. And there was some big bruiser came up over the trail to Calgary, was running a saloon, and he'd get these fellows to work for him all winter, and then when the time came to settle up with them, he'd get into a fight with them, and beat them up. He tried it on Longbow, but he got the worst of it. Longbow just put his hand on the bar and hopped over, and when his feet hit the ground there was a gun in this other fellow's stomach, and he coughed up the money right away.

And that's when Longbow went south. He went down to Montana, and met up with Butch Cassidy and those fellows. He was raised in Sundance, Wyoming. That's how he got the name of The Sundance Kid."

TRAILING PIGS AND YEARLINGS   "I don't know where the cowboys really came from, but they used to show up riding across the country with a horse behind them and their bedroll on the back, and they wouldn't try to get a job unless they had their own horses. These cowboys, they were willing to do a day's work, which is awful hard to find today. Most of the men that came, stayed, and they didn't get paid very much. We had a few fellows there in 1928 that got paid twenty-five dollars a month from the government and twenty-five dollars from us. The government brought men over from Hungaria or somewhere — they imported them, you know — and the top fellow, the guy that worked for us for thirty-five years, got thirty-five dollars a month. It was the top wages then.

At one time you know we had four thousand sheep on one side of the river and four thousand cows on the other side, and four hundred pigs in the yard. I don't think anybody ever saw this before, but we trailed four hundred sows sixteen miles over the hills, you know, and you can't believe what that looked like.

We used to trail fifteen hundred yearlings every year. It was Billy MacIntyre the famous rancher and my father, but we used to trail fifteen hundred of these yearlings and go through the farms with them, a hundred miles every spring. It was a pretty tough deal because you could run into these farmers, and they'd want to charge you two bucks a load if you stopped overnight, and then every once in a while you'd pick some of theirs up, you know, they'd crawl through the fence, and we got in trouble with the police a few times.

You can take a herd of cattle safely and make them gain on the grass about twelve miles a day; if you're going to take them any further, they're going to start to lose weight. And you know those old cows can smell that water, and if they get a mile away, they'll smell her and they'll go to the water."

THOSE FELLOWS ALL GOT CHURNED   "When I was a boy, I wanted to break horses, and I made it a point of working with some of the old-time bronco riders and horse breakers, and a little of their lore rubbed off on me, I'd say. They were pretty skookum men —

they'd take six or eight raw broncs and ride them out every day in a narrow fork saddle, and they didn't have anybody to help them. They just had to saddle them and get on them themselves and ride them and bring them back into the corral. Sometimes they'd front-foot them, rope them by the front feet and throw them down and hog-tie them—which meant tying three legs together—and saddle them on the ground, and get on them, and then somebody would let them up; and other times they'd let them up with a pair of hobbles on, or tie a hind leg up around their neck, just pull it up a little off the ground, and roll them around like that; but they'd take those horses—wild as hawks—and step right up on them. They didn't need anybody to drop them down into the saddle—they would just step right on. If they got the foot in the stirrup and the hand on the horn, well, they was supposed to be able to go up and stay there, and most of them could do it.

You learn a lot from these fellows. They show you how to handle them, how to hobble them, and how to tie a hind leg up or how to blindfold them, how to saddle them and how to get on them and off, and just what to do. I mean it's practically forgotten today because the wild horses aren't in the country any more, and these old range broncs are not here, and there's nobody left now that can do that kind of work. You just have to get on them and get bucked off until you learn to ride them. It was just practice makes perfect.

The old-time bronc riders, they'd probably be riding six horses, maybe eight a day, and these horses, they wouldn't all buck, but some of them would buck pretty hard, and these fellows all got churned. Everybody that did that, after they'd been at it ten, twelve, fifteen years, well, they got what the old cowpuncher used to call churned—shaken up inside.

Herb Miller was one of the great bronc riders here at the Bar U in the early days. He was spitting blood all the time, vomiting blood. He'd get off a bucking horse and just vomit blood. It was pretty rough on him and he was an iron man. He got to quit riding broncs. He didn't live too long, about ninety . . . eighty-nine he was. He was eight-nine when he died, would have been ninety in a couple of weeks. He quit riding broncs, but he very nearly died from it . . . every now and again somebody would get killed.

Some of those horses—what they called the fallback horse—just threw themselves over backwards, and if your belt caught up on the horn, well the horn punched you in the stomach and probably killed you. Some of the good riders were killed that way, but not too many of them.

I broke horses for about fifteen years, and I finally got churned and I couldn't ride for a year or two. But it was in the Depression, and my bread and butter was breaking these horses, and if a horse bucked with me, I'd be tired the next day — and I was getting shaken up inside and I should have quit, but it was all I had to live on. I had to keep riding, breaking these horses to live. That's just what it amounted to—my bread and butter.

And after you get confidence in yourself that you can handle these horses, well . . . you don't mind it much. I guess sometimes you get a little scared, all right, when you think a horse is maybe going to run through a barb-wire fence or buck down over a cut-bank or something like that. And finally a horse threw himself in the corral, and shook me up inside, and bruised my bladder, and I couldn't ride any more for a year. I was in bad shape. I'm all right today."

A WONDERFUL RECOVERY   "In one of the very early Stampedes, there was a young cowboy who had a reputation of being a little bit of a malingerer; and George Lane, who was one of the big four, came along when this young man had failed to get up after being thrown from his horse. So George Lane came along, opened up his knife and said:

'We'll just bleed him and that will fix him up.'

And the cowboy really made a wonderful recovery."

THE FRENCHMAN'S MOTHER   "The story is often told of a Frenchman that settled around here, that had a horse ranch. And apparently he was something of a playboy, and his people in France were well off, and they kept sending more and more money out to keep this ranch going.

And finally his mother, who was quite an astute business head, decided she should come out to see, really, where all this money was going. So she made a visit out and was met by her son.

And she wanted to see all these horses that he'd been raising. And of course he'd been so busy having a good time, he hadn't had much time to raise any horses. So he got in touch with his neighbours and said: 'Well, my mother's here to see all these horses, so can I borrow yours?'

And they said: 'Oh, yes, that'd be fine.'

And his ranch was situated in such a way that there were a number of hills, and he arranged with his hired hands to drive the horses around the hills, into the corral, and send them round again — plus his neighbours' horses mixed in with his bunch. And he parked his mother in a buggy in a strategic place, so she could get a good view of these horses. And so he felt that he'd managed to convince her that he'd really done a job in raising these horses.

But his mother was very astute, and she remarked to him that there was a great similarity in the horses which she kept seeing go by."

DIPLOMACY   "I remember a story about a bunch of these cowhands, who were playing poker in the old hotel, and there was a glass-eyed poker shark from Calgary there. And one of these cowhands figured things weren't quite right and he pulled his six-shooter out and laid it on the table forcibly and he said:

'Now, I don't want to accuse anybody of anything crooked, but there is some funny work going on around this table, and if it doesn't stop, somebody is going to lose his other eye.'

It stopped."

HEADED FOR BOOT HILL   "When I was a kid we had quite a few cowboys around, and on a Sunday, or an evening, they would line up bottles on the fence posts and then they'd run races and see how many bottles they could shoot off the fence posts, with the horse on the dead run. Some of them were good. Some of them — well, we had the odd one that shot himself in the foot, but he didn't come back when he healed up."

FANCY SADDLES "Some of the fancy saddles at this particular time are still in existence among some of the early people who have restored their grandfather's saddle and kept it in their families. And these saddles at that time might have cost sixty-five to eighty-five dollars, where the average saddle that was being built for the average rancher or the average ranchhand was in the thirty-five-to-forty-dollar class. Then after 1912, it became a new era when the Stampede was accepted in Calgary, and then our local ranchhands took up competitive cowboy . . . well, let's call them sports. They were. They went to Calgary to compete in calf roping and bronc riding to show their ability as ranchhands to the public who were there.

Then we had to develop saddles that were of a very much different type. We would find that the bronc rider would come in and he would say: 'Well, I want a saddle built much like you built for Pete Knight, but I want it a shade different.'

So we brought in great big saddle trees with very short seats, high cantles, big fronts, small horns. Then we took hacksaw blades and these saddles were cut to fit the individual rider. Through that came the Gibson Saddle, the Calgary Red Saddle, and all the rest of them. They became really a mantrap. When you got into these thirteen- or fourteen-inch seats you were in there really secure, and the only way you could get out of there was to get bucked clean from that. We called them a mantrap because you were fitted into these with the front swelling back over your thighs with a terrific height of cantle well dished to set you upright in the saddle and compact in there.

When you were in there your whole legs were embodied into the saddle, so if there was any way that you had to go out, you had to go out over the top. But if a horse were to fall on you, there was no quick exit out of this. So as a result, a few years later, they decided to adopt what they call the Association Saddle, and this saddle is used today, and I imagine we'll still be using it in the contest world of bronc riding from here on. And it was a saddle with an average front, an average cantle, and was a type of saddle that could be used by an average rider if he wished to. The roping saddles, I would say, stayed pretty much the same with the big Mexican horns for dally roping, which continued on for years, with the lower cantle and the very, very slight A-forked type of a front, with rigging going to double rig, where your Association Saddle was a three-quarter rig.''

AN EAR IN HIS MOUTH "A lot of these broncos are pretty tough, you know, and they're pretty light on the front end. Their front feet are liable to paw you. And old Jack . . . he'd drag a horse out with a lasso rope, and as soon as he could get close enough to it, he'd walk up alongside of it, he'd reach his left hand up under the horse's jaw, and then he'd get that left ear in his mouth, and he'd twist that ear till you'd think it would come off, and then he'd get it into his teeth. And that took the attention of the horse so that he'd really stand there. Sometimes they would just stand there and quiver. That's when they were saddling the horse.

Well, as soon as they got the saddle on, somebody would say okay. A fellow would crawl up onto the horse, and old Jack would give the horse a kick and let a whoop out of him—he was just like an Indian, he really was. He used to make some awful noises, but they finally were glad when he quit coming to the Calgary Stampede, because he would get drunk over at the barn and break all rules.

They still do that. If you go out to one of these ranches and they're going to break a colt, generally there will be somebody on the place that is good and tall, and he'll reach up under that jaw, and get that ear in his mouth, and I'll tell you, the horse wonders what the heck has hit him.''

NOT A STAID EVENT "The very early balls were the greatest social event in the year's activity in Calgary, and all the very best people went there, and they all had their very best clothes on. And at that time, the gentlemen were expected to drink whiskey and the women were expected to have a claret cup. But some young, enterprising fellow put a whole bunch of gin in this claret cup, and the women just had a wonderful time.

And this one gal, on their way home sometime late in the evening, she took off her stays and put them on her driving horse, and drove up and down Eighth Avenue with her stays on the horse.

And of course for weeks afterwards, no young children were even allowed to discuss this because the parents didn't think it was the right thing to do."

STAMPEDE!   "The only stampede that I know of happened on the Bar U Ranch, when they were rounding up one year, in the Squaw Coulee district where there had been an old buffalo jump. For some crazy reason, a cattle buyer came out driving the first automobile that anyone had seen in that country. And that stampeded about seven hundred head of cattle, and they took off. And some of them went over the buffalo jump, and there were about twenty-five or thirty of them killed in the process. But that's the only stampede that I know of in this country."

RANCH WOMEN   "Ranch women in the early days had a pretty rough time. I have a yoke that was made for my mother to carry water in two five-gallon coal-oil cans. And as far as breaking horses was concerned, why, she could hook up a bronc and break it to work as well as any man. And my sister also was a very good rider."

A MASTER RUSTLER   "Actually there are more rustlers now than there were in the early days. Now they can load up cattle into a truck and be a couple of hundred miles away come daylight. And it is done right along. As a matter of fact, there have been several cases where they have slaughtered animals in the feed lots, loaded them onto a pickup truck, and would be gone before anyone knew anything about it.

I knew of a rustler in the early days, who unfortunately lost his life in the First World War. And he was a master at it. As a matter of fact, he came by our ranch one day and stayed overnight. And he was leading an awful nice roan horse, which my dad said that he wouldn't mind buying. And he said: 'Well, I don't think you want this horse: there's no brand on him.' So we knew then that he'd picked it up some place, and likely just along the road allowance, and was getting out of the country with it.

And he went on up and he sold it to a homesteader neighbour of ours. And Davis, the man that bought it, didn't have a brand at the time, so Dad said: 'You'd better brand that horse, Davis, 'cause it's a good one, and someone'll take it on you.'

And he said: 'No, I don't want to hurt him. I don't want him hurt.'

So that winter, Davis's horse came up missing. Along towards spring, why everybody was looking for Davis's horse, when along came the same fellow, leading a roan horse. 'Course he was thin by this time. And he took it back up and sold it to Davis for a mate for the first one he had. And actually he sold that man the same horse three different times."

OLD JACK MORTON "We were all at the Stampede Dance at the Palliser, and old Jack Morton was there of course, in fact he had a room up there. Then there was a little fellow ... oh, he was from Pennsylvania, and he had a big farm out in the Rosebud district, and he was an insignificant little devil. He was always going around with his nose up in the air; and they were making an awful racket ... Jack always hired two rooms, and everybody'd get in there because he'd hauled in a whole wagonload of booze and everybody went to Jack's room to get a free drink.

Well anyway this little fellow, they were making an awful racket and his room was next to Jack's. He come to the door and knocked at the door and in fact I was in there and I heard him say it. He says: 'Mr. Morton, I wish you would quiet down, because if you don't, I'm going to have you thrown out.'

Jack said: 'You and who else?'

And he grabbed him by the nape of the neck and he took him over to the window ... oh yes, he got him on the floor and held him down with one foot, and he opened the window and then he took the sheets off the two beds and made a rope out of them, and Jack tied them around this guy and hung him out the window, and let him down a floor or two. This little guy, he was yelling his head off, of course, and the police could see him down below, and they really had trouble to find out which room it was, you know, on the whole side of the Palliser Hotel. But this old Jack Morton, he was a case all his own."

TWENTY-TWO

Ranching II

So Many Brands . . . A Chore Man . . . Awful Nice Fellas . . . Horses Were a
Part of Our Life . . . Rattlesnakes . . . All the Help They Could Get . . . A Car
in the Corral . . . "Gravedigger" . . . Lassoing . . . Mountain Oysters . . .
The Old Way . . . Chinooks and Walking Eagle . . . All You Could Eat at
Breakfast . . . Six Weeks . . . A Rustler in Rubber Boots . . . Our Fireflies

B ert Sheppard came to my hotel room in High River to talk to
me about ranching. He'd been a bronco-buster by profession
in his early days until his stomach was churned by all that pitching
and tossing. The story of his life is the story of ranching in Alberta.
To me, it's an intensely dramatic story, and woven into it are many
elements: the famous ranches, such as the Bar U, and men like
George Lane, who are legendary.

Bert has written one of the best local histories ever turned out in
this country: Spitzee Days, about High River and the ranches and
ranch country around it. Bert Sheppard is quiet and well-spoken
and, naturally, he has the native drawl of the ranch country. I was
born in Calgary and he's the kind of Canadian I admire most: he
embodies the history of the ranching West, he's a man of obvious
courage and principle, he's tough and resourceful and not the kind
of man who will take any nonsense from anyone. He's courteous,
nevertheless, and pleasantly old-fashioned. He only uses horses
on his ranch. He doesn't like machinery.

I met other ranchers, I must add, that I admired and liked
immensely: Lloyd Nowlin and Bud Anderson, for example.

I thought, though, I'd just tell you a little about Bert Sheppard: he
is what ranching has been all about.

SO MANY BRANDS "Look at this old wagon seat. It has some of the old and very interesting brands on it.

This Lazy FC Bar is a Nowlin brand which was registered in Alberta in 1908.

The Circle was a large outfit that came in from the States, and their main headquarters was out at Queenstown.

The Rafter Six is a well-known dude ranch out near Banff.

The Flying U was also a large outfit, and was eventually purchased by Mr. Burns, the same as the ML.

The Circle L was the Lyndon brand, one of the first settlers in the Claresholm area.

The Forty-Four is another Claresholm brand that was eventually purchased by Mr. Burns, as well as the WR.

The T Bar Y is Tommy Stewart's brand, of Nanton.

The SN Half-Diamond was a ranch that was started by my father and a man by the name of Sitton. And it was located in the Porcupine hills, west of Claresholm. Sitton was a cowboy that came in from Oregon: there was never a better one.

The Anchor P. It was owned by Rod McClay, who ranched in the hills west of Nanton. And also was at one time out on the Red Deer River.

That's the Rocking Chair.

And this one over here is my wife's brand, I Lazy 2P.

They dreamed up all manner of characters, numbers, and letters for brands. And sometimes when you'd see a cow, she would have so many brands on you couldn't tell where they'd missed."

A CHORE MAN "There was a young chap that was working for my father at the time. And I thought he was going to stay all winter and do the chores which I had been doing, and give me a break. At least that's what Dad had told me.

But we were saddled up early in the morning and it was snowing hard, and Dad told me to go ahead and open the gates, and he and John would bring the horses. So I opened the gates and started. And there was John still standing by his horse. And I yelled and told him, I said: 'Get on your horse and let's get going.'

He said: 'I can't.'

And I said: 'Well, why can't you?'

He says: 'He's standing on my foot.'

So then we were out a chore man. My old man fired him. I had to do the chores all over again.''

AWFUL NICE FELLAS   "The cowboys that I knew were awful nice fellas. They were good men, good horsemen, and their word was their bond and if you hired a good old cowboy, he'd look after your stock just like you would yourself. Most of these men worked at big ranches and they'd do their best for the men they were workin' for. A good man from a big ranch would never get fired, they'd just naturally quit.

They had their own saddles and good equipment and took care of it. And a lot of them liked to have a horse or two of their own, pet horses, they'd cut a cow out of a field or anything, you know. And that made it nicer for some of these big ranches, they didn't have to mount them on so many of their own horses. These cowboys, they'd generally pack a horse and ride around from ranch to ranch. They liked to change their districts now and then and meet new people and see new country.

Cowboys in the early days had their own bed, a big canvas with rings. When they went on roundups they'd put it on their extra horse with some blankets and tie it down like a pack, you know. And they had a little sack with their going-to-town clothes in it, a pair of clean pants and a shirt or two.

They chewed tobacco and could spit through the eye of a needle. Mostly cigarette rollers, though. Bull Durham. You could see the bull hanging out of the shirt pocket on the string of the little sack of Bull Durham.

They were shy with women, you betcha, but they were always polite and nice. They never started a fight but they could stand up and fight if they had to.''

HORSES WERE A PART OF OUR LIFE   "One of my first memories really is of a bunch of horses that had been out on the range coming in. Probably my dad bringing them, but galloping down a lane not far from the house. My mother telling me to get out of the way of those horses, but I wasn't afraid of them, I loved them, with their tails flying, their manes, the sound of their hooves, as they came pounding down the lane.

Then Dad would work in the corral with them, cutting out the younger stock; and he had a snubbing post in the middle of the corral and would work with them. The snubbing post is a very strong post sunk deep into the ground and put in the middle of a corral around which a man can put a rope to handle a horse, to bring the horse up closer. Dad was very patient with horses, and he would work for hours in the corral just driving a horse around with lines and using a blanket or a coat. He'd put it against the horse till he had him so gentle that he'd stand there while Dad would throw this blanket or coat all over him, he knew he wouldn't be hurt. He'd like to break a horse in this way so he'd never buck.

I can remember, too, there was a marshy, swampy place not far from the house, and I remember Dad riding a colt down into the swampy place; he was a bad one, bad to handle, and of course, he wore himself out trying to buck in this swampy place.

Horses were very much a part of our life at home, in fact through the whole district. As a matter of fact, I think through all the foothills country, you could say that the horse was king. A man was judged through that area by the quality and the condition of the horse he rode and by his expertise with horses, and I know at home that the horses were personalities. When a horse died it was a matter of great mourning, it was almost as though one of the family were gone.

There is an excitement about horses, about the very feel of a horse's soft nose, and the feel of riding the fields, muscles of a horse under you and the wind in your face. There is an excitement in riding, and the smell of the sweat, and the smell of the blankets, and the leather and the squeak of the leather as you ride. All this is exciting, and it's a part of life that I'm very glad that I didn't miss.

I never really hurt myself very badly going off a horse — never broke a bone . . . oh, well I did break some ribs once, but I didn't really come off. I was chasing cattle through the brush — we had a lot of fairly heavy brush at home — and I was riding this horse, Rock, and he was a really good horse too, and he would go through paths through the brush in such a way as to miss your knees—you know you can get your knees badly battered going through a path through brush. But on this occasion he was going quickly and we were trying to head off some cattle and it was muddy and he slipped—I was leaning sideways to miss the brush and the horn of the saddle hit me in the ribs and cracked a couple of ribs, but I rode about fifteen miles after that, so it was pretty sore by the time I got off. I wasn't laid up for long, they just strapped them up and they healed pretty quickly."

RATTLESNAKES   "Rattlesnakes have been very common in the Medicine Hat–Empress country. And for some unknown reason, a horse seems to be able to smell a snake. And before you even see them or hear them, why, he'll start sticking up his ears and stepping sideways and dancing along. Many a cowboy has been bucked off while being spooked by a snake.

I knew a man—in this country his name was Dick Smith—what his name was before he came here, I don't know. But he could lean over, off a horse, pick up a snake by the tail, and pop it like a whip and pop its head off. I tried it once and the snake wound up riding the horse along with me, and I got bucked off."

ALL THE HELP THEY COULD GET   "It makes me think of a story that I heard one time about the easterner that come out and bought a ranch, and of course he had two boys that was going to take a part in this, and they had read all these books, and the first thing they do is go down the street and get themselves dressed up in what we call a Rexall Regalia.

And the old fellow that run this ranch, operated it for a good many years, he was now out of a job. And he was riding out of the yard, leading his pet horse, and the dog following. (By the way, this family that has now acquired this ranch were rather of the religious type.) This old fellow threw one last question at this operator, he said: 'How are you going to gather these cattle off all this rough land, Mister?'

And the easterner looked at these two boys with their Rexall

Regalia on and he said: 'Well, with my two sons and the help of God, I think we'll get them gathered.'

And this old cowpoke he said: 'Well, you know, I never knew much about this man, God — but I'll tell you, you'd better mount him on a damn good horse.'"

A CAR IN THE CORRAL   "I grew up on a ranch near Maple Creek, and my father, along with his ranching, decided to sell Model T cars to his ranching friends. And he went out into the hills to sell a car to this rancher.

And so he gave him a demonstration around the yard, and finally the rancher said: 'Oh, I'd feel much happier if we took the car into the corral and took the rough off it in there; and once I feel satisfied that that's happened, you can open the gate and let me go.'

So they went into the corral and did quite a few circles round. And the old rancher felt that he could now handle this wild mustang, and so he said: 'Okay, Jake. Open the gates. We're all ready to go.'"

"GRAVEDIGGER"   "We raised a horse one time, and when we were branding him as a colt, we got a little careless or something, and he got away with the rope on. And he ran for about a month before we finally caught him and got the rope off, and finished the job of branding.

When we went to break this horse, we found it was practically impossible. He not only kicked, but he'd fight and everything else. And he turned out to be one of the best bucking-horses that they ever had in the Calgary Stampede. They called him 'Gravedigger'. And he sure was."

LASSOING   "Ranch boys usually learn to ride as soon as they learn to walk. Well, in order to learn to ride, you had to catch a horse. So in order to do that, you had to learn how to rope or lasso a horse. And some of the kids picked it up easy.

Some of the rest of us—it was a little hard to learn. But if you can swing a rope around your head, and you know when to let go, why you can usually catch him. But if you can't, why you can snare him.

In other words, set a loop and run the horse into it, which some of us had to do at times.

I got a lasso over here that is made of rawhide, that I made myself. And they were an exceptionally good rope, but they weren't as strong as the Mexican ropes, which were made out of, well, the century-plant was what the best ropes are made out of. And the Mexicans knew how to use them. Any place where there are cowboys, even in South American and Australia, why, they use some type of a rope, and the original ones are made of rawhide, which is the hide off a cow and then cut into, usually, four strands, and braided together. Which this one is."

MOUNTAIN OYSTERS "So every spring, I can remember we would castrate the calves, before they went out on the range. I was about ten years old when I castrated my first bull calf, which was quite a feat for me. This experience of castrating a calf actually was normal as far as I was concerned, because all the kids were doing it, taking our turns. The calf would come in the chute and we'd just castrate him, throw some flour on the testicles that were in the sack, and they'd tied it up and let the calf go. And this was an everyday routine amongst the kids.

Of course all the bull calves are castrated because we wanted them to become steers; we didn't want a whole crop of bulls. And the half-breeds would cook these testicles — they were called mountain oysters—and this would be part of the diet. I didn't know what these mountain oysters were, but my father knew and he wouldn't eat them. They were really good.

But the thing that bothered me most was the branding of cattle. You'd hear them yell when you put a hot brand on them. My dad had a brand that was zero—a great big 0—and his brand was the 0 brand, and all the cattle had this burnt into their side. This bothered me more than anything else, with the screaming of the young calves."

THE OLD WAY "Personally I don't like machinery, and I refused to learn how to start a tractor. A horse is good enough for me. I'm getting old now but I can still ride, and I ride with the cowboys on the ranch and help all the time. We handle all our cattle with horses. There's four or five of us there on the ranch now, and we've all been riding every day pretty well, moving cattle and taking calving cows and cows out, stuff like that. And I suppose now we've got about thirty horses. We used to have quite a few more. I had about fifteen quarter-horse mares at one time, but I sold them.

We work cattle the old way, the way these old cowboys taught me to do it. Most of them now, they work the cattle in cutting lanes and stuff like that. We work our cattle right out in the open range mostly. Some of the old ranches are doing it just about the same as we; some of them aren't. We rope the calves for branding. They've got these metal branding traps now, branding tables, but I think it's hard on the calves. You've got flesh and blood and muscle against steel. The other way, when you rope them there's a certain amount of give, and the calf wrestlers pulled them down, and I think it's better.

But we've got a pretty open range; we don't have to feed much in the winter till spring. Usually our cows are not fed until the first of March. We've got Hereford cattle, and they've got good thick coats and curly hair. We are very careful about that, and they're good rustlers.

Personally, I would much prefer the old-time ranching where there weren't any fences. I like horses and I like saddle horses and cattle and roundup work — this sort of thing — but today the problems are increasing all the time. We've got far more diseases to contend with, and we're big enough so that we have a bookkeeper do all our bookwork for us. If I had a small ranch where I had to do all my bookwork, fool around with all this unemployed insurance and pension things, well I wouldn't do it. I'd sooner go and live in a tepee somewhere."

CHINOOKS AND WALKING EAGLE "After you have put in about twenty-five or thirty days of below-zero weather, and you see that chinook or arch in the west, and you wake up about four o'clock in the morning with the water running off the roof, it's the most grandest feeling that you can ever imagine. 'Cause you know that the old cows'll be gettin' the hump out of their back, and you won't have to haul half as much hay.

You can always tell when a chinook is coming because there's an arch across the western sky above the mountains. Some of the old-timers used to say if it was down close, it would be two days before it got here; if it was up high, it'd be there by morning. And it always seemed to work out that way.

We had an Indian in the Rocky Mountain district that was quoted many times on the weather. And he could invariably hit it at least as close as some of our smart boys. An Indian friend of mine asked me one day if I happened to know how he got the name of Walking Eagle. I said, no. 'Well,' he said, 'He's so full of bullshit he can't fly.'

ALL YOU COULD EAT AT BREAKFAST   "The main meal on the ranch was breakfast, and you usually started it off with hot bread of some kind—either biscuits, hot cakes, or flapjacks. And they were of the very best, along with ham and eggs or bacon and eggs, lots of strong coffee — or if you happened to be working for an English rancher, you got tea, which the American cowboys didn't cotton to too well. If they were going to have tea, it was green tea. But practically everybody had lots of coffee, plenty of hotcakes and bacon and eggs. And all you could eat.

And as a matter of fact, I worked on a ranch where every breakfast they served prunes. Prunes were on the table all the time, and you had apple pie for breakfast. 'Course you didn't have any lunch, unless you stuck a couple of biscuits in your pocket. But you'd have roast beef and all the trimmings at night."

SIX WEEKS   "I was out hunting on the Coldstream Ranch, well, actually we call it here the Bald Peak, and it's up fairly high, oh, thirty-five hundred, four thousand feet. The grass is very lush, and these horses went up there in the summer, in August, to get out of the flies, and out of the heat. And they got into one of these cabins that these soldier settlement boys had built just after the First World War. And somehow they kicked the door shut. Six of them.

So I come and was hunting, as I say, come along to this cabin. And I heard a noise in it. And so I come up. And you could see right away that there's been something terrible had happened around there, and I kicked the door open. And the sides of the wall was chewed, and the edge of the windows. It just looked terrible. Here was four or five of them layin' dead. And when I kicked the door open, there was two of them that hadn't died yet. And so I pried it around, and the one that was laying dead against the door, I had to move its feet a bit to open the door, and they got out. These two staggered out. And they stood for about fifteen minutes—and this I'll never forget — after they got out they stood as much to say: 'Well, Lord, what a relief it is to be able to get a breath of fresh air.'

I went on hunting and left them, and came back and they'd got down to water and they had a drink. But they didn't eat. And so I told them at the Coldstream Ranch, and the manager went up a couple of days after, and they were still alive. Two or three months after, I saw the horses and they looked quite normal. They'd come right back, recovered, right from a bag of bones, they were back to looking like a horse again. They were really tough.

You might think there'd be an awful stench when I opened the door. But those animals had dehydrated and wasted away till, actually basically, there was nothing to smell. When they died, they were absolutely dry. They must have been in there six weeks.

You figure, well, there may be five or six or seven of them or eight off in a little pocket that you didn't see, so you don't pay too much attention to it. And that's why they weren't missed—in that time of year, in August, they're in the shade. And most of the time when we're riding in the summer for cattle, if you don't get away at four o'clock in the morning or just break of daylight, by the time the sun is up, all the cattle and everything are back into the shade again, in the timber. So you don't see them.

And quite easily you could miss them. And you may miss them for a month. And then all of a sudden they show up. So I guess that's where the Coldstream were—they figured their horses would show up in a month. While those poor things were in this building, and they'd stomped the door shut and that was it.

If you don't find an animal, you don't know whether you've missed it, whether it's dropped dead or in the brush pile or in the timber and you don't find it. Or it's got drowned in a lake or stolen, so there's lots of things you can't tell what's happened."

A RUSTLER IN RUBBER BOOTS   "I was running some cows—a cow-calf operation. And come a holiday, there was some friends of ours, out at the ranch. And along in the middle of the night we could hear a cow bawling her head off. And she didn't stop.

So early the next morning, I got on my own horse and rode out into the field. And the cow was in a field that she shouldn't have been. And I rode around and I could see where there had been a struggle. And it was very wet, and here, where the hay and grass was tramped down, I found a rubber boot that someone had ran right out of. But this cow was wanting to get out and get back across another field, so I opened the gate and let her out. And then she went over to some thick brush, and her calf came out of the brush, and crawled through the fence, and was home again.

But the rubber boot — unfortunately I knew the guy that owned it."

OUR FIREFLIES   "I have never been able to get away from the country although I've spent a lot of my time in the city. I own a little ranch not too far from Calgary, and I also own an old buckskin horse, and he and I are growing old together. But I do like to get on him in the early evening, and ride out to a spot where it hasn't failed me yet, in the summer, where the air will be full, just after dark, of fireflies. And it used to spook him to start with, but now he tries to grab them with his mouth. And I don't know whether he's ever caught any or not. But the air will have thousands of fireflies in it.

But unfortunately we got a spruce budworm in that district, and the country was sprayed for the spruce budworms, and that was the end of our fireflies."

TWENTY-THREE

The Joys of Farming

No Two Days Are the Same . . . Night Music . . . A Man from Goderich . . . The Picnics Were Great . . . Outdoors . . . Damage to the Crops . . . Eggs in the Mow . . . Snow-bound . . . The Simple Things . . . Always Helping a Neighbour . . . An Evening in May

T*he senses could have full play on a farm. People were alert to the sky and to changes in the weather, and it wasn't just a weather lookout, it was because the sky was part of the total environment and one looked at it and enjoyed it.*

Farmers don't go in for poetical descriptions of nature, but they love the land deeply, although they would look at you sternly if you said so.

NO TWO DAYS ARE THE SAME   "I certainly have a strong feeling for the old farm where I was born, lived all my life, and if I was out to make money out of farming, there'd be an auction sale called here just as quick as they could get it, because you might as well nearly forget about ever becoming a wealthy man on a small farm. I have a hundred and fifty acres here, but it's not all first-class land. It's a beautiful farm; the Saugeen River runs through it and we have a nice maple bush, a lot of cedar swamp, but I think I'd be very lucky if I have ninety acres workable, that I can farm. We keep some cattle, some sheep, and some pigs, as well as a few chickens and geese. I think one of the main attractions to the old farm is the variety.

You know, you never have the same job hardly three days hand running. A factory man works at the same machine day after day after day. Where we live . . . we'll start in the winter, well, we're cutting wood and there's all the animals to look after. If you can do it, you're drawing manure out to the fields, and the odd time, you go and visit with your neighbour and maybe have a game of cards with him on a stormy afternoon, and no two days are the same.

And of course we all get a bit itchy when it gets into March; the days are getting longer and the sun is warm and you get tramping around and wondering how soon you can be on the land. You start cleaning grain and getting prepared, and of course it's great when you can walk across the fields and feel that the land is ready to start working on it. Well even that isn't too monotonous, you sit on a tractor for some pretty long days, but it's the discing and the harrowing and the sowing and so on—it's not monotonous.

And of course there's other spring work. You've got to get the wool off the sheep and . . . well, the first thing you know, it's pretty nearly time to get the mower out and start haying. And I always say that is the heaviest job of the whole year, I don't care how you do it, whether you went back to a hay loader or pitched it by hand, or baled it or . . . I don't care how you do it, there is a lot of hard work involved in haying. I'm always glad when that job is done. I like working at it, but I mean it's tiring work.

Well you might have a day or two to do some hoeing or something like that at the potatoes, and then if you have fall wheat, it's ready to cut. And for ourselves, I guess we're old fashioned, we use a binder and a threshing machine, but again it's not monotonous; you change, you're cutting grain one day and you're stooking it the next, and then it's the oat harvest and then the threshing. Nowadays we don't have the big threshing gangs because nearly every farmer has an old thresher around. Or a lot of them have their combines, and we don't do nearly the exchanging of work, but still a neighbour is always ready to take the time off to give his next-door neighbour a hand if he needs it, and that's very common to this day in this area.

Well, then we're getting on into the fall of the year, and we start the fall ploughing. And all through the year, you may have some fencing to do, and if you're a livestock farmer, there's an enormous amount of manure to draw, and that's a job that can be done pretty nearly any season. And get the wood in if you're still a wood burner, and by that time you're pretty nearly around the time to put the cattle back into the stable again. So it's just one continuous circle, and yet it never gets monotonous.

And my wife and I we've been together here on this place thirty-four years, and you know I don't think there's been a week altogether that we've been off it in thirty-four years, and I don't think she finds it dragging, and I certainly don't, because there's something to interest you all the time. Another thing I should say to you is we have the best neighbours; at least there couldn't be better anywhere. It's a real locality through here for visiting, and there isn't such a thing as a poor neighbour in the settlement. I never heard anyone mention one yet."

NIGHT MUSIC   "I think what I remember most about noises was, on a still frosty night, there would be a great deal of crackling in the barn, like as if the rafters were going to crack, from the expansion and contraction, I guess, in the cold weather. And there would be also the sound of mosquitoes, and you'd hear those at night in the bedroom and they'd get on your nerves, and of course, we also had a lot of hawks that would take chickens, and they'd make a very loud squawking noise. And coons, coons are dreadful things on corn, and they make a crying sound, and we still hear those. They don't eat field corn; they eat garden corn, because it's sweeter, I presume. And the frogs in the spring, yes. If you had a little bit of water in a kind of swampy area, you'd hear a lot of frogs."

A MAN FROM GODERICH   "I loved the farm life from start to finish. We had a bush, a forty-acre bush on the back of our farm, and when you walked back through the hall in the morning, that's what you saw, a beautiful bush back there. We had a man come out from Goderich and he said:

'You know, if I lived here, I'd never want to die.'"

THE PICNICS WERE GREAT "The picnics were great — the social life of summer. For the picnic, you prepared several days
ahead. First thing, you had your date, so you were anticipating it
for a whole week, maybe longer; and everything again was home-
prepared, so there was baskets of sandwiches, and all the very best
of course, of the cakes. If your cake wasn't good, why you just made
another one quick. You'd store all this into the buggy so that
somebody wasn't going to put their foot on something that they
shouldn't be and spoiling some of the prepared food. We didn't
have pop or anything in those days, they'd have lemonade, fresh
lemonade, and raspberry juice, with a little vinegar in it, or maybe
black-currant juice, that'd be chilled, you'd have it in the well, in
these glass jars for a while. So then you'd wrap it up in paper, in a
brown paper bag like, so then that would keep it cold. And of
course, they played games.

   And usually they tried to get to the lake three or four times during
the summer, that was pretty much your social life; or sometimes
we'd go over to Grandpa's creek and have the party there, all the
different members of the family, and the relations, we'd picnic over
at Grandpa's. But usually the highlight of the summer was the Lake
Huron Picnic, and I can still see the buggies going all the way down
this long lane, just one person after the other."

OUTDOORS "I just love being out on the tractor, or maybe when
we were baling or combining or just cultivating; the only part was
having to come back into the house and face the mess there and to
clean up later. I think I would have been quite happy just to do that
type of work if somebody else had been here tidying the house and
getting meals for me.

   I felt when I was out on the tractor, you know, you could just be
thinking about things and looking around and enjoying nature and
the fresh air, and there was a sense of rhythm, just going up and
down the fields with the tractor, working. To me it was a real outlet.
Of course I like being outside, and this is part of it. I just enjoy
the outdoors."

DAMAGE TO THE CROPS   "We used to lay in bed at night and count the distance between the thunder and the lightning. We'd count the time, and I was never frightened of thunder and lightning, and to this very day, I try to bring my children up so they won't be frightened of thunder and lightning, because I just loved thunder and lightning storms and when the wind would howl at the door. And it was quite exciting for me during the hailstorms to watch them bouncing off the ground. They bounced just so high, they'd be hitting so hard that they bounced six feet off the ground. I enjoyed that.

But that wasn't enjoyable to the farmers, because it beat all their crops down. But, you know, I never thought of that in those days. I have only thought of it now, when I'm older, and realize that things that I enjoyed like hailstorms and the windstorms and thunder and lightning, these were doing damage to the crops, for the farmers. But I never thought about that in those days."

EGGS IN THE MOW   "Our children used to thoroughly enjoy going up the ladder and being in the mow when the hayfork came across to dump a bundle, and they'd even ride back on the fork down onto the wagon. It was rather risky, but usually the men knew that they were doing it, and it was a real thrill for the children to do that.

Another enjoyment they had was hunting for eggs in the mow. Once the fresh hay came in the hens seemed to like to burrow into a corner of the mow and make nests, and the children always enjoyed finding a nest of eggs in the mow. One way I used to try and see if the egg was fresh, I'd put it up to my ear and shake it, and if I could hear or feel a movement, that one was quickly tossed.

I think the easiest way to tell a bad egg is just drop it in a hot pan and you'll know immediately."

SNOW-BOUND   "Years ago we were snow-bound for a whole week, and you know it was quite wonderful. There's a very cosy feeling about being snow-bound as long as you've got enough food and enough heat. And we had a coal furnace in those days, and believe me the people with the coal furnaces were the lucky ones, because you always had a big pile of coal — you usually had enough for the winter. But the people with oil, they were really desperate because the snow on the roads was something like eleven feet high, and I'm not fooling — I measured some of these drifts. And everyone was trapped.

We had coal, we had no electricity, we used candles, and everyone sort of sat around and chatted, and the kids thought it was marvellous. We couldn't cook on a stove because we had no electricity, so we used to stick potatoes on the end of a stick and put it in the furnace and turn them, and we'd have roast potatoes. This and a bit of toast was about all that we could dream up to cook that was hot, but it gave you this cosy feeling that Whittier the American poet dealt with in a long and wonderful poem I've always liked called 'Snow-Bound', when the family sat around and they told stories to the kids and they made sure the animals were warm in the barn — they always cut a trail out to the barn and that sort of thing — and you had the feeling of a totally self-enclosed, happy little world."

THE SIMPLE THINGS   "Memories don't cost a lot of money, you know. We had a brook running through the front of our property, and quite often on a Sunday my aunt would pack a lunch and we'd go down and sit by the brook, and put our feet in the brook, and that would be a big day. Just to take the lunch and go down by the brook and sit and watch the little fish.

It was the simple things that made our life so worth while, and those memories are still vivid, because they are the most important things."

ALWAYS HELPING A NEIGHBOUR   "In retrospect, when I look back on the farm, I would think that the most reliable part of it was the closeness of the people in the community, how they helped each other, how we made our own good times. In the summer we had a ball team and we'd walk two miles in the evening after a day's work to play ball. In the winter we'd go five or six miles with a team and sleigh with our skates and shovels and shovel off a bit of ice on the Pipestone River and play hockey, and then come home and do chores. But we didn't do it ourselves only — the neighbours' boys and girls would be with us — kind of a fun time, a lot of hard work making the fun possible. They helped each other. Now it's dog-eat-dog, every man for himself, and more so anyway than it was then. You were always helping a neighbour."

AN EVENING IN MAY   "The best day I've had on the farm this summer, it made me filled with the most contentment. I was cleaning up under the willow trees the muss that the trees had dropped for about fifty years, and I had a bonfire all to myself. The sun was going down. It was a beautiful sunset and the birds were giving their last call in the evening. It was so calm and peaceful; even the air was still. This was the middle of May when the leaves were just coming out on the trees, and the silhouette against the background of the deep blue sky is just beautiful, and it makes country living all worth while."

TWENTY-FOUR

One Man's Story

One Man's Story . . . Getting Started

Denis McCarroll and his wife Mary live two concessions away from us, and that's about fifty miles northwest of Toronto. Denis always longed to farm; single-handedly he has made a monkey of the theory that it's impossible to start farming on your own without a large bankroll. Denis had some money, but not much, and he had this devouring ambition to be a farmer. Although he knew next to nothing about farming, he made it his business to find out. How he became a farmer and what happened to him in the process of starting to farm is what this chapter is all about.

Denis McCarroll is sturdily built, has a cheerful outlook and a fabulous grin, and his wife Mary is as self-reliant as he is and as eager to make a go of their farm. Where Denis used his head is that he never pushed his luck too far: he learned to crawl before he tried to walk. He's getting along fine now, thank you. Like many small farmers, he has a job near home for a few hours a day that brings in some money. But essentially he's a farmer, and a good one.

I take my hat off to a rare breed. The homesteader and the pioneer is still around: Denis McCarroll!

ONE MAN'S STORY — GETTING STARTED "My farm is at Beeton, Ontario, which is about fifty miles northwest of the city of Toronto. I grew up in the city, except maybe for two years that I lived up in this country when I was thirteen and fourteen years of age. I left, went back down to the city, went back to school, finished my schooling, became an offset printer for two years, and then I joined the railway. The railway was fine for eighteen years, but I always wanted to farm.

With farming it's the satisfaction of seeing things grow and knowing that you accomplished something, seeing the hay come up where you've planted it, seeing sick animals that you've treated become well. It's this gratification that has led me to the country, the country that I love—I would never go back to the city if I could help it.

Nature does have a great appeal to me. It's the birds or the trees, the animals and the forest that we have around here that we see, the different birds that you'd never see in the city. Also at night, you can go out and you can see stars; in the city you don't see the stars any more because of all the lights. But it's just being out close to nature that I think is why I actually came to the farm.

I wanted to move up around Beeton — this is where I went to school for a couple of years, and I got to be very good friends with this chap I went to school with, and when I was in the city, he'd come down on weekends and I'd come up on weekends. Finally I'd come up every weekend to be at his place and I'd keep looking for property up here, but oh, property got to be so expensive, I felt I'd never be able to afford anything.

And then in June of '71, we came along the 7th Concession and here was a sign: ten acres for sale. I went into the real-estate office, and of course it didn't turn out to be ten acres, it turned out to be twelve acres. We came back and we had a look at the house. The house was not vacant at the time. I think there were two school-teachers, a husband and wife, that were living in here, and they wanted to sell the property. It was a nice property.

The barn is one of the most important things on a farm. The barn is the most important, or the fencing is the most important part. Now there was no fencing because all the property around here had been broken up into ten-acre lots, and there were no fences at all. The only fence I guess would have been around the original hundred acres, the line fence, but as for other fences, no, there weren't any fences at all. The barn was in good shape, stone, a regular stone-banked barn that is, oh, I guess thirty-six feet wide and fifty-two feet long, it's a big enough barn, but not a real big one. That barn was built back in around the 1880s or the 1890s, solid, a very good barn, and I thought: 'Boy, this is it.'

So I made an offer to purchase, and those people, one day they wanted to sell and the next day they didn't. They'd take back a second mortgage. I think the real-estate man, it took him two to three weeks before he finally had the deal settled. And I was getting to the point that I said: 'The heck with it, if they don't want to sell it, nuts!'

And he phoned me one night at twelve o'clock and said: 'They finally made their minds up and have signed and it's yours now.'

I bought it for thirty-one thousand dollars, which is a house, a barn, twelve acres, a garage, and on the back of the garage is a workshop, and it's thirty feet long, and it's in good shape. Back in '71 where would you even get a house for thirty-one thousand dollars? Any place in the city or in the country — it was a very good bargain, and one that I could afford.

So I got my own little farm, about twelve or fifteen acres; the neighbours who have ten-acre lots don't use the backs of their property, and there's quite a few of them, so we ended up with seventy acres that we work. I rent the land from these neighbours and we don't pay too much for it because it's useless to them, they haven't got the tractors or the machinery. These people have ten-acre lots. They've come out from the city to live out in the country, and they don't use the land, and it's a shame, all these houses or these people, all they should do is have a half-acre of land around the house instead of having ten acres just going to waste.

When I worked for the railway and I wanted to come out to the farm they often asked me: 'What the devil do you know about farming? You don't know a darn thing. You were raised in the city . . . well, granted, you spent two years on the farm, but two years isn't very much.'

But I had friends in the country, and they helped me. I did lose quite a bit, yes, I learned from experience. Even though you have neighbours that will help, they can't be with you twenty-four hours a day. Reading also has an awful lot to do with how you go about it, but reading is all right to a certain extent. It's the neighbours who help an awful lot, and good luck.

And there are the disasters. It's not all apple pie and ice cream, it's disasters, and I had quite a few disasters. Three months after I bought this little farm, I went out and purchased twelve ewes or sheep and one ram. I figured we had sheep when I lived on the farm with this man when I was thirteen or fourteen. He didn't have any problem with them. I was working for the railway in the city and I thought, well, buy the sheep, just stick them out there, no problem at all, maybe bring them in when they're going to have lambs and they'll be fine in the barn. Well, it certainly didn't end out that way.

The first ewe started to come in around the twenty-first of January, and it was cold, it was twenty, twenty-five below zero, and I walked out in the barnyard on the Sunday morning, and here was this ewe with baby lambs, twins. Where did she have them? In the middle of the barnyard during the night, and they were frozen, frozen dead. Sheep are the stupidest animals you can ever want to meet. They had a place they could have gone in to get out of this cold, but they wouldn't: they had their lambs in the middle of the barnyard. There was the barn they could have gone into that was fairly warm, out of this cold, but no, they wouldn't: they'd have them in the middle of the barnyard. Three ewes had lambs, five lambs altogether; five lambs froze to death in the barnyard before I got them into the barn to sort of look after them better because I didn't figure they'd be having lambs until later on in March or April. The cold weather doesn't bother the older ewes at all, and actually the lambs, if they're out of the cold at all, the first couple of days, it doesn't bother them, and then when they get out, they're fine. So I'd lost the first five lambs and I thought:

'Boy, isn't this a beautiful start for the first year I've been out here. There goes five lambs right down the drain.'

Out of that first year for the lambs, I think I had ten out of approximately twenty or twenty-one lambs. I had ten lambs for about a month, and then one day I came home and I walked into the barn, the ewes and the lambs were still in the barn. I have a watering trough in there for the lambs to water and the sheep to drink. One lamb is in the watering trough, he is dead, drowned. I guess he jumped in and didn't have enough sense to get back out. However, I thought: 'That's not bad, I still got nine left.'

The next day I came back home from work, there were two of them that had died. I never did just find out what, I think it might have been the white-muscle disease. So now I guess I was down to about six lambs out of twenty or twenty-one, which isn't too good at all. But these six, finally they did live.

It was no killing on the market when I sent them to the stockyard ... thirty-nine and a half cents a pound. And then you go into the store and you pay a dollar forty-five or a dollar seventy-nine for lamb. I don't know where the justice is.

The sheep survived that winter; they survived right up until this year, and last fall the dogs got into them, and they killed one and scared the rest of them. We had the vet come out and look at the ewe the next day, but he said there wasn't much sense in getting her fixed, sewing her up, she was mutilated so badly; probably she wouldn't have any lambs again, and probably with the rest of the ewes, I'd have problems next spring in lambing. And sure enough, out of, I guess, eleven ewes, we only had eleven lambs, and out of the eleven lambs, ten died. So I was left with one lamb, I think ten ewes, and lots of worries. And I said: 'I'm not going to have any more worries with the sheep.'

And all the sheep and the one lamb went to market. I figured that year for the one lamb that I sent to market — it was a nice fifty-pound lamb and I got seventy-two cents a pound — I figured there were ten lambs that died; if all ten had weighed fifty or sixty pounds apiece, we would have got seventy or seventy-two cents, there's three hundred and sixty dollars just on lambs alone that we lost in the one year.

I didn't have any cows until, oh, I guess it was 1973. My neighbour up the road had been kicked by a horse, ended up in the hospital for about two months; and while he was in the hospital—

it was in November he went into the hospital—he had his cattle pastured over about three miles from home. He's got eighty or ninety head of cattle. He has thirty or so head of horses, Clydesdales, so he doesn't keep the cattle at home. He pastures them at one place in the summer and at a different farm in the winter. Now he was in the hospital, the neighbours all got together and decided we had better move the cattle from the summer farm over to the barn that he keeps them in in the winter, where there's hay for them.

So we moved them one cold December Saturday afternoon. It was five miles I guess from one place to the other. We just drove them down the road like they did in the old days, except we had cars, we didn't use horses. We were a little more advanced then . . . I don't know whether we should say advanced or what, in those days when they had horses, it didn't cost them anything to run, but it does cars. But anyway we drove them down with cars and walked beside them, and there was one little calf there that had been born, oh, I guess a month or six weeks before we started to move them, and by the time they got down to the barn where we were going to keep them for the wintertime, it was just about out on its feet.

So I took and brought that calf home and looked after it, and the neighbour said when he came out of the hospital, he said: 'Well, you might just as well keep him: you've raised him.' That was my first calf. She's a good calf, or was a good calf until the following spring she decided she wanted to go over with the neighbour's cows, so she went over with the neighbour's cows and stayed there all summer. I picked her up in the fall and the neighbour said: 'Well, I've got a calf here that was born and only has one eye, you might as well take that with your own.'

So I got that, and there were two calves that I had now and then the next . . . I got married then . . . I don't know whether it was because I had so many cows or because I was lonesome that I wanted a wife, but anyway I finally married this girl that I had known for quite a few years.

She loved the farm. She came out before she was married a couple of times and just loved it out here, and she knew that she was going to marry me long before I knew I was going to marry her, but she said she knew it, and eventually I did, I guess. . . . I know I did.

So now I have two calves, one is about a year old and the other one is four or five months old, I guess they're called a yearling now, just about a yearling, and the calf, but I always call her a calf. We call her Red and the other one, we call her Henrietta, and we still refer to them as calves. They're two and three years old now, but they're still calves to us.

Later on, it wasn't until the following spring . . . I'm trying to think of what happened that winter . . . anything happen in that winter, dear? When we were first married . . . Oh yes, yes, yes.

With our sheep we had a ram, the original ram came with the twelve ewes. After a year or so I thought: 'Well, I'll get rid of him and get a new ram.'

A neighbour across the road had a young ram and they called him Rammy — he was a pet. They got him I guess when he was only a couple of weeks old and they looked after that little ram and he grew up to be a big ram and when he was small they used to have him in the house all the time. They'd even let him get up on the bed with them, and he loved to be petted and to have his head rubbed and to have a fuss made over him. If you didn't do this, if you ignored him, you were liable to end up with a shot in the rear end when you weren't looking.

Mary, my wife, went out to the barn this afternoon to check on the sheep, to make sure that everything was all right; some of them had lambs; some others were coming in. Mary got down to the barn and she gave the ram a little tap on the head and said: 'Hello and good-bye and get out of the way.' That sort of thing.

She opened the barn door and as she did that she walked in, and one of the lambs got out. So she kept the ewe in and closed the door and went out and tried to get hold of the lamb that got out through the door on her. As she bent over, bent over and picked the lamb by his foot, that ram came up behind her and let her have it right in the rear end, and knocked her head over heels right into the manure pile.

It was funny. When I came home she told me this, I laughed and thought it was a big joke, but it turned out that the ram did break her tail bone. She wasn't laid up, but it was awfully sore, and she hobbled around for a month at least — it still bothers her now. From then on we took extra precautions against this ram. We always went out with a stick in our hand and gave him a bat on the head. A bat on the head to a ram, you might just as well bat the side of a brick building. We used to hit him across the nose with a stick and that would keep him a fair piece. But he was a sneaky . . . he'd come up beside you and if you did pet him and rub his head, he was fine, but if you didn't or you didn't bother with him, then he let you have it. He'd give you a butt, on the side of the leg or the side, just to get your attention. And you'd come hobbling back then with a bruise on your hip or on your thigh.

I've lost my temper at that ram so often, because he nailed me one day when I wasn't expecting it, and I wasn't in the greatest of humour when he hit me. I had an old cane that I found around here some place, and I used to use it, and I gave him a wallop over the nose with that. I broke the cane, which didn't make me too happy. I picked up the pitchfork . . . I was mad, but I was still smart enough not to stick him with the pitchfork. So I hit him with the end of the pitchfork, broke the pitchfork, which made me even madder, so I got ahold of him and I hoofed him down in the snow and I gave him a couple of clouts across the nose with my fist. But that didn't even faze on him. He'd come back and he'd still do the same thing. The fate of that poor ram, I guess he ended up on somebody's table. He went down to the market and he ended up, I guess, as lamb chops or mutton or something else on somebody's plate some place.

I worked for the railway up until 1975, April, when I finally quit. I should say I was still getting up at six o'clock, a quarter to six. The first six months when I was up here, when I moved up here in '71, I was working in the Union Station, and I'd commute right down to Union Station, leave here at a quarter after seven and be down there at Union Station by eight-thirty. I used to leave Union Station at a quarter to five and get home here at six-thirty at night, do the chores, make my dinner, and then most nights go back out to the barn. I put up with that for six months.

Since I've left the railway, I don't get up near as early. As I said, when I was with the railway, I would get up at a quarter to six, six o'clock. Now we get up at eight o'clock, a quarter after eight. Granted, we will work later at night, but it's easier to work at night, especially in the summertime, bringing in hay, than working out in that sun when it's eighty or eighty-five degrees, it's hot, dry, and the hay is dusty. It's no sense in going out in the middle of the day killing yourself. A lot of farmers do. They say they have to. This year, between my neighbour and myself, we brought in pretty close to four thousand bales of hay.

We didn't work in the daytime. He has another job outside, so we would work at night. On my own place here, when he was at work, I'd bring my own hay in. In the real hot weather, my wife would help me, she'd drive the tractor. We would get up early — we'd get up at six, work from six until ten, and then have our breakfast and do chores and come in the house and have a sleep during the day, and then go back out at six o'clock and work when it was cooler, in the cool of the evening, until ten, ten-thirty at night, which was an awful lot better.

And it has come out all right. We're better, we're healthier, and we haven't minded the heat as we would have; even if we were in the city we would have been complaining about the heat. But now we don't do anything in the daytime.

So as I say, we will get up around eight or eight-fifteen, and we'll work through till . . . oh, seven or eight o'clock at night now that the hay is finished. We'll do the chores around six-thirty, a quarter to seven. At night there's about an hour's chores to do; milk the cows, feed the pigs — get all the water pails filled for the next morning for the pigs. But that is the way that we have found it. We have this routine where we get up at eight or eight-fifteen.

In the evenings, we'll go up and visit the neighbours, we'll stay at home, watch television. I like to read mystery books, police stories. I always like detectives and westerns. This is what I'll do with my evenings when we're finished all the work.

Now we have a good relaxed life; farming is the greatest, and never, I hope, will we ever go back to the city."

TWENTY-FIVE

Just Fond Memories

I am inordinately fond of farm auctions, and I go to as many as I can and come home with the back of the car overflowing with what my eldest son refers to witheringly as "that junk". Actually, some of it is very useful — the tools he used to clean out the old shed were bought at auctions.

Every farm auction means that someone's giving up farming. A widow may be going to the old-folks' home. Or a family may have had enough of farming, or have found that it just can't get along farming any longer. More often, it means that a farmer is retiring and buying a house in a nearby community, where he and his wife may well grow the best flowers in town.

I said in the introduction to this book that I am ready to argue that the family farm is not finished. I do agree, however, that the great days are over. I greatly hope that the memories and stories that have been documented here will stand as a record of a long and most honourable era that, to a great extent, made Canada the vigorous nation it is and Canadians the distinctive people they are. Much of the character of Canada comes right out of our farm past.

In a sense, then, I suppose I should end by saying hail and farewell to that fine Canadian institution: The Family Farm!

THE OLD FARMHOUSE "When the old farmhouse was torn down it was a very sad thing to my grandmother, who was my mother's mother. And we took her out one time for supper, this was to the farm, and this was in the new house which was a beautiful, big house. And she could hardly look out the window to see where her farmhouse had stood.

And to me the memories in that farmhouse are just fantastic. I can remember my grandfather used to have to eat his limburger cheese downstairs in the basement, because my grandmother wouldn't leave it upstairs. And I used to go down with him and have some. And to this very day, the smell of limburger cheese brings back memories of this farmhouse."

A CERTAIN AMOUNT OF SADNESS "We suspected that, living in Granby and being away from the farm, Grandfather would miss it. We had a very huge garden and everything, but I think once a farmer, always a farmer. I mean, he just loved it, and to this day he talks about it. I know he wants to be buried in that part of the country, because it has great meaning to him, and he has a great many friends there, and he talks about them all the time, and he tries to visit once a year and enjoys seeing his old friends. Unfortunately, they are all aging at the moment. We all do, I guess, but there is a certain amount of sadness for him when he hears that certain farms are being sold or certain friends of his are no longer farming or the boys did not continue. That bothers him, and I think it must go through his mind at times that none of the five boys he had stayed on farms or decided to buy. But I haven't given up yet. I'm thirty-three and I have another twenty years to decide whether I can still get into farming, and I may end up on a farm in British Columbia some day, so there may be another chance for a Pozer ending up on a farm . . . but in western Canada, not in Quebec."

BUYING AN ELEVATOR "Sometimes the elevators are not pulled down. For instance some of the larger farmers have purchased these older smaller elevators and hauled them to their farms and use them for storage. We have quite a few Hutterites in Manitoba, and they have purchased a number of elevators that have been closed out, hauled them to the Hutterite colonies, and used them for grain storage facilities."

A MORE ACTIVE PART   "I'd be happy to live on a farm, but I don't think I'd just want to hold the role that my mother did. I'd want to be more active on the farm itself. I feel I've grown up too ignorant of the farm and the things that happen, and I'd like to learn more about them. I mean planting the crops; there's so many technical things — setting up a planter, and how do you set to have a certain number of seeds for each crop. Everything is different. And how do you get the sprays ready? You have a spray concentrate, and how much water do you put in with it? And when is the best time to spray? When is the best time to harvest? There's so many little details that I don't know. Maybe on some farms women do have a more active part than my mother. More women should have a more active part, and I know if I had the opportunity of living on a farm, then I certainly would like to go to school to learn more about it."

IN JULIE'S HARBOUR   Like every other native Newfoundlander, I go back to Newfoundland regularly, and one summer day when I was enjoying myself there, Joe Simms and his boy hove by in their punt.
    I said: 'Is ya hungry, Joe?'
    'Yes, bye, we is.'
    'Wouldja like a bit of fried baloney and a cup of tea?'
    'Yes, my son, dat would be foine.'
    Joe was sixty or so and a great storyteller. After the fried baloney, he said: 'Didja ever know what happened to dis place?'
    'Tell me,' I said.
    'Well, sir, way back before I wuz barned, fellers come in dis cove an settled down to farmin' and fishin' . . .'
    And Joe took his time and, with that stutter that he had, told me about the people of Julie's Harbour on Notre Dame Bay, Newfoundland. This is what happened:

Almost two centuries ago a few families settled in this beautiful cove and did a bit of farming and a bit of fishing, and didn't get along too badly at all. They cleared the surrounding forest and built log cabins, and they planted the meadows and farmed enough to feed themselves. But they were terribly isolated—from October until April they were completely cut off. But they survived. They survived until about the 1920s when diphtheria swept through the little colony. Almost all the children died. The tombstones in the grove where they were buried give their ages . . . eleven months . . . two years . . . four years.

However, there were two little girls who somehow or other escaped the contagion, and they both grew up and became lovely and lively. Then when they were just sixteen they went off one day for an outing and, at a nearby pond, they found an old punt and got in it to cross the pond—and the punt sank and they were drowned. At first they weren't missed, but then, gradually, people became panicky and a search was started. A mile from Julie's Harbour their bodies were found in what is now known as 'Deadman's Pond'.

Their bodies were brought home, and the nearest priest was summoned. He well knew the tragic history of the community and he said, 'I will not bury these children in this accursed place!' The bodies were taken out along the coastline and interred in a secret place that no one knows to this day. And the community was abandoned by the ten families who had lived there, and it is abandoned today. It was 1933 that the people who had been farming and fishing at Julie's Harbour left it.

But there's a postscript to the story. Years later, two fishermen set up a tent there one summer, and then they put up a shelter, and then the next year a shack, because the fishing was good in the cove. One night at midnight they were playing cribbage, and one man said to the other, 'D'ye hear what I hear?' And his friend said, 'I do indeed!' From the grove where the children were buried there came a wailing noise and a sound like 'Help!'

They were brave men and they went outside into the solid dark. There seemed to be an apparition floating above the cemetery, just a loose mass, a greenish glow, of the colour you'd call 'Cat's Eyes'.

The sobbing and the wailing continued, and the apparition moved back and forth over the graves.

The men were terrified, but one of them said, 'And who might ye be? And what is it that ye seek from us?'

And the other man added, 'Either ye states yer case, or ye gets da hell out!' There was no answer except the crying and the word, 'Help!'

The two men were horrified, and before dawn came they had packed up and left. They sold the shack and it was removed.

And there is no more farming or fishing there at all in Julie's Harbour.''

WHAT AM I MISSING? "I was happy growing up on the farm until I got to school and started learning about all the other places. And then I began to get this awful sort of feeling of 'what am I missing?' And that is accentuated up in the Peace River country because you are so far away up there; there's a whole day's travel to get out. And so, yes, I was really happy until I got this feeling of 'I must know what's beyond.' And now that I know what's beyond, I would be happy up there again, in the Peace River.''

TOSSED OUT OF FARMING "One day I decided I would go to be with my father, who was working with the horses. I was never supposed to be in the farmyard or near the animals. So I went away out around the field and came in behind my father. The cattle were in the farmyard. They had never seen me, and they just didn't know who I was and what I was. I would be about seven years old. And this cow picked me up in its horns and tossed me into the yard. I don't remember whether I was hurt or not. I know I was scared, and my father hadn't seen me come, and when he heard me yell, he turned around, picked me up, of course, carried me to the house. Now, whether they were annoyed or not, I don't know. But it scared me, and that was one good lesson. I never went back to the farmyard.

I married a newspaper man and I live in a small town; I'm very happy here. I just love the small town. I like to go to the city for a

day, but I want to get home again. But when we go out driving in
the country and it comes dark, I want to get right back to the small
town. And so many times, I said to my husband:

'How thankful I am I never married a farmer.'"

YOU WISH YOU WERE BACK "I remember this one particular
day. I think I was seventeen and we were harvesting at my sister's,
who was just a mile away, and this one day I shovelled fifteen
hundred bushels of wheat, and I'm telling you I was dragging
when ten o'clock at night came. At the time you do think this is
hard, why should you have to do this, you know, and things could
be easier, and you think of the bright lights of the city and all this
stuff—that's the place to be. But as you grow older and you do get
to the city, you do wish you were back on the farm.

I think you have a slower life; things aren't so hectic. Sure, you
work hard, and there's more to do on the farm. Sure, you don't
have as many places to go, but I think people on the farm are more
satisfied with going to a show maybe once a week, curling in the
winter; and now they can skidoo. The air is fresher; you've got a
place to plant a garden.

That day that I worked so hard, I thought, I'll never marry a
farmer boy if this is what you have to do, I'll marry a city guy —
and that's what I did.

But I love the farm. I go back now that I'm older and smarter."

SOMETHING A LITTLE BETTER "I was never encouraged to
stay on the farm. I was never encouraged to be a farmer. This in
part may have been a result of growing up on sort of a co-operative
farm where the farm wouldn't naturally have passed on to myself.
But my parents always encouraged me to go to university and to
get an education and to do something else, possibly related to
agriculture, and consequently I took a degree in agriculture. But
they didn't have the strong Protestant work ethic that would see
me take over where they were. They wanted, I think, something a
little better for me.

And farm prices weren't as good then as they are now. Perhaps
if they had been I would have got more encouragement to go into
farming. But they didn't encourage it."

THE GOOD OLD CHEESE FACTORY "Years ago, before the McKinley tariff was put on barley, the farmers used to grow barley for a dollar a bushel and send it to the States. Well, the McKinley tariff was put on it and the farmers had to do something else, so they went into more cows, and then the cheese factories sprung up all over the province, and there were maybe three or four in each township. Here in Prince Edward County, there must have been twenty-five or thirty, because there were at least three or four in our township.

That was cheddar cheese, it was all cheddar cheese. My good old uncle, a cheesemaker, he'd say: 'The good old cheese factories that paid off every debt on the farm'. Now there's only two or three cheese factories left now, possibly not that — a good bit of them has closed up and are idle."

SWEET MEMORIES "In the spring of the year, we always tapped and made maple syrup, which my husband had done for years, and sold syrup all over the country. That was a great experience, gathering the sap and boiling it down in the big evaporators and keeping the fires going.

When we left the farm I brought some with us and I only finished the last pint of it . . . saved it for years because I wouldn't use it. I think it was about two years ago I finished it, but it was getting a little bit sugary. That maple syrup was about twenty years old."

THE CENTRAL MEETING PLACE "The closing of the rural schools has destroyed our community life. There's no central meeting place for the district. Now it's all . . . it's destroyed. It's about eight years since they started closing out the small schools. It will never come back—it's gone.

I think it's a shame. I know we have to give way to progress, but the little children always went to Grade One, and the little red schoolhouse was their second home, and they thought the world of it. Now they have to come in on buses. They're in most of the day and when they get home they're tired, and to me it seems that there should have been some other way to phase it out. It really has meant a great deal to us. Everything went on — you had your

Christmas concerts, you had everything — in the schoolhouse. Now they all have them in town, and as a result they don't even have a Christmas concert. These were the things that mean so much to the parents, to see their little youngsters get up and give a recitation or do a little dance. You were pretty proud of them, but that's all gone.

Actually, the same thing is happening to our rural churches in many areas, and this is having the same effect exactly as with the closing of the smaller schools. The community life is more or less lost."

A CITY AND A COUNTRY KID   "Now when I first come to Winnipeg I was a real greenhorn, I'll tell you. But fortunately I had a few friends in here, and they sure helped me adjust, so it didn't take me too long to adjust to the city life after growing up on the farm. I think when I was younger there was a big difference between city and country kids. The city kids knew more than the country kids did. But now I think the circle has completely changed. I really don't see there is any difference between a city and a country kid. They all do the same thing, have their cars, they go to shows, they skidoo, they go to parties, they have money — and possibly a lot of them have more money than city kids do right now."

A VERY WEALTHY MAN   "I think one of the saddest things I experienced in my auctioneering up to the present was when a very wealthy man had purchased three farms in the Albion Township area, and had assured this elderly couple, when he purchased their farm, that they could live there as long as he was owner. And of course they thought, well, it would be the same as theirs, a lifetime. They thought this was great, we'll sell him this.

Then he combined these three farms and then sold them at a good price, and they had no alternative but to get out. And this had bothered them to the point where she had got a little bit mentally disturbed.

The party that lived on the other farm was an elderly couple too, and he had taken their stove out the night before and left them in the cold that night with no heat, so it would be ready for sale in the morning.

And before the sale came up the first lady, who was very upset to start with, she had lost her husband, and he said to her: 'Well, the best thing you can do is to move the stuff into the farm where the sale will be on.' And as I was selling her property, she followed me around and was crying the whole time, about her merchandise being sold, you know. I felt very sorry for her. And this was a bit of a sad thing."

WHY FARM?   "With the older way of farming with the teams, there was less rushing, hurrying, and we weren't trying to do as much; we were getting along with a smaller acreage and we could get along with fewer cows and make a living much easier, I think, than we can today. And if I was young today, I doubt very much whether I'd be looking to a farm or not. It's such a change from the old way of doing things that it's just almost unthinkable for me for to carry on the way it's going now.

It seems to me nowadays that there's getting to be so much money required to run a farm, keep it up with implements and stock and all such things like that, and the value of your land, that you're getting so much money invested before you can farm, then why farm? You might just as well invest that and live on the proceeds of the money rather than farm. So this is the way I look at it now."

SOIL MINERS   "Farming has changed. You've got a few great big farms now. You know they're farming ... well, I don't say they're farming, they're soil miners. They roar in with huge machines and rip up acres and throw down acres of fertilizer and weed killers and plants and up they sprout, and they tear them all off again. Haven't got the old farmer's feel for the land, you know, the land for their sons. They're developing the land ... they're using the land right now to pay off the huge loans they probably got from the bank or somebody else. And it's a different way of doing business.

It wasn't farm 'business' when you had time to talk to your cows and you had a mixture of things. If the pea crop was bad, well, you had corn; if the corn was bad, you had pigs. If the pigs were bad, you had chickens; if the chickens were bad . . . well, you don't put all your eggs in one basket. But now it's mass, large crops, large machinery, huge acreages, all just in and out, bang, bang, and it's roar, roar, rush, rush, don't think of anything but get it in, get it out, get the money in, get the money out back to your bank, pay off your loan to get more money to borrow more money to . . . you know it's a big rat race.

And you've got all these people coming in diluting the old farms, the old alliances, the honest web of families and friends and neighbours and self-help. And this is being diluted all the time, and not only by people coming in who are living here just for the weekend. You know, they can sell their house in Toronto and take half the money and buy a place in Prince Edward County, live here, and some of them commute back and forth until they can afford to find something here and set up an antique business or something."

DISAPPEARING FENCES "The stone fences, or stone bottoms or stone corners as we used to call them, are gradually disappearing. In those days a ten- to fifteen-acre field was a large field; now farmers are getting bulldozers in and trucks and either burying these stone fences or loading them and disposing of them so that they will have larger fields for their bigger machinery. That seems to be the trend, and I think it will continue too, that the fences will disappear as we go to different types of farming, where we have housed livestock, where they're not pastured. Bigger fields to work in—eventually these fences are going to disappear."

THE FARM ALL RUNS IDLE "The farm that I was born and raised on, there's not one furrow ploughed in the last ten years on it. There hasn't been one bushel of grain growed on it, there hasn't been one bag of potaties grown on it, I don't think, nobody bothers with them. They have a house on it; they drive to work, the farm all runs idle. When my dad lived on it and us boys lived on it, we went out and we dug the potaties with a fork. We'd have a cellar full of potaties; when the fall come, we teamed out the potaties; we paid the threshing; we paid the taxes."

WONDERFUL MEMORIES "I still call the farmhouse my home. Not so much now because the grandparents are gone from there, but up until just a few years ago, I really said that was still my home.

The road was cut off in the wintertime, you know, it just didn't get ploughed by horses. You didn't even get it ploughed at all, and you were really isolated in the wintertime. Being so young, I didn't realize the seriousness of being isolated, because if you ran out of something, you just didn't get it until you were able to get the horse through to get to town.

So therefore my memories are mostly good, and I wish that my children could have these wonderful, wonderful memories, out playing in the hayloft, in the garden, and could have come to love the woods. But in my fondest memories are these beautiful fields of golden wheat, just floating in the breeze. Something that I'll be able to see forever in my mind."

THE DAY OF THE SMALL FARMER "I don't know what will happen to the place when we get too old to run it. I still hope Walt will take it over, but he's been a trucker ever since he was able to crawl into one, and makes long hauls out to the West, hauling cattle. I'd have no trouble selling the farm; I could sell it next week if I wanted to, but I'll bet it goes to a city man instead of to a farmer. At least the city man could pay more for it. At one time, with the river running through here, this would be called one of the poorer farms, too much waste land. But now it's possibly worth more than a really productive farm. A farm like mine today, it would be no trouble at all getting anywheres from eighty to a hundred thousand dollars for it. And there's the problem, for any young chap to buy a farm, and try to make a living out of it farming, he'd die of a broken heart before he'd ever get it paid for.

Now that's a tragedy, because there's several of the old farms that have been sold, and, well, they're really not being worked too much. Schoolteachers, professors, somebody comes up and they buy a farm — well it's just a recreation place really — and while some of them will rent the land out, others aren't very particular about doing it. It's private property and some of them are going back, weeds and stuff gets growing up. I really believe that the day of the small farmer is pretty nearly over, that is, the fellow that will still stick right on the farm and make his living entirely off the farm. I think it's too bad when I see so many of the neighbours have to take a job in a factory so that they can meet the payments. It's really not right when a property is worth a lot of money that you can't make a living off of it."

JUST FOND MEMORIES   "But when it comes right down to the nitty-gritty I think a lot of people, when they get right back to the farm, they miss the pavement, they miss the bar, they miss whatever. They can't really appreciate the natural things that you can get a lot of enjoyment out of. You've really got to have a terrific love of nature and the outdoors and just the natural things to be really happy there. And I think a lot of people, when they were kids it was great, but now they're grown up, and even if they did get back, maybe it wouldn't be the same. Maybe they're just having fond memories of something that's entirely gone."

The Storytellers

This is a list, chapter by chapter, of the names of the people who contributed to this book. In almost every case, the location mentioned after the person's name is where the story took place, or where the person telling the story grew up, or lived at the time, and is not necessarily where the storyteller lives now.

I want to say a word about accuracy. As I worked I tried to keep a careful record of the spelling of people's names and of the locations they gave, but occasionally in the rush of interviewing I overlooked this. Also, some few people did not want their names used. My greatest difficulty of all, and it was a devilish one, was trying to sort out people's voices on tape when I interviewed a group of people rather than just one person; people's voices on tape can sound rather similar. What I'm saying is that a handful of stories may be wrongly attributed and I apologize to those involved. I must point out, though, that almost all the identifications are accurate. Putting this list together was the only onerous part of an otherwise engrossing task. *ALLAN ANDERSON*

Chapter 1: All Kinds of Farms, All Kinds of People

The New House: Nancy Miller, Dixonville, Peace River country, Alta.
The Barking Dog: Frank O'Brien, Saint John, N.B.
On the Buzz Saw: Brian Hoole, Saanich area, Vancouver Island, B.C.
A True Rancher: John Cross, near Nanton, Alta.
I Miss the Farm Very Much: Joan Finnegan, Shawville, Que.
A Bunch of Hicks: Mike Dolinski, Selkirk, Man.
Born in a Sod House: Saskatchewan farm
High in the Pecking Order: Peggy Holmes, 140 miles N.E. of Edmonton
Politics and Ploughing: Elgin Thompson, Brucefield, Ont.
An Evening's Fun: Marjorie Jean Pentland, near Goderich, Ont.
Last of the Big Spenders: K. K. Dawson, Auburn, Ont.
Who's in Charge Here?: Marjorie Jean Pentland, near Goderich, Ont.
Respect for Mother Nature: Jim Dawson, Lougheed, Alta.
An Awful Character: Ron Oswald, Chesley, Ont.
Stone Houses: Ron Oswald, Chesley, Ont.
Just a Two-Holer: Peggy Sproul, Viscount, Sask.
Full of Fun: John Cross, near Nanton, Alta.
Grandfather's Kettle: David Meyers, near Quebec City, Que.
If It's Not One Thing, It's Another: Dan Ness, Lougheed, Alta.
Moonlighting: Hugh Hill, Ben Miller, Ont.
I Hated the Farm: Alice Dunlap, Harris, Sask.
Deep in the Hay: Ron Sera, near Lethbridge, Alta.
Dousing: K. K. Dawson, Auburn, Ont.
Always Look for the Best: John Cairns, Ameliasburg, Ont.
A Little Dip: Gordon Kirkpatrick, Ridgeville, Man.
A Wonderful Feeling: Saskatchewan farm
Very Efficient with Her Work: Ruth Busby, farm near Regina
A Lesson: Dorothy Hett, Hidden Valley Road, near Kitchener, Ont.

Chapter 2: The Weather Controlled Our Lives

The Weather Controlled Our Lives: Nancy Miller, Dixonville, Alta.
No Salvaging of Anything: Ernie Severn, Hockley, Ont.
Better Luck Next Time: Bill Chykaliuk, Derwent, Alta.
There's a Flood Coming: Beth Kirkpartrick, Manitoba farm.
Ice on Their Noses: Jack MacDonald, Virden, Man.
Hail in the Butter: Peggy Sproul, Viscount, Sask.
A Really Dumb Thing To Do: Mike Dolinski, Selkirk, Man.
The Joys of Farming: Elmer Arnt, near Larivière, Man.
An Act of God: Ethel Taylor, N.W. of Drumheller, Alta.
Gumbo: Fred Fetterman, Starbuck, Man.
Darkness at Noon: Lloyd Nowlin, Porcupine Hills area, Alta.
A Visit from a Tornado: Bertha Rose, Larivière, Man.
Sophisticated City Fellows: Marion R. Smith, Rainier, Alta.

Chapter 3: Schools and Schoolteachers

A Very Good School: Olga Brygadyr, Primrose, Alta.
The Schoolroom: Lillian Knupp, High River, Alta.

Boarding the Teacher: Eleanor Wagner, near Regina, Sask.
Around the Bear: Nancy Miller, Dixonville, Peace River country, Alta.
On the School Bus: Cheryl Snider, Tisdale, Sask.
Shells in the Stove: Marion R. Smith, Rainier, Alta.
Christmas at School: Mary Almond, Belmont, Ont.
The Fence Post: western Manitoba farm
Chester: Ethel Taylor, Drumheller, Alta.
The Schoolwork Slipped: Mike Dolinski, Selkirk, Man.
Like One Big Family: Tottenham, Ont.
Hats Off to the Teacher: Gord McClung, Neepawa, Man.
The Inspector Calls: Eleanor Wagner, near Regina, Sask.
The Last of the Little Red Schoolhouse: Cindy Cairns, Ameliasburg, Ont.
Quite a Nice Girl: Steve Churchill, Chegoggin, N.S.

Chapter 4: The Kitchen
The Stove Was the Centre of the Kitchen: Mary Mair, Chesley, Ont.
Wood for a Winter's Burning: Andrew Mair, Chesley, Ont.
Chimney Fires: Andrew Mair, Chesley, Ont.
Our Smokehouse: Dorothy Hett, Hidden Valley Road, near Kitchener, Ont.
Cooking on a Wood Stove: Mary Mair, Chesley, Ont.
Very Good Food: Dorothy Hett, Hidden Valley Road, near Kitchener, Ont.
The Spirit of All the Home-Cooked Things: Marie Henderson, Unionville, Ont.
Rabbits All Over: Frank Gilbert Roe, homestead near Red Deer, Alta.
Too Fond of the Cream: Elizabeth Davis, Tottenham, Ont.
Canning Sausage: Elmer Arnt, Larivière, Man.
Well-Cooled: Bernardine Kinney, near Goderich, Ont.
Gingerbread with Whipped Cream: Bernardine Kinney, near Goderich, Ont.
Moose in a Barrel: Nancy Miller, Dixonville, Peace River country, Alta.
The Mountie's Dinner: Eleanor Wagner, near Regina, Sask.
The Native Fruit: Jane Fetterman, Grosse Isle, Man.

Chapter 5: To Every Thing There is a Season
Such a Variety of Things: Marie Henderson, Unionville, Ont.
A Harvest Excursion: Howard Dulmage, Cherry Valley, Ont.
The Back End of the Train: Allan Best, Stanley, N.B.
The Harvest Crew: Gordon Kirkpatrick, Ridgeville, Man.
Stooks: Gordon Kirkpatrick, Ridgeville, Man.
Harvest-Time Refreshments: Donalda McClure, Chesley, Ont.
The Lindsay Syrup: Ida Jean Lindsay, Caledon, Ont.
A Real Winter Storm: K. K. Dawson, Auburn, Ont.
Hunting the Mud: Lester Wallace, Alberton, P.E.I.
Beautiful Apples: Steve Churchill, Chegoggin, N.S.
In the Fishing Season: Steve Churchill, N.S.
Learning to Plough: Marie Henderson, Unionville, Ont.
A Showing on the Field: Willie Clark, Dunvegan, Ont.
Priming Tobacco: Les Churchill, Delhi, Ont.

Hand-Knit Drawers: Allan Best, Stanley, N.B.
Ukrainian New Year: Mike Dolinski, Selkirk, Man.
Auctions: Graeme Gibson, near Alliston, Ont.
The Day the Mountie Came: Eleanor Wagner, near Regina
The Manure Spreader: Tommy Douglas story about Chaplin area, Sask.
Every Vote Counts: Bill Oswald, Chesley, Ont.
Berry-Picking Expeditions: Peggy Sproul, Viscount, Sask.
Christmas Shopping by Mail: Nancy Miller, Dixonville, Peace River country, Alta.
The Christmas Parcel: Peggy Holmes, 140 miles N.E. of Edmonton
An All-Night Session: Lou Hartsook, Richlea, Sask.
A Toboggan for Christmas: Jim Dawson, Lougheed, Alta.

Chapter 15: Coo-Boss!
Cows Have Personalities: Grace Moses Copeland, near Sidney, B.C.
The Chihuahua Cow-Chaser: Ron Sera, near Lethbridge, Alta.
Such Good Friends: K. K. Dawson, Auburn, Ont.
Little Squirt: Harry Walsh, Old Kildonan, Man.
A Wonderful Memory: High River, Alta.
Cattle on the Ice: Andrew Mair, Chesley, Ont.
Cow and Calf: Florence Watkins-Jones, Lucky Lake, Sask.
Cows Are Smarter: Steve Churchill, Chegoggin, N.S.
Robbing the Dead: Peggy Holmes, 140 miles N.E. of Edmonton
Guernseys Are Lovely Cows: Steve Churchill, Chegoggin, N.S.
Riding the Cow: Eileen Burgess, near Windsor, N.S.
The Herd Boy: High River, Alta.
We Refused Twenty Thousand Dollars: Steve Churchill, Chegoggin, N.S.
A Working Dog: Mary Almond, Belmont, Ont.
Blue Cow, Chocolate Dessert: Helen Stanbury, near Saskatoon, Sask.
Your Turn to Name the Calf: Bernardine Kinney, near Goderich, Ont.
Coo-Boss!: Olive May Blake, Ashfield Township, Ont.
Bringing in the Cows, City-Style: Marjorie Jean Pentland, Goderich, Ont.
Friends: Beatrice Butcher, Marshfield, P.E.I.
Never Trust a Bull: Richie Davis, Tottenham, Ont.
Tony the Bull: Jack MacDonald, Virden, Man.

Chapter 16: If It Wasn't for the Neighbours . . .
Neighbours: farm in Glengarry County, Ont.
The Colour of the Horses: homestead near Maple Creek, Sask.
Help at a Fire: Bernardine Kinney, near Goderich, Ont.
Too Heavy for Six Men: Russ Stone, Beaver, Man.
Sharing Food: Fred Hamilton, Baldur, Man.
I Had to Keep Going: Olga Brygadyr, Primrose, Alta.
Two Inches of Land: K. K. Dawson, Auburn, Ont.
Farm Forum: Elgin Thompson, Brucefield, Ont.
A Great Help: Eleanor Wagner, near Regina, Sask.
The Peeping Tom: Ann Robbins, Thompsonville, Ont.
Indian Neighbours: Olga Brygadyr, Primrose, Alta.
Not a Registered Nurse: Florence Watkins-Jones, Lucky Lake, Sask.

A City and a Country Kid: Bertha Rose, Larivière, Man.
A Very Wealthy Man: Ernie Severn, Hockley, Ont.
Why Farm?: John Cairns, Ameliasburg, Ont.
Soil Miners: farm in Prince Edward County, Ont.
Disappearing Fences: Ron Oswald, Chesley, Ont.
The Farm All Runs Idle: Fred Dermott, Beeton, Ont.
Wonderful Memories: Peggy Sproul, Viscount, Sask.
The Day of the Small Farmer: Andrew Mair, Chesley, Ont.
Just Fond Memories: Jim Reiger, Elstow, Sask.